ECONOMICS AND SOCIETY: No 3

Problems of
Economic Policy

ECONOMICS AND SOCIETY SERIES
General Editor: Professor C. D. Harbury

ECONOMICS AND SOCIETY SERIES

Problems of
Economic Policy

by

KEITH HARTLEY

Reader in Economics
University of York

London
GEORGE ALLEN & UNWIN
Boston   Sydney

First published in 1977
Second impression 1978

ISBN 0 04 339008 0   Papercased
     0 04 339009 9   Paperback

Printed in Great Britain by
Unwin Brothers Limited
The Gresham Press
Old Woking, Surrey

Preface

This book arose out of the author's experience of the difficulties of teaching economics to first-year social science students. Instead of teaching theory in a vacuum, where students inevitably and understandably have difficulty in seeing its relevance, the author adopted a problem-oriented approach in which theory was introduced wherever it was required for an understanding of UK policy issues. In this way, students can see the relevance of theory to policy and, in the process, they (hopefully) learn-by-doing and improve their understanding of theory. Thus, this is an introductory applied economics text in which the basic theory of any first-year university economics course is applied to a whole range of UK macro- and micro-economic issues. Applied economics is concerned with the application of theory, including its empirical verification. Inevitably, limitations of space mean that the text cannot outline the details of all the relevant theory: it is assumed that students are familiar with a standard first-year economics text, although in each chapter efforts are made to summarise the relevant theory. The topics have been selected because they are familiar UK policy issues and provide opportunities for the application of basic macro-, micro- and welfare economics. An introduction is also provided to some of the newer developments, especially in micro-economics. These include the economics of politics and bureaucracies; human capital, search and learning theory; transactions and information costs; utility-maximising and labour-managed firms; X-inefficiency and the economics of subsidy policy. The text is designed for both first- and second-year students who are already familiar with basic theory. Those without prior knowledge of economics will find it most useful to read this book alongside an introductory theory text.

The book is divided into three parts. Part I introduces the methodology of economic policy which is applied throughout the text. The stress is on specifying policy objectives, using theory to identify the causes of policy problems and considering alternative policy solutions. This methodology is outlined in Chapter 1 which also considers the debate about predictive accuracy and the realism of a theory's assumptions. Chapters 2 and 3 consider why governments need economic policies: are they trying, in some sense, to make people 'better off'? Chapter 2 considers the concept of 'better off' and an 'improvement': it introduces Paretian welfare economics and market failure as well as the compensation principle and second-best. Welfare economics is not the easiest of subjects but it is hoped that Chapter 2 will provide students with an introductory survey and a broad outline of its policy relevance. Alternatively, policies might be explained by a concern with votes, interest groups and advice from budget-maximising government departments. Chapter 3 outlines the economics of politics and bureaucracies which students usually find to be a more attractive explanation of policy; it also provides a good example of the application of utility theory to voters and of the theory of the firm and market structures to political parties.

Part II concentrates on macro-economic policy, although the micro-economic foundations of macro-economics are always present. This part is based on the standard British government concern with full employment, price stability, balance of payments and growth objectives. Chapter 4 introduces search theories of unemployment, and considers what the unemployment statistics actually measure and the effectiveness of monetary policy as an employment-creator in a standard Keynesian model. Policy towards the regions and lame ducks is considered in Part III. The controversy over the Phillips curve and conflicts between employment and price stability objectives provides a useful link between Chapter 4 on unemployment and Chapter 5 on inflation. Chapter 5 is concerned with the debate about the importance of money and unions as causes of inflation: the natural unemployment rate and short- and long-run Phillips curves are explained; the evidence is critically assessed, especially on the effects of pay policies; and the chapter ends by predicting the micro-economic effects of profit controls on utility-maximising firms. Chapter 6 specialises on the balance of payments and assesses the theory and evidence in relation to exchange rate, domestic deflation and tariff policies. For example, is a deflation an appropriate solution to Britain's balance of payments problems? This chapter will be of interest to those who have followed the debates in the mid-1970s about import controls. Chapter 7 on growth uses a production function approach and refers to such policies as the Selective Employment Tax and proposals for the Regeneration of British Industry; the latter provides an appropriate introduction to many of the micro-economic policy issues analysed in Part III.

Income distribution is a recurrent theme in policy debates. Price controls are sometimes advocated as the 'best' solution, especially in such 'key' markets as housing and 'essential' food. Others emphasise the need to fix a minimum wage or introduce equal pay or make cash payments to relieve poverty. But will cash payments, such as a negative income tax, affect the incentive to work? Some of these issues, and other arguments for price controls, are presented in Chapter 8 which uses standard demand, supply and indifference curve analysis. The chapter also provides predictions about the effects of price and wage controls as elements in a pay policy. Chapters 9 and 10 are concerned with mergers, monopoly and UK policy. The economies of scale, technical progress and capital market failure arguments for bigness are presented and the evidence is considered. Are large firms successful and do takeovers improve efficiency? Monopoly is a source of market failure and Chapter 10 analyses UK monopoly policy. Does theory offer any guidelines for a policy towards mergers and monopoly? X-inefficiency, second-best, transactions costs and the economics of politics are each applied to the monopoly problem. Evidence is presented on market and aggregate concentration and on the effectiveness of British policy. Bureaucracies can also be regarded as part of the general monopoly problem and they are analysed in Chapter 11, which also contains a critique of government contracting policy. This is a subject on which there is little published material by British economists, but which has been extremely topical in criminal proceedings in the mid-1970s relating to local government contracts. Chapters 12 and 13 deal with subsidy policy. Human capital theory, location of industry measures and the Regional Employment Premium are considered in Chapter 12. More recently, British subsidy policy has been directed at firms and 'lame ducks'. In Chapter 13, the shadow pricing, externalities and marginal cost pricing arguments for subsidies are presented and then reinterpreted using the economics of politics. Nationalisation and labour-managed firms (workers' co-operatives) are presented as alternative policy options. In trying to write a readable text discussing these and other policy issues, it is difficult to be totally impartial: answers can only be given to questions. A statement of an economist's value-judgements can contribute to understanding. My values are individualistic which leads me to prefer market-improving state intervention which promotes opportunities for individual choice.

To those who feel that my choice of policy issues is limited, I can only remind them that within the limits of 75,000 words I have selected major topics based on the objective functions of successive British governments and each topic has been chosen for its potential in illustrating the application of theory. Hopefully, if the text achieves its aims, students will be able to apply the methodology to other policy issues such as taxation and the distribution of wealth, agricultural subsidies, Britain and the EEC, and underdeveloped nations.

Many have contributed to this text, some knowingly, others unwittingly through their advocacy of alternative policies. Colleagues and students at the Universities of York and Illinois have forced me to simplify and clarify economic concepts. I owe much to Professor Jack Wiseman, who has been especially influential both in discussion and in joint teaching of applied economics, although I suspect that this effort will further reveal my confusions (especially on costs!). I am deeply grateful to Professor Colin Harbury, who exceeded the normal duties of a series editor: he commented on each chapter and repeatedly reminded me of my audience and the aims of the text. Janet Cubitt helped with Chapter 11. The usual disclaimers apply. Perhaps the greatest costs have been borne by Winifred, Adam, Lucy, Cecilia, Ivy and Walter who remain convinced that economics is about money and that more is preferred!

KEITH HARTLEY
University of York
September 1976

Contents

Part 1

Methodology

Chapter 1

The Economists' Approach to Policy Problems

INTRODUCTION

Economic policy leads to a great deal of controversy between economists. Disagreements arise about the aims of public policy, the importance or 'weights' to be attached to various aims, the relevance of alternative theories in explaining the causes of policy problems and the appropriateness and desirability of particular policy solutions.[1] The problems which confronted the British economy in the 1970s illustrate some of these controversies. In this period, unemployment and inflation were major issues but politicians and others differed in the emphasis which they were willing to place on each of these. Some emphasised, or valued highly, the maintenance of full employment whilst others preferred more price stability. Disputes also arose over the precise causes of the inflation and the nature of unemployment in this period: an area where economic theory and the evidence on the predictive accuracy of alternative theories is relevant. For example, is inflation always a monetary phenomenon or do trade unions matter? Disagreements appeared over the choice of policy solutions, especially the appropriateness and desirability of deflation and incomes policies. Worries were expressed about conflicts in policy objectives such as the likely effects on inflation and the balance of payments of policies aimed at maintaining full employment. But policy debates were not confined to macro-economics. Micro-economic policy, embracing product and factor markets, was also controversial.

In the 1970s, there were disagreements about Britain's membership of the European Economic Community, subsidies to lame ducks, trade unions, the housing market and rent control, merger policy, the nationalised industries, worker's co-operatives and the extent of state ownership, to name but a few. Criticism surrounded such policy instruments as the Selective Employment Tax, the Regional Employment Premium, the National Board for Prices and Incomes, the Industrial Relations Act, 1971–4, and the National Enterprise

Board. The list is illustrative rather than comprehensive. Debate has also intensified over the distribution of income and wealth in the UK. The distributional implications of such alternative policies as deflation, incomes policy, lame ducks, rent control, agricultural support policy and wealth taxes are consciously assessed and compared with some criteria relating to an 'ideal' distribution. Inevitably, disagreements arise since on each policy issue everyone has an opinion and these differ. This book aims to identify the general contribution of economic theory to current debates about British economic policy.

METHODOLOGY: HOW DO ECONOMISTS APPROACH
POLICY PROBLEMS?

In approaching policy problems, economists seek answers to three questions:

(1) What is the problem? For example, in the 1970s, successive British governments were concerned with inflation and unemployment: hence price stability and full employment were two policy targets.
(2) What are the causes of the problem? Economists use economic theory to explain the causes of events which are of concern to policy-makers. For example, inflation might be explained by demand-pull and/or cost-push theories. The acceptability of a particular theory of inflation will depend on whether it fits the facts.
(3) What can we do about the problem? Frequently, theory suggests alternative policy solutions or instruments. Once again, inflation provides examples with the debate between such alternatives as monetary, fiscal and pay policies. In this situation, theory can be used to predict the likely effects of alternatives and the results presented to the policy-makers. The politician is then faced with a classic problem of choice between alternatives: the situation is similar to that confronting utility-maximising consumers and other economic agents. Standard utility-maximising behaviour requires the policy-maker to choose the least-cost method of achieving the aims of policy (see Chapter 4). Least-cost is thus related to the decision-maker's preference function. It means that costs are subjective in that the policy-maker will attempt to minimise the sacrifices, including the sacrifice of other policy aims, involved in pursuing a particular course of action. For example, in choosing between alternative policies to control inflation, he will act according to his preferences and select the policy which *he believes* will have the minimum of adverse effects

on the other policy targets such as employment, growth and income distribution.

Each of these three general questions will be expanded in the remainder of this chapter. Consideration will be given to the policy objectives of governments, the relevance of economic theory to policy, and the relationship between policy objectives and instruments. The technical equipment used consists of production possibility boundaries and some general principles of economic methodology.

WHAT IS THE PROBLEM? THE OBJECTIVES OF
ECONOMIC POLICY

Any logical assessment of economic policy in the UK must start with the basic question of the Government's policy objectives: What is the Government trying to achieve? What is its objective function? What is it trying to maximise?

In the post-war period, the various British governments have been concerned with six objectives relating to:

     (1)   Employment.
     (2)   Price stability.
     (3)   The balance of payments.
     (4)   Economic growth.
     (5)   The distribution of income and wealth.
     (6)   Efficiency in the use of resources.

Whilst various British governments have accepted these broad objectives, they have differed in the importance or the 'weights' which they have placed on each aim. Labour governments have traditionally emphasised employment, growth and distributional objectives whilst Conservative administrations appear to have attached greater importance to price stability and balance of payments objectives. Similarly, the two political parties have differed in their approaches to efficiency in resource-use, one emphasising state intervention to replace or limit the operation of private markets, the other believing more in the virtues of private enterprise, competition and individual consumer choice.

Most of the above objectives are widely known, although a concern with efficiency probably requires some explanation. A requirement for economic efficiency is that it must be impossible to raise the output of one good without producing less of another. On this basis, inefficiency in production exists if, for example, a re-allocation of labour or capital will increase total output. The inclusion of the efficiency objective arises from the observation that various British governments have attempted to raise output through improving the efficiency with which resources are used in the economy. For example, governments have been concerned with the allocation of resources, especially labour, between regions and industries and with promoting a re-allocation of labour from the declining to the expanding sectors of the economy. The coal industry is a classic example, where there has been a long-run decline in employment and a re-allocation of labour both within the coal industry and to other industries. Govern- ments have also been interested in the structure of industries and the organisation of markets. For example, the Labour Government's Industrial Reorganisation Corporation supported mergers to en- courage the formation of larger firms capable of obtaining economies of scale and so reducing unit costs (see Chapters 9 and 10). Competi- tion policy also exists to regulate any mis-allocation of resources due to monopoly. Finally, government support for productivity bargain- ing, as occurred in the 1960s, is a further example of the general concern with efficiency in resource-use. In these ways, governments have attempted to reach the economy's production possibility boundary.

Once an economy's resources are fully and efficiently employed, it will be operating on its production possibility boundary. A simple example, assuming constant returns to scale, is shown in Figure 1.1.

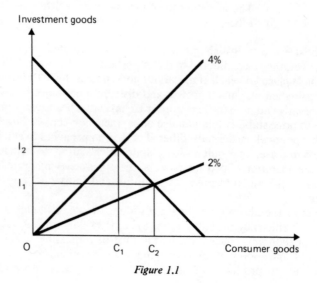

Figure 1.1

The production possibility frontier in Figure 1.1 shows the various combinations of consumer and investment goods[2] which can be produced when an economy's resources are fully and efficiently employed. With the unemployment which existed in the mid-1970s, the UK was clearly operating at a point within its production possibility boundary. Even at full employment, it is likely that some inefficiency exists in all economies. Information might be inadequate and firms might not be profit–maximisers, so that markets might 'fail' to work properly. Questions then arise about the additional costs of reducing inefficiency in relation to the expected benefits. In a world of scarcity, where public policies are not costless, it will probably be too costly to *completely eliminate* all inefficiencies: there will remain an 'optimal' (positive) amount of inefficiency.

Once the boundary is reached or approximated, resources become scarce and have alternative uses. Consider the case of economic growth, which can be represented by an outward shift in the production possibility boundary. If the Government's preference function is such that it prefers to raise the growth rate from, say, 2 per cent to 4 per cent, more investment will be required. As Figure 1.1 shows, present consumption of C_2C_1 is sacrificed for the extra investment required to raise the growth rate. In other words, where resources are scarce, governments have to choose between alternatives. They have to choose between, say, more or less growth with the implications for consumption levels amongst present and future generations. Such a choice involves a distributional judgement. Policy-makers cannot avoid choices. Defence or schools, *Concordes* or hospitals, and space programmes or houses? In each case, choices are required and the ultimate decision will be based on what a government is trying to achieve. For example, decisions might reflect a government's beliefs about the likely results of its policies in making people 'better or worse off'. This explanation of government behaviour will be critically assessed in Chapter 2.

So far, we have identified the broad objectives of UK economic policy. But, before the economist can proceed to analyse policy issues, he requires a much clearer specification of the objectives. Answers will be required to questions about the objectives:[3]

(1) What is meant by a government's commitment to maintaining a 'high and stable level of employment'? Is an unemployment rate of, say, 2 per cent to 3 per cent consistent with a 'high' level of employment? Does 'stability' require unemployment rates to fluctuate within some relatively narrow range, say, 1·5 per cent to 3·5 per cent and how tolerable are departures from these targets?
(2) What is meant by the frequently claimed objective of maintaining

price stability? Does it mean no increase in domestic prices? Or is an increase in prices of, say, 5 per cent per year consistent with stability? Alternatively, are governments concerned with relative price stability, namely, domestic price movements in relation to price changes amongst the UK's major foreign competitors?

(3) What is the meaning of a 'strong' balance of payments? For example, in the mid-1950s the aim of policy-makers was to achieve a current account surplus of between £300m. and £350m. per year, whilst in the early 1960s the target was raised to about £450m. per year.[4] In addition, until the early 1970s, the balance of payments targets of successive governments was associated with a desire to maintain the exchange rate for sterling.

These are the type of questions which economists have to ask about policy objectives. The answers enable the economist to identify the problems which concern policy-makers and also to assess whether a government has actually achieved its declared objectives. Governments are understandably vague and reluctant to quantify both their aims and the importance they attach to each one. Policy objectives are frequently expressed in terms which bear a marked resemblance to the health of some ideal individual ('strong', 'healthy', 'vigorous'). In the circumstances, a start can be made in assessing government performance by considering the evidence on unemployment, prices, the balance of payments and growth for the UK, as shown in Table 1.1.[5]

For 1964–75, unemployment fluctuated between 1·5 per cent and 4·4 per cent. After 1945, unemployment of 3 per cent was accepted as consistent with full employment, although the target was later reduced below 2·5 per cent. On this basis, the employment record in the 1970s was below target. It is, however, possible that the nature of unemployment has changed compared with the 1960s, requiring a revision in the full employment target. Alternatively, the employment target might have been sacrificed for other policy ends. As for prices, at no point in the period has there been price stability in the sense of no change in the retail price index. Both prices and wages have risen continuously, with the annual increases being at a minimum in 1966–7, and an unprecedented maximum in 1974–5 – each being periods of rising unemployment! The balance of payments has also fluctuated widely. It varied between a surplus of over £1,000m. in 1971 and a deficit of £3,650m. in 1974, much of which was due to the rise in the prices of oil and raw materials. Only between 1969 and 1971 did the UK achieve the target of a current account surplus of over £300m. per year and this period followed the devaluation of 1967 and was characterised by unemployment rates of 2·5 per cent and over.

Table 1.1

Year	Growth GDP at Factor Cost (£m., 1970 (prices)	Unemployment		Prices		Balance of Payments Current Account (£m.)
		Rate (%)	Numbers (000)	Retail Prices (1970 = 100)	Weekly Wage Rates (July 1972 = 100)	
1964	37,678	1·7	354	76·3	56·3	− 355
1965	38,633	1·5	305	80·0	58·4	− 27
1966	39,402	1·5	292	83·1	61·2	+ 100
1967	40,401	2·3	539	85·2	63·6	− 301
1968	41,864	2·5	553	89·2	68·4	− 275
1969	42,452	2·5	581	94·0	72·1	+ 462
1970	43,252	2·6	618	100·0	79·4	+ 735
1971	44,216	3·5	799	109·4	89·3	+ 1048
1972	44,954	3·9	886	117·2	101·5	+ 128
1973	47,334	2·7	630	128·0	114·6	− 835
1974	47,630	2·7	631	148·5	134·3	− 3650
1975	46,970	4·4	1,014	184·4	174·4	− 1702

Source: Central Statistical Office, Economic Trends: Annual Supplement, 1975, (London HMSO, 1976). Figures for the UK.

Growth, as measured by real GDP, generally showed an upward trend, with a large increase in 1972–3: this increase was associated with substantial reductions in the unemployment rate and a deterioration in the balance of payments. In fact, a distinction has to be made between variations in resource-use and changes in long-run productive potential. The latter is a more accurate indicator of the economy's growth performance and might be approximated by comparing periods of similar unemployment rates. If the National Plan's target growth rate had been achieved, GDP in 1970 would have been some £47,000m., a figure which was not reached until 1973. Table 1.1 also shows the changing magnitude of the problems confronting British governments in the 1970s. Compared with the 1960s, the scale of the unemployment, inflation and the balance of payments problems was unprecedented.

ECONOMIC THEORY AND PUBLIC POLICY: WHAT ARE THE CAUSES OF THE PROBLEM?

The emphasis so far has been on identifying the problems which confront policy-makers. Once identified, these problems can be subjected to economic analysis. Theory can be used to explain why governments need public policies towards, say, full employment or inflation or lame ducks or the regions. Theory can also be used to predict the consequences of proposed policy solutions.

A major task for the economist is to identify the general theoretical issues which are usually concealed in the detailed controversy surrounding a particular government policy decision. Consider the example of government support for mergers in the aircraft, car, engineering, shipbuilding and textile industries. Each is an example of a more general issue, namely, does economic analysis suggest any policy 'rules' for the formation of mergers and for the control of monopolies? Are these 'rules' applicable to both product and factor markets including trade unions? Similar questions can be formulated for other policy issues. State aid has been given to the British Aircraft Corporation's Concorde, British Leyland, Burmah Oil, Chrysler and Upper Clyde Shipbuilders, and for such industries as aircraft, computers and nuclear power. What is the economic 'logic' of state support for private firms and industries and for the regions? On price controls and the regulation of firms, does theory offer any 'guidelines' on the 'appropriate' pricing policies for private firms and nationalised industries? Within the labour market, does analysis predict that if left to itself the economy will not necessarily achieve full employment? What are the economic arguments for state intervention in industrial training, geographical mobility and for the provision of a state employment service? On international trade, does analysis suggest when the UK's balance of payments position constitutes a 'problem'? Each question involves the application of economic theory to a policy issue (see Chapters 4–13).

Economic theories are designed to explain facts and to offer predictions about the likely results of a course of action. They consist of a set of definitions and assumptions which generate logical deductions about behaviour. Theories are retained so long as they are consistent with the facts and continue to offer accurate predictions. On this basis, the acceptability of a theory depends on its empirical validity rather than on the realism of its assumptions.[6] This is a controversial area and it raises the question of what is meant by realism. In one sense, assumptions have to be unrealistic: they have to be abstractions, generalisations and simplifications because the world is so complex. For example, economic theory uses such abstract concepts as utility and expectations (how many readers have seen these 'things' as distinct from their consequences?) and in the theory of demand the problem is simplified by ignoring the clothing and hair styles of consumers. Yet, there is a sense in which assumptions have to be realistic: some assumptions might be regarded as conditions which have to be satisfied for a valid test of a theory.

Consider an economic theory of British government behaviour which assumes the absence of inflation. This could mean that the analyst only intends his theory to apply when inflation is absent. However, the controversy about the realism of assumptions is something of a non-debate. Ultimately, if economists wish to introduce more realistic assumptions into theories, then, as scientists, there is a standard procedure for resolving controversy. We compare the *alternative* predictions of the different models and see which is more accurate.

Theory which is consistent with the facts is relevant to public policy in three ways. First, when a government is confronted with a specific problem such as inflation, the lack of economic growth or a balance of payments deficit, theory can be used to show the factors causing the problem. What is it that determines the general price level and aggregate employment in the economy together with its balance of payments and growth performances? At the micro-level, questions arise about the determination of prices in different product and factor markets and the effects of an increase in wages on employment in an industry. A concern with regional employment requires a model of the location decisions of firms and the mobility of labour. For growth targets, it is necessary to understand the contributions of different factors of production, alternative market and economic structures (for example, oligopoly and manufacturing or services) and varying sizes of firms. Worries about the balance of payments require an understanding of why nations trade, the role of exchange rates and why firms export. Policies towards the distribution of income and wealth lead to questions about the determinants of factor payments. If, for example, investment in human beings through training leads to higher incomes, why do some firms train and others not? These are examples of the questions which economic theories have to answer. Once a government understands the causes of an event, it can formulate policy solutions. The difficulties arise where there are alternative theories and, at the time when a policy solution is required, it might not be at all obvious which is the more accurate explanation.

Secondly, once a policy measure has been selected, theory can be used to analyse and to predict the likely results of the policy. Predictions can be made about the possible consequences of reducing the money supply in the economy, changing the foreign exchange rate, introducing minimum wage legislation and abolishing tariffs and rent control (see Chapters 5, 6 and 8).

Thirdly, theory can show the possibilities of conflicts between policy objectives. Conflicts might arise between growth and balance of payments objectives, with higher growth rates and fixed exchange rates being associated with deficits. Both price stability and a balance of payments surplus with fixed exchange rates might require large-scale unemployment. Theory can be used to identify and to explain these conflicts or 'trade offs' and to suggest the possibility of formulating policy measures which might reduce such conflicts (see Table 1.1 and Chapters 4 and 6).

POLICY OBJECTIVES AND INSTRUMENTS: WHAT CAN GOVERNMENTS DO ABOUT THE PROBLEM?

Policy objectives are achieved through policy measures or instruments. British governments have available a whole range of macro- and micro-policy instruments. Macro-policy instruments affect the broad aggregates throughout the economy: consumption, investment, government expenditure, exports and imports, together with the general level of prices and total employment. The macro-policy instruments include monetary, fiscal and incomes policies as well as national economic planning. Monetary policy changes the money supply, the rate of interest, HP controls, and the liquidity of government securities (debt management). Fiscal policy varies the level and composition of government expenditure and changes taxation and subsidies. Prices and incomes policy involves the Government in the process of determining prices, costs and factor payments in the private and public sectors of the economy. National planning involves a government statement of policy objectives, especially a growth target, over some time-horizon, say five years, together with a list of the measures which the state proposes to implement to achieve its targets. Governments also possess a variety of micro-policy instruments which involve state intervention in individual markets. These instruments affect market prices and the structure and operation of markets. Examples of the former include rent and profit controls, tariffs, minimum wages, 'free' or subsidised milk, and the pricing policies of the nationalised industries. Examples of market structure measures include policies towards monopolies, the size of firms, entry conditions and competition in its price and non-price forms (for example, advertising). Planning Agreements (1975) between the state and firms affect both prices and the operation of markets. The Agreements aim '... to ensure that the plans of companies are in harmony with national needs and objectives' (see Chapter 7).[7]

Micro-policy instruments can be readily related to macro-policy objectives. State intervention in individual markets such as industry and labour policy forms the micro-economic foundations of macro-policy targets. To achieve full employment objectives, governments have supported (for example, through loans, subsidies, tariff protection and defence orders) firms which would otherwise go out of business and industries and regions which would otherwise contract: Rolls-Royce, British Leyland and the shipbuilding and textile industries are examples. To assist the re-allocation of unemployed labour, grants are available for mobility, training is provided in Government Training Centres, and subsidies are available for firms which move to the Development Areas (see Chapters 12 and 13). For the price-stability target, micro-policy has included investigations of monopolies and the general outlawing of restrictive trade practices and resale price maintenance (see Chapter 10). More recently, various pay policies have introduced price and profit controls with the National Board for Prices and Incomes (1965–71) and the Prices Commission (1971) as 'policing' agencies. As a result, some firms have been prevented from raising prices so that they might have been 'shocked' into increased efficiency: an outcome which depends on the existence of organisational 'slack'. The balance of payments objective has involved state intervention in industrial structure through the Industrial Reorganisation Corporation (1966–71), which aimed to create larger firms (mergers) capable of obtaining economies of scale and competing more successfully in world markets (see Chapters 9 and 10). Government support for British projects such as the domestic agricultural and aircraft sectors has often been explained in terms of their import-savings and foreign exchange contributions. Hire purchase controls, especially for cars, have been used to reduce the domestic demand for vehicles and so induce British firms to expand exports. For economic growth objectives, the UK joined the EEC and the state has supported research and development in advanced technology industries like aircraft, computers and nuclear power. In the labour market, the Industrial Training Act (1964) and the Selective Employment Tax (1966–73) were tax-subsidy measures designed to raise the growth rate. The former provided firms with fiscal incentives to train more skilled labour, while the latter was designed to promote a re-allocation of labour from services to the higher-productivity manufacturing sector (see Chapter 7).

Finally, various micro-policy instruments contribute towards distribution of income and wealth objectives. Examples include the introduction of equal pay and productivity-raising investments in human beings in such forms as the raising of the school-leaving age and public policies towards training and re-training. Distributional objectives became increasingly important in the early 1970s, culminating in the Social Contract of 1974 and the 'flat rate' pay policy of 1975. Both embraced policies towards rents, housing, food subsidies, the lower paid, job preservation, pensions, family allowances and taxes on capital transfers and wealth. They represented a commitment to distributional aims as a means of achieving full employment and the control of inflation.

Whilst policy instruments are a means of achieving objectives, difficulties arise because of conflicts in aims. At the macro-level, there might be conflicts between, say, employment, income distribution and growth objectives. Policies which aim to preserve jobs might interfere with the allocation of resources to more productive alternative uses (growth). Profit regulation might reduce entrepreneurial incentives for risk-taking, with adverse effects on investment and efficiency. Trade offs exist between defence expenditure on the one hand and balance of payments and growth targets on the other. At the micro-level, a policy which aims to maximise the gains from domestic and international trade might conflict with regional employment, defence and agricultural policy objectives. Policies which tax or nationalise the profits of North Sea oil companies might reduce the incentives to further exploration and self-sufficiency. The introduction of price and wage controls in markets will result in shortages and surpluses and affect the allocation of resources within the economy. Redundancy pay and earnings-related unemployment benefits might adversely affect an individual's willingness to work. Conflicts might arise between mergers and competition policy, and between public ownership and internal efficiency. Where there are conflicts in objectives, there is no such thing as a costless policy. Each involves sacrificing alternatives with the inevitable controversies over the relative importance of policy goals. Policy-makers cannot avoid choices. They are required to choose between alternative policy targets and between alternative policy instruments as a means of achieving chosen objectives. If, for example, policy-makers choose to concentrate on the removal of a balance of payments deficit, they will still have to choose how to do it. Should they deflate, devalue, adopt floating exchange rates or use tariffs and quotas to control imports (see Chapter 6)? A decision to maintain armed forces requires governments to decide whether to buy weapons from domestic or foreign sources of supply and whether to allocate resources to land, sea or air forces. Self-sufficiency in energy supplies requires choices between coal, North Sea oil and gas and nuclear power. Thus, policy-makers cannot avoid the standard economic problem, that of choice, and choices will reflect value-judgements.[8]

The relationship between policy objectives and instruments and the existence of conflicts has been formulated into a well-established principle of economic policy.[9] To achieve a stated number of objectives, a government requires at least an equal number of policy instruments. Only in exceptional circumstances is it possible for one policy measure to secure the attainment of more than one objective. Take the example of a country with inflation and a balance of payments deficit. If a government uses aggregate demand measures, such as monetary and fiscal policy, to achieve its employment objective, some other policy instrument such as a pay policy, will be required for its price stability target and a further policy measure, such as a floating exchange rate, will be required to achieve the balance of payments objective. Additional instruments will be needed if the state also has economic growth targets. Applied to micro-economic policy, the principle suggests that if a government encourages mergers for balance of payments reasons, some other instrument such as a marginal cost pricing 'rule' will be required for economic efficiency, whilst a further policy measure, say labour mobility, will be needed for growth objectives. An implication of this principle of economic policy is that the post-war economic performance of successive British governments can be partly explained by the simultaneous pursuit of a variety of conflicting policy objectives in a situation where there has been an insufficient range of policy instruments. The exchange rate is a classic example. Until 1972, British governments committed themselves to maintaining the exchange rate as an objective of policy with the inevitable sacrifice of domestic employment and growth targets. The situation changed in 1972 when the Government seemed willing to regard the exchange rate as a policy instrument rather than an objective. The Chancellor in his 1972 Budget Statement announced that '. . . the lesson of the international balance of payments upsets of the last few years was that it was neither necessary nor desirable to maintain unrealistic exchange rates, whether they were too high or too low'.

CONCLUSION

This chapter has shown some of the general issues which arise in the study of economic policy. In particular, it has provided a basis for answering the question raised by all students: why do economists disagree about policy? It has been shown that disagreements arise because opinions and views differ. Economists disagree about the 'desirable' aims of public policy. Like all scientists, there are genuine disagreements about the 'correct' explanation of the facts. Such disputes are likely to continue until competing hypotheses have been satisfactorily tested and one has been refuted.[10] Finally, the preferences or value–judgements of economists are likely to be a source of dispute over the 'appropriateness' or 'desirability' of specific policy solutions. Even if economists agree about the predicted consequences of rent control they are likely to disagree about its desirability.

One of our tasks is to distinguish between these sources of controversy, separating testable propositions from beliefs. We shall explore
this point by considering the question: why do governments need
economic policies?

Chapter 2

Why Do Governments Intervene in the Economy?

INTRODUCTION

Policy-makers cannot avoid choices. One economic theory of government behaviour (a theory of choice) postulates that policy-makers' choices between targets and instruments will be based on their beliefs about the likely results of policies in making people 'better or worse off'. On this view, the objectives of policy are a means of improving, and ideally of maximising, the utility or welfare of individuals in the community. Thus, if governments are social welfare maximising agencies, the model explains state intervention in the economy as a means of contributing to the welfare of the community. What is meant by policies making people 'better or worse off', so contributing to their welfare? When is a change desirable? Welfare economic theory helps with these questions.

WHEN IS A CHANGE AN IMPROVEMENT?

Any introduction to economic policy cannot avoid welfare economics. We shall confine ourselves to an elementary treatment of the criteria used to determine whether a particular change is 'desirable'. Should the Corn Laws have been abolished? Is competition preferable to monopoly? What should be the pricing policies of the nationalised industries? Will British membership of the EEC make us 'better off'? To answer these questions and to provide a benchmark, economists *start* by postulating an ideal situation called a Pareto optimum or an optimum allocation of resources. Such an optimum is achieved when it is impossible to make one person 'better off' without making someone else 'worse off'. 'Better off' means a movement to a higher level of satisfaction and 'worse off' to a lower level of satisfaction or utility.

Consider the example of an economy producing only two goods, cars and colour TVs.[1] The initial (non-competitive) allocation of resources to the production of these two goods results in a price for cars of £1,400 which is greater than the additional costs of £1,200 for producing an extra vehicle. The price of a colour TV is £200 which is less than the £300 of costs required to produce an extra unit. In other words, price is greater than marginal cost for cars and less than marginal cost for TVs, a situation which departs from the competitive outcome where profit-maximising firms sell their products at a price equal to marginal cost. In this initial situation, the value or utility to consumers of another car as measured by price exceeds the value of resources required to make it whilst the consumer utility of another TV is less than its extra costs. Here, the costs of a car are opportunity costs or the utilities sacrificed by not producing more TVs. This is not an optimal allocation of resources. Consumer satisfaction can be raised by re-allocating resources from the television to the car industry. If £1,200 worth of resources were transferred from TVs, consumers would lose some £800 worth of TVs but they would gain about £1,400 worth of cars. Further gains are possible so long as prices are not equal to marginal costs. Only when price equals marginal cost in the production of both cars and TVs will it be impossible to further raise consumer satisfactions by the additional shifting of resources. Thus, if the interests of consumers and society are identical, an optimal allocation of resources requires that, *at the margin*, the value to society of each good must equal the costs incurred by the community in producing the good. We now have a general policy 'rule' which suggests that optimum resource allocation requires the equality of price and marginal cost throughout the economy: a result which arises under perfect competition.[2] The 'rule' is widely applicable. It provides policy 'guidelines' suggesting that monopoly is undesirable and that marginal cost pricing is appropriate for private firms and the nationalised industries. For 'lame ducks' the 'appropriate' policy would be state subsidies for any losses due to marginal cost pricing, otherwise a re-allocation of resources is required. With regional policy, the 'rule' suggests the desirability of re-allocating resources from low- to high-productivity regions (see Part III). The acceptability of these policies depends on society wishing to achieve an optimum allocation of resources. The implications of such a policy objective can be understood by considering the distinction between positive and normative economics.

POSITIVE AND NORMATIVE ECONOMICS

The Paretian model of optimum resource allocation and its criterion for a desirable change forms the subject area of normative economics. This is the study of what ought to be. To state that price *should* or *ought* to be equal to marginal cost is a normative statement which reflects a particular value-judgement. In the Paretian model, the value-judgements on which the system is based are clearly stated. They start with the proposition that the individual – and no one else – is the best judge of his welfare or well-being. Next, the welfare of the community is assumed to depend on the welfares of the individuals comprising it. On this basis, it follows that if one person is made better off, no one else being made worse off, the society as a whole is better off. Whether or not everyone agrees with these judgements, their specification ensures that the sources and nature of any disagreements can be identified and that alternative assumptions and models can be developed.

Perfect competition is one economic model which would lead to resources being used to produce the most desired mix of goods and services. It is one solution to the basic choice problems confronting any economic system: *what* to produce, *how* to produce it and for *whom* (distribution). Under competition, firms will respond to consumer preferences. Output will be produced and supplied at the lowest possible cost, and firms which fail to meet this test will not survive. The resulting distribution of income will depend on the ownership of resources and the relative scarcity of factors as reflected in market values. Yet again, not everyone will accept the desirability of a competitive organisation of the economy.

The desirability of competition and marginal cost pricing is a different issue from the factual problem of whether the British economy *is* competitive and whether prices are equal to marginal cost: the latter are part of positive economics or the study of what is. A few examples will help to clarify this distinction. In the field of policy, normative statements suggest 'desirable' policy objectives and policy measures: they suggest what governments ought to be trying to achieve and how. Examples include those who urge governments to control inflation or who advocate British membership of the Common Market or the desirability of price controls. On the other hand, positive economics is concerned with predicting the effects of, and with assessing the evidence on, various policy objectives and instruments. Thus, predictions can be made about the effects of controlling inflation, of Common Market membership, and of equal pay without any attempt being made to pronounce upon the desirability of the proposals (see Chapters 5 and 8). In this way, the distinction between positive and normative economics provides a conceptual framework for assessing the sources of controversy over economic policy.

THE SOURCES OF MARKET FAILURE: IS THERE A ROLE
FOR THE STATE IN CAPITALIST ECONOMIES?

Why does the state intervene in the economy. Why cannot markets
be left alone? Actual markets in private enterprise economies may
fail to work properly. They may not resemble the competitive 'ideal',
so that they will fail to respond to consumer preferences, with adverse effects on the utility or welfare of individuals. Market failure
can arise from two general sources, namely, externalities and imperfections. Each results in an 'incorrect' output of goods and services.
Externalities, including public goods, mean that markets provide 'too
much' or 'too little' of a commodity.[3] External costs are harmful and
arise when costs are imposed on society additional to those incurred
by individual buyers and sellers. Examples include pollution and
traffic congestion. Similarly, external benefits occur when the gains
to society from an activity exceed the benefits to individual transactors. Education, immunisation against infectious diseases, and
street lighting are examples of beneficial externalities. Where there
are externalities, market prices will not accurately represent society's
valuation of a commodity. Markets can also fail because of imperfections due to monopolies, oligopolies and restrictive practices. Imperfections in the form of price rigidities can mean that prices fail to
clear product and labour markets, thus resulting in surpluses and
unemployment.[4] Entry barriers can prevent additional resources
flowing into expanding activities. Some markets might only be able
to support one firm. Utilities such as gas, electricity and telephones
are examples of technical or natural monopoly. Both imperfections
and externalities as sources of market failure might justify state intervention in a private enterprise economy. Such intervention in the
form of macro- and micro-policies are the means by which governments can correct market failure and so raise community welfare.
    Although a variety of policy instruments exist, it is possible to
classify the various forms into market-improving or market-
displacing. This classification uses the market failure analysis and the
choice of policy will depend on the value-judgements of the decision-
maker. Market-improving policies aim to improve the operation of
private markets and to promote opportunities for consumer choice.
Examples include the provision of more labour market information
to individuals, cash subsidies to the poor and a vigorous anti-
monopoly policy designed to reduce entry barriers and expand competition. Such policies are likely to be preferred by those who favour
consumer sovereignty and the dispersion of economic and political
power in a society. In contrast, those who believe that individuals are
not the best judges of their welfare might favour market-displacing

policies which aim to restrict, replace or prevent the operation of private markets. British examples include nationalisation, planning agreements, the state education, employment and health services as well as policies on pornography, prostitution, drugs, abortion and immigration. An advantage of this market classification scheme is that it separates the positive and normative issues in policy debates: a distinction is made between the *technical issues* concerned with the potential sources of market 'failure' and the *policy issues* relating to the most 'appropriate' solution.

WELFARE ECONOMICS AND THE OBJECTIVES OF POLICY: A SOCIAL WELFARE FUNCTION

What about the idea of government policies' making people 'better' or 'worse off' – of contributing to their welfare? This approach to policy suggests that we might regard the objectives of government policy as contributing to the welfare of society. In other words, for the UK we might formulate a social welfare function showing the set of variables which affect the welfare of the community. An example is given below, where the welfare of society (W) is shown to depend upon employment (E), price stability (P), the balance of payments (B), economic growth (G) and the distribution of income and wealth (Y):[5]

$$W = W(E, P, B, G, Y)$$

Whenever economists try to assess the welfare effects of public policy, the standard starting-point is Paretian welfare economics. How is it possible to relate the social welfare function outlined above to the Paretian principle? Such a link can be made by regarding the targets of employment, price stability, etc. not as goals or 'ends' but as a means of raising, and of maximising, the utility of individuals in the community. On this basis, the above social welfare function becomes

$$W = W(U_1, U_2, \ldots, U_n)$$

where W is social welfare and $U_1, U_2, \ldots, U_n$ are the ordinal utility levels of each of the n individuals in the society; utility is assumed to depend on goods and services or real income. On this basis, full employment and efficiency targets are methods of reaching an economy's production possibility boundary (more goods) which allow some individuals to raise their utility without making anyone else worse off. Similarly, growth targets aim to shift outwards the constraints on individual choice, so raising utility levels. Pareto optimality can be achieved through domestic and international trade, and policies which promote exchange improve welfare. Money facilitates trade and a stable domestic currency is required for optimality. Thus, control of inflation through some domestic price-stability target is required to prevent a loss of confidence in money with its adverse effects on exchange. However, whilst optimality requires a policy on inflation, it is not at all obvious what the policy should be. Is the optimal rate of inflation positive, zero or negative or simply a matter of correctly anticipating inflation? International trade can also improve welfare by promoting mutually advantageous exchange between nations with different relative costs. This requires reductions in trade barriers, and exchange rates which reflect each nation's relative cost-price position: hence the possible relevance of a government's balance of payments target and associated exchange rate policy. Controversy exists as to whether flexible exchange rates might adversely affect international trade as well as parts of the domestic economy (see Chapter 6). Distributional objectives raise further difficulties. The Pareto criterion is concerned with efficiency in resource allocation and not with income distribution objectives. There are distributional implications of various optimal allocations but these might differ from the distribution which society regards as desirable. The Pareto model does not provide any criterion for determining an optimal distribution of income and wealth: this requires an additional distributional judgement which has to be incorporated into society's welfare function. Inevitably, conflicts are likely to arise between distributional targets and policies aimed at full employment and efficiency in resource allocation. If, for example, the price system, including wages, is used to allocate resources it cannot be used for distributional 'ends'. A policy which subsidises 'lame ducks' interferes with prices as an allocative mechanism and so maintains full employment at 'distorted' relative prices for distributional aims.

THE COMPENSATION PRINCIPLE: WHAT CAN WE SAY
ABOUT POLICIES WHICH BENEFIT SOME PEOPLE AND
HARM OTHERS?

The Paretian model provides a starting point for defining a 'desirable' change. A change is an improvement when one person can be made 'better off' without making anyone else 'worse off'. In this case, the Pareto model concludes that the community as a whole is better off. This criterion for a 'desirable' change is only a beginning. Policy changes usually make some groups 'better off' and others 'worse off'.

Examples include imports, the debate on the location of the Third London Airport, and the construction of reservoirs in Wales and urban motorways. Difficulties arise because welfare economics has no objective or scientific and universal standard for comparing the utility levels of different individuals: we are unable to make inter-personal comparisons of utility. To resolve this problem, economists have introduced the principle of compensation. At its simplest, the compensation principle states that a desirable change occurs when the potential gainers from the change can *overcompensate* the potential losers.[6] Consider a proposed change in which individual A is made £100 better off and individual B is made £5 worse off. In other words, individual B is only willing to pay A up to £5 to prevent the change. Such a change would be an improvement. Individual A could offer £5 to B, so that he is no worse off, whilst A would still be better off even after offering compensation. Thus, the construction of inner ring roads and urban renewal in historic cities such as York might be regarded as desirable if the potential beneficiaries (for example, road users) are capable of more than compensating the potential losers. The criterion is also used in cost-benefit studies, for assessing such issues as the desirability of British membership of the Common Market and whether the Industrial Revolution was an improvement.[7] Even so, the compensation principle is not without its problems. Inter-personal comparisons of utility (gains and losses) are effectively made by using money as a measuring rod. In addition, what if the potential gainers from a change are rich stockbrokers, property developers and 'speculators' whilst the potential losers are poor workers, pensioners and large families? Distributional issues cannot be avoided.

THE THEORY OF THE SECOND-BEST: CAN WE APPLY THE PARETO MODEL IN SOME SECTORS BUT NOT IN OTHERS?

A further difficulty arises in using the Paretian model. It requires that all the conditions for a Pareto optimum are simultaneously satisfied throughout the whole of the economy. For example, prices must be equal to marginal costs *everywhere* in the economy. However, consider the case where marginal cost pricing applies in only a limited part of the economy, say the nationalised industries, but not in the private sector. Assume also that there is a constraint in the form of at least one private firm where price can *never* be made equal to marginal cost. In this situation, it does not follow that policy efforts to introduce marginal cost pricing into some, but not all, of the private markets will necessarily move the economy towards an optimum position. It might, but it might also affect welfare or efficiency by lowering it or leaving it unchanged. In other words, if there is a constraint so that the rules for optimum resource allocation cannot be satisfied throughout the economy, then it becomes necessary to resort to a 'next-best' or 'second-best' solution, in which efforts are made to make the best of the resulting situation. A second-best solution involves a complete departure from the conditions required for optimum resource allocation. Thus, in the example given above, the second-best pricing rule might require the abolition of marginal cost pricing in the nationalised industries. Similar examples apply to other 'piece-meal' policy recommendations involving proposals for more competition or more centralisation or more free trade.

The theory of second-best can be expressed more formally. It states that if one of the conditions for a Pareto optimum *cannot* be fulfilled, then the other Paretian conditions – even though they can be achieved – are, in general, no longer desirable.[8] Second-best considers what is the best we can achieve when constraints prevent the attainment of the first-best. Two types of constraints might exist. First, nature-dictated or technical constraints such as indivisibilities and increasing returns to scale. Secondly, policy-created constraints such as a government's reluctance to break up monopoly unions or to change legislation on industrial relations or its support for a higher-cost domestic defence industry. Such constraints are not unknown in the UK! For policy purposes, the theory of second-best suggests that piece-meal policy recommendations based on Paretian principles may well reduce welfare. Second-best is a major blow to Paretian-type policy recommendations which suggest the desirability of marginal cost pricing for a nationalised industry or a public utility. It seems to be a blow to policies recommending the regulation of individual monopolies and mergers on grounds of resource mis-allocation. In other words, second-best refutes partial Paretianism.

CONCLUSION: CAN ECONOMISTS MAKE POLICY RECOMMENDATIONS?

It has been shown that policy recommendations involve value-judgements, some of which might not be universally acceptable. The Paretian model provides a useful conceptual framework for approaching policy issues and for identifying sources of controversy. Within this framework governments are regarded as agencies for maximising social welfare, and public policies are the means of achieving this objective. State intervention in private enterprise economies is required to correct market failure and policy can be either market-improving or market-displacing. Two issues limit the general applicability of Paretian welfare economics. First, controversy exists about some optimal distribution of income. Secondly, there are the implications of second-best. These are not necessarily separate issues since second-best constraints might reflect a government's distributional policies. For example, for distributional reasons, a government might introduce an incomes policy in which some labour received a wage greater than the value of its marginal product: this would create a second-best constraint.

Second-best seems to reduce drastically the applicability of welfare economics. It tells us what economists *cannot* do when making policy recommendations. It tells us that it is false to believe that it is better to fulfil some of the optimum conditions rather than none. Also, it is false to believe that it is better to depart from the optimum conditions to a *uniform* extent rather than by different amounts. For example, the second-best position may require price to greatly exceed marginal cost (MC) in some firms, slightly exceed MC in others and in some cases price might have to be less than MC. Once we recognise the existence of second-best, what is the economist's role in policy formulation? A number of responses are possible.

First, economists could try to estimate a second-best solution. The difficulty is that whilst the conditions for a Pareto optimum are straightforward, the corresponding requirements for a second-best solution are complex even in the simplest model. There are no simple *a priori* rules for establishing a second-best position: it is a complex, costly task and we almost certainly do not have sufficient information.

A second possibility is simply to ignore it. This is essentially a pragmatic position which asserts that we do not know enough about the workings of the economy to be able to handle second-best problems with any degree of confidence. In such circumstances, some argue that it is better to leave bad alone.[9] Others suggest that the more we apply second-best 'rules' the less likely we are ever to achieve a first-best since we shall be moving the economy further away from the first-best position.

A third possibility is to consider the relationship between the constraining sector and the rest of the economy. If the constraining sector is totally *independent* of the rest of the economy, we can ignore second-best and apply Paretian 'rules' to the remainder of the economy. For example, if we are interested in formulating policy 'rules' for the steel industry and the constraining sector is the baby-powder or the Harris Tweed industry, we might ignore the constraint and apply the Paretian welfare 'rules' to the rest of the economy. A similar result would apply where the constraining sector is a geographically remote region. Such a region would be completely independent of other areas and could be treated as a separate economy.

A fourth response is to act solely as a positive economist, predicting the likely effects of policies and leaving policy-makers to determine the desirability of the changes. In this way, economists can avoid second-best issues and the welfare implications of policies.

Finally, it might be possible to act on the second-best constraint and try to remove it. If it is a technically-created constraint, this might be removed by new technology. Where the constraint is policy-created, it can be removed by changing public policy. This latter possibility does, though, raise a more fundamental question: why does the policy constraint exist in the first place? If the policy constraint (for example, government attitude towards unions and industrial relations) reflects a desire to maximise the life of the government, it would seem that an alternative theory of economic policy is required embracing voters, political parties and governments. Such an economic theory of politics is outlined in Chapter 3.

Chapter 3

An Alternative Explanation of Public Policies: An Economic Theory of Politics

INTRODUCTION

The analysis of British governments as social welfare maximisers is not without its critics. The approach ignores the existing voting, political party and bureaucracy arrangements in a democracy. Difficulties inevitably arise in compiling a social welfare function which reflects the individual preferences of British voters and which contains no 'dictatorial' decisions. Who, for example, has ever seen a social welfare function for the UK? What does it look like? A simple majority voting rule does not clarify the issue since it is subject to the paradox of voting.[1] Let three individuals (1, 2, 3) rank three alternative policies (A, B, C) in order of preference. The policy context could be a vote on alternative regional policies, such as more labour mobility (A), greater mobility of capital (B) or do not intervene (C). The resulting votes might be:

	1st choice	2nd choice	3rd choice
Mr 1	A	B	C
Miss 2	B	C	A
Mrs 3	C	A	B

A majority prefers A to B and B to C. If preferences were transitive, a government would conclude that the community prefers A to C. This would be incorrect. A majority of voters prefer C to A so that the social outcome is intransitive! The simple majority-voting rule breaks down when society has to choose between more than two alternatives. Elections are also based on equality of voters so that voting is not 'weighted' by the strengths of individual preferences for alternative policies. Furthermore, since elections are general, an individual cannot reveal his 'feelings' for any single item within the 'mix' of issues presented to the electorate. Also, the social welfare model of British governments implies that politicians have no private motives and faithfully respond to the 'will of the majority'. These aspects of the political system raise doubts about the explanatory value of the orthodox social welfare maximising view of governments. Since the constitutional arrangements are likely to affect the behaviour of governments, an alternative model is required which incorporates assumptions about the behaviour of voters and political parties. The choice between the two models of government behaviour and policies will depend on which yields the more accurate explanations and predictions.

AN ECONOMIC THEORY OF POLITICS

An economic theory of democracy has been constructed by Anthony Downs.[2] It assumes that voters are utility-maximisers and that political parties are vote-maximisers. Each citizen will vote for the political party which he believes will provide him with a higher utility from government activity. Political parties behave like profit-maximising firms in capitalist economies. Just as firms produce in response to consumer demands and expected profits, so will political parties aim to supply policies which will gain the most votes. New political parties might enter the market if the established parties are not satisfying the preferences of a substantial number of voters (for example, nationalist parties for Scotland and Wales). In the Downs model, politicians are assumed to be motivated by self-interest and the desire to hold office. As a result, they formulate policies as a means of achieving office rather than seeking office to carry out preconceived policies. From these assumptions, Downs derives a number of testable propositions, three of which are especially relevant to explaining the macro- and micro-economic policies of British governments:

(1) In a two-party democracy, both parties agree on any issues favoured by a majority of voters. In such a system, party policies tend to be vague and similar (for example, concensus politics). A party which suffers drastic defeats will modify its ideology to resemble that of its more successful rival.
(2) Democratic governments tend to redistribute income from rich to poor.
(3) The policies of democratic governments tend to favour producers more than consumers.

The Downs model explains the logic, form and extent of state intervention in the British economy. *Governments and political*

parties need economic policies to obtain votes. In the two-party democracy of Britain, where the mass of voters seem to have been concentrated at the centre rather than at the extremes of the political
spectrum, the Downs model predicts 'consensus politics' and, hence,
similar economic policies between the major parties.[3] There are many
examples from the 1960s and 1970s. For employment objectives, both
parties have adopted similar approaches to the management of
aggregate demand and to regional policies. Attempts to control inflation resulted in both parties introducing incomes policies and
'policing' agencies in the form of the Labour Government's National
Board for Prices and Incomes (1965–71) followed by the Conservative
administration's Prices and Pay Commissions (1971–4). On industrial
relations, the major parties developed remarkably similar policies
during the late 1960s. For balance of payments targets, the consensus
of the 1960s favoured deflationary policies and fixed exchange rates.
Efforts to raise the economy's growth rate in the 1960s involved the
major parties in planning, with a Conservative Government establishing the National Economic Development Office which was retained by the subsequent Labour administration. Within the field of
micro-economic policy, the major parties have adopted similar
policies towards industrial training and the labour market (for
example, the 1964 Industrial Training Act and the 1974 Manpower
Services Commission); towards monopolies and restrictive practices
as expressed in the continued existence of the Monopolies Commission and the Restrictive Practices Court and the development during
the early 1970s of state support for private firms. Parties do, of
course, attempt to differentiate their policies but movements towards
the extremes of the political spectrum are likely to be constrained by
the potential losses of 'moderate' voters. On this basis, neither party
is likely to move towards the policy extremes of, say, complete
laissez-faire or total collectivism.

   Income distribution issues are recurrent in applied welfare
economics. Such issues also dominated the 1970s with debates about
the 'shares' of labour and capital in the UK's output, the taxation of
wealth and incomes policies. The Downs model explains government
policy towards distribution. Governments have the power to redistribute income through taxation or inflation. In the Downs model,
governments will have distributional objectives and will redistribute
income whenever it helps to maximise votes. Market economies are
likely to produce substantial inequalities with a few persons receiving
relatively large incomes and the majority relatively small incomes.
With one vote per person, vote-maximising governments will act in
favour of the most numerous income groups: those with relatively
low incomes. A government can gain votes by redistribution from the

wealthy few, so losing their votes, making the income available to
many persons, so gaining votes. 'Thus, the equality of franchise . . .
creates a tendency for government action to equalise incomes by redistributing them from a few wealthy persons to many less wealthy
ones.'[4] Interestingly, though, the Downs model suggests that vote-
maximising governments will not move towards complete equalisa-
tion of incomes. For example, a policy of equality might adversely
affect the economy's output. Low-income voters might believe that
their incomes from a large output distributed unequally are likely to
be greater than under complete equality. Low-income voters might
also believe that one day they too might be wealthy. Such beliefs
mean that voters are likely to oppose complete equality, with vote-
maximising governments responding to this preference. The opposition to complete equality might be reinforced by wealthy voters using
their resources to form an interest group to influence governments.
Interest groups are a major feature of the Downs model.

   Government policies will tend to favour producers more than
consumers. This appears to be a surprising and counter-intuitive
prediction. Surely, for vote-maximisation, would not a government
favour consumers? In fact, a characteristic of a theory is that it provides insights which are not immediately obvious. In the Downs
model, the costs of transactions and information explain the role of
interest groups. Producer interest groups (that is, management and
trade unions) are dominant in democracies because they have the
most to gain from trying to influence government policy in their
favour. Since most voters earn their incomes in one activity but spend
in many, the area of earning or producing is much more vital to them
than the area of spending or consuming. Producer interest groups
can afford substantial investments in information to influence
governments (for example, on the employment effects of price controls or cancelling, say, *Concorde* or a major weapons system) and
the potential returns are likely to make the investments worthwhile.
Consumers are in a different position. They cannot afford substantial
investments to acquire information on, say, the price effects of
monopoly, tariffs and agricultural support schemes. Nor do consumers usually form an integrated group since their interests are dispersed over many product markets so that there are substantial
transactions costs in organising a consumer group.[5] Thus, with the
Downs model, the economic policies of successive British governments are a means of maximising votes. Such vote-maximisation will
not necessarily result in maximum welfare for the community: votes
are likely to be maximised at a sub-optimal Paretian welfare position.[6]

THE ECONOMICS OF BUREAUCRACIES

The economic model of democracy can be expanded to include bureaucracies in the form of Ministries, government Departments and state agencies. Examples include the Ministry of Defence, the Departments of Industry, Employment and Education, the Monopolies and Manpower Services Commissions, NEDO, the Training Boards and the National Enterprise Board. Once state agencies have been established, the model assumes that they will behave as budget-maximisers. Larger budgets enable bureaucrats to satisfy their preferences for salaries, promotion, job security and such non-monetary advantages as power, prestige and opportunities to allocate contracts (see Chapter 11).[7] An implication of such behaviour is that state agencies frequently appear to be decreasing-cost activities. In pursuit of budget-maximisation, an agency's costs are likely to be based on its estimates of the buyer's (government's) downward-sloping demand curve for the activity rather than revealing the 'true' marginal cost conditions. Thus, apparently decreasing costs for state agencies might be the logical outcome of budget-maximising behaviour rather than evidence of market failure due to technical monopoly.

An economic theory of democracy which embraces political parties and bureaucracies suggests that British governments need macro- and micro-economic policies to obtain votes and that within this framework policy is likely to be further influenced by the budget-maximising aims of the Departments, Ministries and state agencies involved in public policy. The model is widely applicable, a classic example being defence and the military-industrial complex. Since defence is frequently an election issue, vote-maximising politicians have an incentive to be well-informed of 'public opinion'. However, median preference voters are likely to be uncertain in their assessment of defence. On the one hand, voters will favour civil goods and 'free-riding'; on the other, they will probably require some minimum level of protection. For vote-conscious politicians, the collection of information on diverse and uncertain voter preferences is costly. In addition, the citizens who are best informed on any specific issue are likely to be those whose incomes are directly affected: producer interest groups in the form of weapons firms (management, scientists and unions) tend to be dominant since, with their relatively favourable earnings, they have the most to gain from trying to influence government policy in their favour. The influence of weapons contractors will be reinforced by the budget-maximising aims of the Ministry of Defence and the Services. To maximise its budget, an agency can under-estimate the costs of a project for a given demand or it can attempt to increase or over-estimate demand (for example, an enemy's missile threat) and it can formulate programmes which are potential vote-winners for the government. Optimistic cost estimates have frequently occurred with major weapons projects such as combat aircraft, missiles and nuclear-powered submarines. On the demand side, the possibility arises that budget-maximising agencies together with producer interest groups have combined to persuade vote-conscious governments that the alleged or over-estimated social benefits of a project are sufficient to make it worthwhile. As a result, government policy is likely to favour producers rather than consumers. Similarly, British government support for advanced technology projects in the civil sector such as *Concorde* and the RB 211 jet engine is more appropriately explained by the economics of politics. With such projects there exists a readily identifiable producer interest group with relatively favourable earnings, employment, technology and other vote-winning attributes supported by a Ministry with a major budgetary involvement. Other examples of interest groups which embrace large government Departments include the academic–scientific–student complex, the road construction–car industry–motorist complex, the doctor–patient–health lobby and the building industry–householder group.

CONCLUSION: WHY DO GOVERNMENTS HAVE ECONOMIC POLICIES?

The economics of politics explains the extent and form of state intervention in the economy. Policies are formulated to obtain votes. They will reflect the preferences of the median voter and the influence of producer interest groups and bureaucracies. Voters are likely to reinforce producer interest groups since the ones who are best informed on any specific issue are likely to be those whose incomes are directly affected by it. In contrast, voters who are well-informed on issues that affect them as income-earners probably have less information on policies that affect them as consumers.[8]

The existence of government Departments influences public policy. Budget-maximising state agencies are likely to prefer state intervention of a market-displacing rather than a market-improving type. The state provision of services provides opportunities for larger budgets whereas the private supply of such activities adversely affects a bureau's budget. With income distribution policies, there might be a bias towards income-in-kind measures, such as government-subsidised housing, education and health. Spending programmes that provide income-in-kind can also obtain votes from producer interests. There is probably a bias against cash subsidies

such as negative income tax and voucher programmes. Such programmes are likely to restrict the role of the bureaucracy and are more
uncertain as vote-winners: they are less likely to yield votes from
identifiable producer interest groups who might otherwise be the
recipients of major government contracts.

The economics of politics is intuitively appealing and seems to
describe the real world. But intuition and description are not
sufficient criteria for accepting a theory. In its present form, the
model provides *ex post* rationalisations of the 'facts' which are too
general to be refuted. It needs, for example, to specify *ex ante* the
producer interest groups in the political market. Which collection of
economic agents constitutes an interest group and have governments
actually favoured such groups? Do governments always maximise
votes? If voters have short memories restricted to pre-election
periods (a testable hypothesis), governments might pursue other
objectives (which?) in the interim years. Much empirical work is
required. For example, do incomes policies and economies in defence
expenditure affect a government's total votes? In other words, work
in the economics of politics is promising but in its infancy. Much will
depend on whether an economics of politics offers alternative and
more accurate predictions than other models of government behaviour.[9]

Part II

Macro-Economic Policy

Chapter 4

Unemployment

INTRODUCTION: WHAT ARE THE POLICY ISSUES?

In the mid-1970s unemployment in the UK exceeded 1·5 million or some 6 per cent, with the rate differing between regions. Also in the 1970s, the average duration of unemployment rose. In the early 1960s about 15–20 per cent of unemployed men had been on the register continuously for over one year; in 1972–3, the figure was between 25 per cent and 33 per cent. These are substantial numbers, creating questions about the definition of unemployment, its causes and the range of policy solutions. What, for example, do the unemployment statistics tell us about the labour market? Is unemployment caused by markets re-allocating resources as consumer demands change and industries acquire different comparative advantages? Can large-scale unemployment be reduced by monetary policy? If so, is the desirable amount of unemployment zero?

HOW DOES THEORY DEFINE UNEMPLOYMENT?

Unemployment is a situation where there is an excess supply of labour at the ruling wage rate. Economists distinguish between involuntary and voluntary unemployment, the former existing where men who are willing to work at the current real wage rate are unable to obtain a job. An example is given in Figure 4.1 which shows an economy's labour market with labour demand and supply curves.[1] At the real wage rate $(W/P)_1$ there is excess labour supply or involuntary unemployment of N_2N_1. Full employment occurs at the market clearing price $(W/P)_e$ where involuntary unemployment is absent, although voluntary and frictional types could exist.

Recent developments in the micro-foundations of unemployment have started from the proposition that the labour market is not characterised by perfect information available at zero price and, by instant, costless adjustment. Instead, imperfect information exists amongst buyers and sellers about available labour, its offer-prices, vacancies and employers' bidding prices. In the circumstances, economic agents have an incentive to search the market. When demand falls in an industry, workers may not immediately accept a

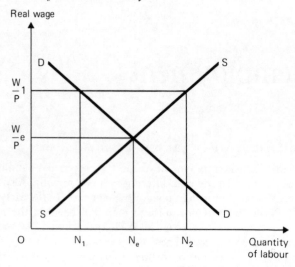

Figure 4.1

wage cut sufficient to retain their jobs, nor will they necessarily accept
the first job offered, since they believe that more attractive alternatives exist somewhere in the market. Thus, some unemployment can
be regarded as part of job search by which workers acquire additional
information about vacancies and wages. Search will be undertaken
so long as it is expected to be profitable. It will continue until, at the
margin, the expected income gains equal search costs in the form of
foregone earnings and out-of-pocket expenses. Private and state
employment agencies exist to provide information and reduce search
costs: they bring together buyers and sellers and so facilitate market
clearing. However, major problems arise when demands in the whole
economy are declining. It takes time for economic agents to learn and
acquire information about the new set of market clearing prices.[2]
Initially, labour will be reluctant to revise downwards its acceptable
wage offer and will prefer to search for a job at its existing expectations. After acquiring more information, workers will slowly revise
downwards their wage expectations. In other words, because of imperfect information there will be a time lag between losing a job and
acquiring a new one as workers search and learn about the changed
market situation.

WHAT DO THE UNEMPLOYMENT STATISTICS MEASURE?

Difficulties arise when the economist's definition of unemployment
is used to interpret the official UK statistics. Unemployment is

measured by the number of people who register as unemployed at the employment exchanges. Registration is necessary for those who wish to claim unemployment or supplementary benefits. As a result, the UK unemployment data are a by-product of the administrative arrangements for paying unemployment benefit. The official total includes the wholly unemployed or those displaced from permanent employment, as distinct from the temporarily stopped, together with the unemployables.[3] The latter consist of those who cannot work because of age, physical or mental difficulties, and those who will not work or who are unwilling to work: for example, they prefer to consume leisure and be voluntarily unemployed.

The official unemployment statistics do not provide an accurate measure of the people who are searching for jobs at the current wage rates. Not all the registered unemployed are in the involuntary category, nor do the figures embrace everyone who is actively seeking work. Some people are voluntarily unemployed. Others, such as married women and pensioners, do not register as unemployed so that they are excluded from the official statistics even though they might be seeking work.[4] In view of such problems, a further indicator of labour supply, namely the activity rate, is sometimes used. Activity or participation rates measure the proportion of the population of working age who are actually in the labour force, either employed or registered as unemployed.[5] However, not all those eligible for employment because they are part of the population of working age are necessarily seeking jobs. Some groups such as university students and married women with children cannot be regarded as potential recruits to the labour force, at least not at the existing wage rates.

SOME POLICY PROBLEMS

Governments frequently wish to raise employment and reduce registered unemployment. How closely associated are these two groups? For increases in employment to be exactly matched by a decline in registered unemployment requires the latter to be the only source of additional labour. This is not so. When employment is rising, there are a number of sources of extra manpower. In addition to reductions in registered unemployment, there might be an increase in the population of working age or variations in activity rates. For example, in the early 1970s it was estimated that to reduce unemployment by one person required the creation of an extra three jobs.[6] This suggests that to remove 500,000 from the UK unemployed register might require a further 1·5 million jobs. Nor is an expansion instantaneous. In the mid-1970s, each £1,000m. of extra aggregate demand due to lower taxation generated between 30,000 and 50,000 jobs, but only after an interval of twelve months.[7] Since expansions of aggregate demand eventually have inflationary and balance of payments consequences, it is necessary to ensure that the official unemployment statistics are a reliable indicator of the state of the labour market.

Critics assert that the official statistics exaggerate the amount of Keynesian involuntary unemployment. If so, increases in aggregate demand will result in inflation rather than in higher employment. It is argued that certain groups such as school-leavers, frictional and voluntarily unemployed, together with the unemployables, should be excluded from the official figures. But what is the economic basis of excluding some of these groups? If, for example, school-leavers are involuntarily unemployed, why omit them from the register? Even if the excluded categories are accepted, how do we distinguish, say, short- from long-term unemployment? One attempt at estimation showed that in 1972, when there was almost one million wholly unemployed, the exclusion of these categories gave a 'true' involuntary unemployment figure of some 350,000.[8] If involuntary unemployment is as low as this, there is little that can be achieved by expanding aggregate demand and a higher margin of unemployment might have to be accepted. Interestingly, since the mid-1960s, the UK appears to have experienced a change in the traditional relationships between vacancies and unemployment, so that given levels of aggregate demand are associated with higher levels of unemployment than previously. One controversial hypothesis explains the structural change in the labour market and the higher unemployment levels as a result of the introduction of redundancy pay and earnings-related unemployment benefit. Both are likely to have reduced the costs of job search and of unemployment or leisure and there is tentative support for the hypothesis.[9] Further results show that earnings-related unemployment benefit might have raised unemployment in 1968 by an average of 12,000 men out of about 500,000 male redundancies. In other words, higher unemployment benefits appear to have had only a small disincentive effect.[10]

WHAT ARE THE CAUSES OF UNEMPLOYMENT?

There are various types of unemployment each reflecting different causal factors and hence requiring different policy solutions. Economists usually distinguish frictional, structural and cyclical or deficient demand unemployment. Frictional or temporary unemployment is caused by short-run changes in the labour market and arises because labour supply does not adjust instantly to changes in demand. For example, workers quit their jobs to search for better ones and there will be time lags in moving from one job to another. As long as information is imperfect and adjustment takes time and costs, some amount of frictional unemployment is necessary for the efficient operation of the labour market. Policy can, however, correct some of the major imperfections and externalities which might cause market failure. Manpower policy might provide more funds to individuals to promote worthwhile job search and mobility which might otherwise be prevented due to imperfections in the human capital market (see Chapter 12).[11] Recent changes in the state's employment service involving new job-centres, self-service and greater circulation of vacancies have created an improved information exchange which is likely to reduce the time and costs involved in job search.[12] None of this should be interpreted to mean that policies are costless. Proposals to reduce frictional unemployment cannot avoid the issue of whether such reductions are worthwhile, or, are there more attractive alternative uses for the resources?

Structural unemployment arises from permanent, long-run changes in the demand for, and supply of, labour in specific industries and regions. It is caused by changes in the comparative cost position of an industry or a region, by technical progress or by shifts in consumer demands. Classic examples of structural change include the UK coal, shipbuilding and textile industries. The resulting structurally unemployed are people who are available for work but their skills and locations are out of line with job openings. Such unemployment can be reduced by manpower and regional policies involving retraining, the mobility of labour and capital, and employment subsidies. Some of these policies contribute to the re-allocation of resources from declining to expanding sectors in the economy, with favourable effects on economic growth. Others, such as employment subsidies and import controls, preserve jobs but at the expense of resource re-allocation.[13] However, if structural unemployment exists and governments wish to save jobs, selective policies aimed at vulnerable sectors might be extremely cost-effective methods of reducing unemployment, especially if the alternative is an expansion of aggregate demand. General reflation is more appropriate for cyclical unemployment.

WHAT CAUSES CYCLICAL UNEMPLOYMENT?

Cyclical or deficient-demand unemployment is economy-wide or macro-unemployment. It is caused by a general decline and deficiency of aggregate demand: hence it can be explained by a model of aggregate demand. A standard macro-model of income, expenditure and employment can be summarised:[14]

(1) Employment depends on output.
(2) Output depends on aggregate demand.
(3) Aggregate demand consists of private consumption and investment, government expenditure and net foreign transactions.
(4) Consumption depends on disposable income and the marginal propensity to consume.
(5) Investment depends on the marginal efficiency schedule and the rate of interest, more being bought at a lower price.
(6) The rate of interest is the price of money determined by the demand for, and supply of, money.[15]

The model shows that policy measures which raise private consumption and investment, government expenditure or net foreign injections will increase aggregate demand and so reduce unemployment. Fiscal and monetary policies are obvious possibilities. For example, fiscal measures such as lower income taxes will raise consumption, whilst greater state expenditure on, say, education or defence will also raise demand. Can monetary policy reduce unemployment due to deficient demand?

Monetary policy operates by changing the available supply or quantity of money in the economy. In a Keynesian model, changes in the money supply eventually change aggregate demand via the interest rate and investment. To reduce deficient demand unemployment, monetary policy has to raise private investment which, in turn, requires a reduction in the interest rate. To reduce the interest rate, the Bank of England can increase the quantity of money through, say, open-market purchases of government securities. With a downward-sloping demand for money or liquidity preference schedule, an increase in the money supply will reduce the interest rate, so increasing investment. And greater investment will, through the investment multiplier, increase aggregate demand and output, so raising employment.[16]

ARE THERE ANY LIMITS TO THE EFFECTIVENESS OF MONETARY POLICY?

Two major problems arise, involving the money market and investment. Each might reduce the effectiveness of monetary policy in creating employment. In the above model, the money supply is determined by the central bank. The money supply consists of coins, notes and bank deposits, with deposits a major component. It is assumed that bank deposits depend on the quantity of reserve assets held by the banking system and the reserve assets ratio. An example is shown in Figure 4.2, where cash is the reserve asset and the banks are required to hold, say, 8 per cent of their deposits in cash.[17] On this basis, deposits will be $12\frac{1}{2}$ times the volume of cash with c_1 supporting d_1 of deposits. The Bank of England can increase the money supply either by raising the quantity of cash held by the banks from c_1 to c_2 or by reducing the cash ratio from a to b.

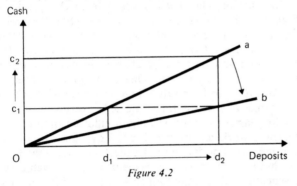

Figure 4.2

An increase in the money supply does not always reduce interest rates. Theory shows the limiting case of the liquidity trap where the liquidity preference schedule becomes horizontal. An example is given in Figure 4.3(a).[18] Over the liquidity trap range, it is not possible to reduce the interest rate through an expansion of the money supply. In other words, in the liquidity trap, there are no prospects

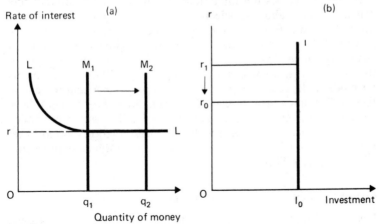

Figure 4.3

of raising investment by lowering interest rates. Thus, theory shows that the economy might not be able to achieve full employment by relying on monetary policy. There is, however, no empirical support for this limiting case. Studies show 'conclusively that the demand for money is stable and inversely related to the interest rate, there being no empirical support for the liquidity trap hypothesis'.[19]

Even without the liquidity trap, monetary policy might be an ineffective employment creator if the investment demand schedule is perfectly inelastic or relatively unresponsive to changes in interest rates. Figure 4.3(b) shows a limiting case such that there will be no multiplier effect on the level of income. In fact, evidence indicates that interest rates have a relatively small effect on investment. It seems that investment responds more to changes in output and capacity utilisation than to interest rates. One study of UK manufacturing from 1956 to 1967 also found that there was a lag of over two years before a change in interest rates affected investment, whereas the corresponding lag for output was about eighteen months.[20] Inevitably, empirical work has its problems. How does the investigator accurately measure entrepreneurial expectations so that he can be confident that he is measuring movements along a given investment demand schedule, rather than joining points on different curves? If uncertainty dominates investment decisions, the schedule will resemble a wide band with an indeterminate range where small changes in interest rates will not affect investment. Furthermore, UK governments have usually permitted only relatively small variations in interest rates, which might further explain the interest-inelasticity of investment.

Because of the possible limitations of monetary policy, doubts were originally raised about its effectiveness in reducing deficient-demand unemployment. Fiscal policy, which permits discretionary state intervention, was advocated as the most appropriate method of achieving full employment. Certainly, the employment experience of the UK since 1945 compares favourably with the 1930s: governments have been able, and willing, to expand aggregate demand to achieve their full employment targets. However, different problems have emerged as full employment has involved conflicts with other policy objectives. Recently, concern with continued inflation has led to renewed interest in monetary policy in the form of the modern version of the Quantity Theory.[21]

CONFLICTS IN POLICY OBJECTIVES

Less unemployment is preferable to more unemployment, *ceteris paribus*. Problems arise and choices are required when reductions in unemployment conflict with other policy objectives, such as the balance of payments and price stability. With a fixed exchange rate, a deficit on the current account of the balance of payments might emerge, as output and employment are expanded to the full employment target. It could be that with fixed parities, international payments are only in balance at less than full employment. Monetary and fiscal policies can raise aggregate demand to full employment but they cannot achieve both full employment and equilibrium in the balance of payments. Some other policy instrument, such as flexible exchange rates, is required for the balance of payments target (see Chapters 1 and 6).

Full employment might also mean less price stability. UK evidence has shown that reductions in unemployment have been associated with rising wages and prices. The relationships are shown by the Phillips curve which remains a useful example of the theory of economic policy and provides a basis for understanding UK economic policy up to the mid-1960s. In Figure 4.4, the Phillips curve (W) shows a relationship between the annual rate of change of money wage rates ($\dot{w}$) and the registered unemployment rate (U). The curve has been extended to show a relationship (P) between the annual rate of change of prices ($\dot{p}$) and the unemployment rate. In

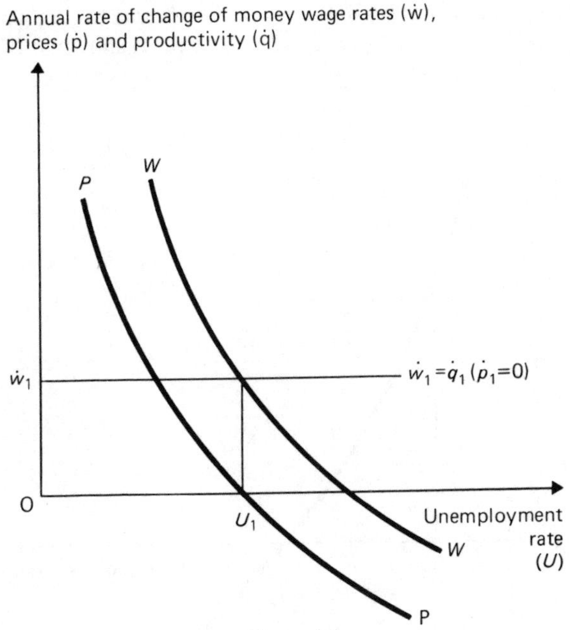

Annual rate of change of money wage rates ($\dot{w}$), prices ($\dot{p}$) and productivity ($\dot{q}$)

Figure 4.4

Figure 4.4, the two curves are related by assuming that price changes depend on changes in wages and productivity. At U_1, with productivity ($\dot{q}$) rising at 2 per cent per year, wages could rise at a similar rate without price inflation. Until the mid-1960s, U_1 was estimated to be about $2\frac{1}{2}$ per cent for the UK. Perhaps the most surprising feature of the original Phillips curve was its apparent success in 'explaining' the association between inflation and unemployment over a long time horizon from the 1860s to 1966.[22] The curve seemed to be stable despite technical progress, wars, changing governments and doubts about the accuracy of the official unemployment statistics as indicators of involuntary unemployment. Moreover, the use of money wage rates has to be reconciled with the traditional emphasis on real wages. If Figure 4.1 is valid, the original Phillips curve requires a reduction in labour's real wage for employment to rise.

CONCLUSION: IS IT DESIRABLE TO REDUCE UNEMPLOYMENT TO ZERO?

Conflicts in policy objectives, as shown by the original Phillips curve, require policy-makers to choose. The targets and optimising approaches illustrate the choice problem. With the targets approach, governments might have fixed ideas about the maximum acceptable inflation and unemployment rates. An example is shown in Figure 4.5

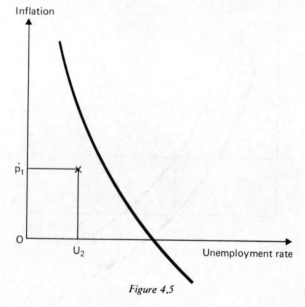

Figure 4.5

where the maxima are $\dot{p}_1$ and U_2. In such a situation, a government has to revise its ideas about the acceptable maxima, since it can only achieve one and not both. At the same time, long-run policies might be used to achieve a leftward shift in the inflation-unemployment trade off. Incomes policies and regional policies have been advocated as methods of achieving such shifts. Pay policies were believed to reduce union militancy and to change the traditional relationship between costs and prices, so reducing inflation at any level of unemployment. Regional policies, by transferring excess labour demand to areas of excess labour supply or vice versa, could reduce aggregate unemployment without accentuating inflationary pressure.

The optimising approach assumes policy-makers have a preference function showing that they will trade, say, a higher inflation rate for less unemployment. Assume that this preference function can be shown by a set of concave indifference curves, such that higher utility is obtained by moving towards the origin, as in Figure 4.6.[23] Efforts to maximise utility will be constrained by the inflation-unemployment frontier (curve P). In Figure 4.6, reductions in unemployment below R involve costs or sacrifices of price stability. The policy-maker will aim his aggregate demand measures at point A where he reaches the highest level of utility on the inflation-unemployment frontier. The reduction in unemployment from R to its optimal level at S involves a cost, in inflationary terms, which is

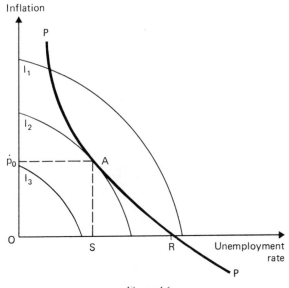

Figure 4.6

acceptable to the policy-maker. Thus, point *A* represents an optimal rate of unemployment and inflation. Although the original Phillips curve provided fairly accurate predictions on the relationship between inflation and unemployment until 1966–7, serious forecasting errors have arisen since the late 1960s. A new inflation seemed to have exploded.

Chapter 5

Inflation

INTRODUCTION

Inflation dominated discussions of British economic policy in the 1970s. For governments, this involved trade unions and industrial relations, various forms of prices and incomes policies, control of the money supply, and general deflation. By 1975, the major issues were clear. Policy-makers were emphasising that 'One man's pay rise is not only another man's price rise: it might also cost him his own job – or his neighbour's job'.[1] Inflation was seen as a cause of unemployment when Keynesian analysis expects unemployment to be associated with deflation. Observers of British economic policy with memories of the 1960s might well ask whatever happened to the Phillips curve? In the circumstances of the mid-1970s, it was claimed that there were no doubts and disagreements about the Government's objective function: the nation was '... united in insisting that the rise in the cost of living must be curbed. There is no difference of opinion about that'.[2] As for the causes of the problem, public policy suggested that no '... reasonable person can put all the blame for runaway inflation on wage rises or trade unions. There are many other causes. There was the steep increase in 1972–3 in world costs of food and raw materials and the colossal rise in oil prices in 1973–4.'[3] Such a statement is consistent with a supply side or cost-push hypothesis of inflation. Vote-maximising governments with a monopoly of the domestic money supply are understandably reluctant to reveal any causal involvement in inflation! To solve the problem, massive immediate cuts in state expenditure were rejected because they '... would have created mass unemployment and set back our chances of economic recovery through industrial growth. There was only one alternative: to tackle inflation by reducing our rate of increase in wages and salaries. Pay restraint will reduce inflation without sacrificing our long-term goals.'[4] Such policy statements raise fascinating and controversial questions related to the methodology of economic policy. What, for example, is the underlying model of inflation and of the economy which can be deduced from such policy statements, especially those which relate to pay restraint and long-term goals? Are there any alternative models and, if so, what is the evidence on their relative explanatory powers and predictive accuracy?[5] If in-flation and unemployment are *positively* associated, has the Phillips curve collapsed? What is the evidence on the effectiveness of pay-restraint policies? Are they the apparently costless policy which is sometimes implied?

THE CAUSES OF INFLATION

Since inflation is concerned with rising absolute price levels, it is usually explained in terms of demand or supply factors, each with different policy implications. If an inflation is due to excess aggregate demand for goods, or an inflationary gap, following a rise in govern-ment spending, exports or investment, it can be controlled by defla-tionary monetary and fiscal policies; but with adverse effects on out-put and employment. Alternatively, if an inflation is due to supply or cost factors, it is frequently concluded that a prices and incomes policy is required to restrain 'aggressive' wage-bargaining and price increases and to change the traditional relationship between costs and prices. Although useful as a taxonomy, this simple distinction is not without its problems. It is a continuation of the classic debate about whether prices are determined by demand or supply alone, and on which Marshall commented that the argument was very much like asking whether the upper or lower blade of a pair of scissors really cuts a piece of paper.[6]

Problems arise in defining inflation. Which is the appropriate price index, especially when there are new and improved products and changes in consumer preferences? Does it make any difference whether rising prices are correctly or incorrectly anticipated? Where prices are subject to state control, should allowances be made for black markets, queues and possible subsidies to 'key' items? Further complications arise for an open economy where some of the infla-tionary pressure is likely to be reflected in greater imports and re-duced exports with consequences for the balance of payments and the exchange rate. With fixed exchange rates, if the UK's inflation rate consistently exceeded that of its foreign competitors, a balance of payments deficit would result, requiring either a domestic deflation and/or a change in the exchange rate. Fixed parities mean that Britain could not indefinitely sustain an inflation rate substantially different from the rest of the world. The balance of payments impli-cations of inflation are considered in the next chapter.

The simple demand-pull and cost-push models with their distinc-tions between product and factor markets, offer alternative explana-tions of inflation. In the demand model, inflation is initially caused by excess demand for goods which results in a rise in the general level of product prices. In the next time period, this price rise will be reflected in an increase in the derived demand for labour, so leading to higher wage rates.[7] Thus, demand inflation is caused by factors on the demand side of the product market with feedback effects on the labour market and corresponding rises in the prices of goods and labour. In cost-push models, the causality is reversed and the initial causal push comes from supply or cost factors. These include trade union wage claims, higher import prices or greater profit margins. Attention is most frequently given to the monopoly bargaining power of trade unions. The wages-push explanation of inflation means that an increase in wages can take place in the absence of excess demand in the labour market, and that subsequently the higher wage costs are passed on to consumers in the form of higher product prices. Tests of these explanations of inflation depend on each yielding alternative predictions. Since both predict rising prices and costs, once an inflation has started, the time-sequence of changes in prices and wages does not readily enable a distinction to be made between demand and supply hypotheses. There are, though, alternative output and employment effects. A demand inflation is associated with either no change or an increase in output and employment, depending on the elasticity of the aggregate supply curve in the vicinity of full employment. Cost-push inflation will be associated with *falling* output and employment. The most telling evidence of such an inflation is a rising price level with output appreciably below its full employment level and continuing to decline. Although the predictions differ, empirical tests are complicated by the Government's commitment to maintain full employment, so that any cost-push unemployment is likely to be offset by expansions of aggregate demand. Of course, once decision-makers in firms and unions incorporate a government's full employment policy into their expectations, conceptual difficulties arise in distinguishing cost-push forces which are truly independent of demand. This raises a fundamental question about the underlying causal factors which the simple inflation models generally classify as demand or supply forces. What are the sources of demand-pull and cost-push?

THE QUANTITY THEORY OF MONEY: IS MONEY IMPORTANT?

Since rising price levels are monetary events, an obvious starting-point is the role of money as a causal factor in demand inflation. The Monetarist school with its modern version of the Quantity Theory maintains that the money value of the economy's output depends on the stock of money and its velocity of circulation.[8] For this to be a theory rather than a tautology, attention is concentrated on the factors determining the supply of, and demand for, money and the associated market clearing process.[9] The supply of money is assumed to be determined by the central bank. The demand for money in real terms depends on expected real income and the cost of holding money as determined by the expected rates of return on money, financial and physical assets and the expected rate of change of prices. If at the ruling price level there is an increase in the supply of money, individuals will try to reduce their excess money balances by spending on goods and securities. With unemployment in the economy the result will be a rise in aggregate demand which will increase output and employment. This happened in Britain in the early 1970s, when the increase in the money supply provided a short-run stimulus to real growth. At full employment, the result of an increase in the money supply would be a rise in the general price level. However, the short-run effects of a monetary expansion on output and employment, on the one hand, and prices, on the other, cannot be predicted by the Quantity Theory.[10] This is essentially a theory of nominal income. It predicts that an increase in the stock of money will raise the level of money national income and the Monetarists have been impressed by the evidence on '. . . the closeness, regularity and predictability of the relation among the stock of money, the level of prices and the level of output *over any considerable period of years*'.[11] For the USA between 1949 and 1968, it has been estimated that a 1 per cent increase in the money supply would raise nominal income by $1 \cdot 1$ per cent to $2 \cdot 3$ per cent, depending on the definition of the money stock.[12] For the UK between 1880 and 1968, the evidence is 'consistent with the hypothesis that the stock of money does have a significant influence on the level of activity in the economy. And for most of the years surveyed the effect of money on prices and incomes is significant and in the predicted direction.'[13] Evidence of the correlation between prices and money in the ten major industrial nations for 1960–74 is shown in Figure 5.1. The peaks in price changes clearly *follow* peaks in the growth of the money stock, with varying lags of between six and nine months and up to three years. Such evidence leads the Monetarists to conclude that inflations are explained by the behaviour of the money supply and that Britain is no exception. Friedman maintains that 'inflation is always and everywhere a monetary phenomenon . . . and can be produced only by a more rapid increase in the quantity of money than in output'.[14] There is a general agreement that inflation is a monetary phenomenon in that it either causes or accompanies rising prices. Not everyone accepts that excessive monetary expansion is the *cause* of inflation. Cost-push, militancy, political-sociological explanations are also popular.[15]

Per cent per annum

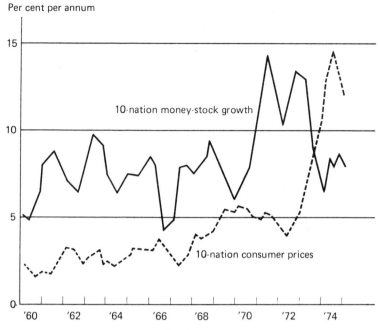

Figure 5.1.   Prices Follow Money's Lead

Note: Plottings represent three-quarter moving averages of the sum of ten major industrialised countries' narrowly defined money-stock growth rates and their inflation rates, measured by the consumer price index, each weighted by its share in their summed gross national products. Information from IMF, Federal Reserve Board, Bank of England, Bank of Canada, Bank of France, Deutsche Bundesbank, Bank of Japan, Bank of Italy.

Source: First National City Bank, *Monthly Economic Letter* (July 1975).

Controversy over the Monetarist interpretation of inflation is wide-ranging, involving questions of methodology and of the analytical and empirical validity of the demand and supply functions in the Quantity Theory. The methodological criticisms centre on whether statistical associations as shown by high correlation coefficients in single equation models are conclusive evidence of causation. An observed association between nominal income and the money supply raises difficulties of determining conclusively whether Y responds to M or the other way round. Some British economists have maintained that the money supply *responds* to economic conditions and is not a determinant of these conditions.[16] Such criticisms are further supported by UK evidence which shows that since 1945, money has been relatively unimportant in explaining variations in nominal income.

Indeed, one UK study found that changes in the money stock explained less than 10 per cent of the variation in Y between 1955 and 1962,[17] a result which appears to provide little support for money supply policies. And, yet, it is plausible that if the central bank's counter-cyclical policies are successful, the observed changes in Y will be small relative to changes in M, so reducing the statistical association between these variables and leading the researcher to the mistaken conclusion that monetary policy was ineffective! Such examples show that for empirical work, observed statistical relationships need to be related to an underlying economic theory with explanations and predictions derived from a set of definitions and assumptions. Using the criterion of predictive accuracy, a famous study by Friedman and Meiselman compared the Keynesian and Quantity theories in an attempt to find the better predictor of consumer expenditure. For the Keynesian model, it was hypothesised that changes in autonomous expenditure[18] would, via the standard multiplier, change income, and induce a change in consumption. For the Quantity Theory, it was predicted that a change in the money supply would directly change consumption. Using single equation models and US data for 1897–1958, it was found that apart from the period 1929–34, the Quantity Theory was by far the better predictor. Although the models yield alternative predictions, controversy arose about the appropriateness of the statistical tests and, in particular, whether the observed association could be ambiguous. For example, a plausible analytical relationship exists between the money supply and the investment component of autonomous expenditure and this interdependence makes it difficult to identify their independent influences on income: money could be capturing some of the influence of autonomous expenditure. Similar problems arise from a two-way chain of causation between, on the one hand, the money supply and consumption and, on the other, investment and consumption. In other words, the criticisms of the Friedman-Meiselman tests were based on the proposition that they used simple, single equations to represent what in 'reality' are extremely complex relationships within the economy. The introduction of lagged variables meets some of these methodological criticisms. When this was done for the UK for 1870–1963, it was found that the money supply was a slightly better predictor of the *level* of consumption expenditure whilst *changes* in autonomous expenditure gave better predictions of *changes* in consumption.[19] At a more general level, studies of different countries over different time periods show that 'practically without exception . . . changes in the money stock appear to lead changes in money incomes . . .' and that '. . . in the absence of evidence to the contrary, a consistent lead is a *prima facie* indication of causation'.[20]

For policy purposes, the modern Quantity Theory is further criticised because it is subject to variable and lengthy time lags, without indicating how a change in nominal income will be divided between output and prices. Such criticisms are in danger of requiring a quantitative, as distinct from the more usual qualitative, specification of theories in economics. The Quantity Theory simply offers qualitative predictions with a general qualification that the relationships operate over a 'considerable period of years'. The precise size and strength of the relationships is an empirical matter. Here, us evidence shows that monetary policy might influence output and employment within six to twelve months, whilst price effects are subject to a lag of from one to three years. In the UK, it seems that monetary policies influence economic activity with a lag of at least three months and no longer than fifteen months.[21]

Similar controversy surrounds the demand for money function, in particular the stability of the velocity of circulation. Critics have argued that velocity is volatile and unstable and that its variability can offset changes in the money supply. These objections are empirical and their resolution requires a clear statement of the predictions of the modern Quantity Theory and their empirical testing. The modern Theory does *not* predict that velocity is a constant, unchanging magnitude. British evidence for 1952–73 shows that even in the long run, velocity has varied between about 2·2 and 3·5 which is sufficient to refute a constant velocity hypothesis.[22] Instead, the Monetarists maintain that the demand for money is such a relatively stable function that predictions can be made about variations in velocity.[23] Briefly, changes in velocity or in the demand for money will result from changes in relative prices, incomes and tastes. If, for example, the money supply is increased, people will *eventually* respond by increased spending so that velocity will also rise. In other words, firms and households take time to adjust, so that the initial effect of an unexpected increase in the money supply will be a short-run reduction in velocity. Economic units will eventually respond by raising their expenditure plans and spending more, so that velocity will rise towards its long-run equilibrium.

This is the sort of predicted behaviour which has to be refuted if the Theory is to be rejected. It clearly recognises temporary disequilibrium variations in velocity as observed in the UK between 1963 and 1971,[24] so increasing the uncertainty of predicting the short-run effects of a change in the money supply and its use as an instrument of 'fine tuning'. Evidence does, though, confirm that the demand for money function is relatively stable, as hypothesised by the Monetarists. Indeed, after surveying the literature, two British economists have concluded that the evidence on '. . . the stability of the demand for money function . . . and the evidence which we have cited on the responsiveness of the inflation rate to excess demand lends considerable weight to the proposition that a sustained expansion of the money supply . . . is both a necessary and a sufficient condition for a sustained inflation'.[25]

Even if it is accepted that money is of some relevance for policy, questions arise as to whether interest rates or the money supply are the appropriate target indicators for the UK. Immediately, there are definitional and data problems. The relevant interest variable is the real rate but the data refer to nominal values. As for the money supply, there are at least three possible definitions which can be used as targets. M1, a narrow definition consisting of currency in circulation and UK residents' current account deposits; M3 which is M1 plus deposit accounts, and M5 which is M3 together with private-sector liquid assets with non-banking institutions such as building societies. Evidence shows that whilst the three measures tend to move together, their average growth and amplitude differ, with the growth rates of the wide definition of money supply being substantially greater than that of the narrow series. Moreover, when changes in M1, M3 and M5 are compared with movements in nominal and real interest rates, the alternative indicators are capable of giving significantly different readings of policy both in the very short run, say quarter-by-quarter, and in terms of comparisons across periods of years.[26] Nor does theory offer unambiguous guidelines.[27]

Assume that the monetary authorities aim to achieve and maintain a full employment level of real income and that this can be approximated by either a target interest rate (r^*) or a target money supply (M^*). At full employment, if the authorities choose r^* as their target variable and the interest rate rises due to increased investment, then efforts to re-establish r^* by increasing the money supply will simply increase demand pressure in the system! In fact, if the authorities use a Keynesian model, a rising interest rate is likely to be interpreted as reflecting a *rising* demand for money. By comparison, the Quantity Theory would interpret a rise in interest rates as a symptom of declining rather than a rising demand for money: economic units may be reducing their holdings of both cash and securities in order to buy more goods, and sales of securities will cause interest rates to rise. Operating on M^* as a target is not without problems. Assume that, through a process of deposit expansion, the money supply will increase in response to a rise in the interest rate. If there is an increase in the demand for money, interest rates will rise, so reducing income below its full employment level. At the same time, the higher interest rates will induce a rise in the money supply above M^* and the authorities will react by attempting to reduce it to its target level; such a contraction will cause a further fall in output and move the system away from full employment. In view of these ambiguities and controversies over the interpretation of evidence, it is perhaps not surprising that economists disagree. Inevitably, such disagreements frequently reflect their values '. . . as there is no view except from a viewpoint and no answers except to questions'.[28]

COST-PUSH THEORIES: ARE WAGES AND
UNIONS IMPORTANT?

Critics of the Quantity Theory argue that it ignores money wages and hence neglects *the* major cause of rising prices.[29] Their criticism appears persuasive since most people recognise that in post-war Britain money wages have continued to rise and that labour costs are the major component of the economy's total output. An example is given in Table 5.1 which shows the immediate contributors to UK inflation, 1973–4. Earnings made a dominant contribution in 1974 with import prices playing a substantial part in the previous period. Profits and indirect taxes do not appear to have been a major factor in 1974. Convincing though Table 5.1 might be, it has to be recognised that simple statistical associations, casual empiricism and intuition are not necessarily evidence of causation. The Monetarists have been similarly criticised!

Trade union pushfulness is frequently hypothesised to be a major source of wage increases and of cost-push inflation. In a pioneering

Table 5.1 Contributions to Six-Monthly Percentage Increase in UK's Market Price Index

	Estimated contributions					
Period	*Employment Income per unit of output*	*Gross profits per unit of output*	*Net indirect taxes*	*Import prices*	*Residual error*	*Total*
1973 Q_2 to Q_4	+2·9	+0·8	+6·3	+2·8	+6·4	7·2
1973 Q_4 to 1974 Q_2	+4·7	−0·9	+1·35	+5·5	+0·65	11·3
1974 Q_2 to Q_4	+6·9	+2·0	−1·3	+1·6	−0·3	8·9

Source: R. G. D. Allen, 'The Immediate Contributors to Inflation', in *Economic Journal* (September 1975).

study, Hines hypothesised that militancy is necessary for a wage-push and that union aggressiveness can be measured by the level and rate of change of unionisation.[30] On the basis of the original UK study from 1893–1961 and subsequent extensions to 1970, Hines concluded that militancy as measured by his unionisation variables '. . . is the most robust and important determinant of the rate of change of money wage rates'.[31] No relationship was found between pushfulness and the demand for labour as measured by unemployment. Other UK studies have also found support for the role of union pushfulness. For example, evidence shows that the unions became more militant under the Conservative Government of 1952–6 compared with the previous Labour administration: wage rates increased by almost three more index points after 1952 than before, *ceteris paribus*. It has also been found that between 1954 and 1970, union activity as reflected in the number of strikes had a significant influence on the rate of wage inflation.[32]

Any assessment of the supporting evidence for variants of the cost-push hypothesis has to start from the underlying model, and especially the assumptions about the behaviour of the economic units. Theory defines a monopoly union as a single seller of labour with no close substitutes. A union which monopolises a previously competitive labour market can raise wage rates, but usually at the expense of lower employment. There are a number of recognised exceptions to this employment effect, namely, monopsony and oligopoly markets, firms with organisational 'slack' and circumstances where the possibilities of factor substitution are relatively low.[33] However, these specific situations are unlikely to be present throughout the economy in perpetuity so that eventually wage increases will encounter employment effects. Thus, if unions continue to push for wage increases there will be an adverse effect on the employment of their members, creating two sets of questions for the strict wage-push hypothesis. First, what is the objective function of monopoly unions: are they maximising wages or membership or some utility function? The wage-push models simply assert that 'when unions are being aggressive they simultaneously increase their membership and bid up wage rates'.[34] No explanation is offered as to why unions become 'aggressive' and how they increase membership. If, for example, union aggression results from a reduction in labour's *real* wage, then models which attempt to explain variations in *money* wage rates are likely to be concentrating on the wrong variable. Interestingly, the original Hines' study gave indirect support for this interpretation when it found that the rate of change of prices was a major determinant of the change in unionisation. Union aggressiveness to defend real wages could also be consistent with explanations of inflation in terms of class-distributional struggles, although the theoretical and empirical validity of such propositions leaves much to be desired. Worker and capitalist classes are never clearly defined; nor does it follow that all unions represent *poor* workers or that the poor are union members; nor does the UK evidence since 1945 show that unions have achieved a long-run increase in labour's share in the national income.

A second set of questions relates to the concept of monopoly power. What is the continual source of a union's monopoly power when increasing numbers of its members are losing their jobs following continuous wage increases? Clearly, there are potential inconsistencies between falling membership and the Hines' unionisation hypothesis. Similar worries arise over the use of the rates of change and levels of *aggregate* unionisation as measures of monopoly power in individual labour markets. This is not to deny that when a labour market is monopolised, there will be a once-and-for-all increase in relative wages and prices; but this cannot be an explanation of *continuing* inflation, especially when it is remembered that there have been periods of rising prices and no unions.[35] As with the Monetarist controversy, correlation-causation problems are present. For example, there might be a two-way causation between changes in wages and unionisation. Unions might also be acting as information and transactions agencies for restoring monetary equilibrium in an economy with an expanding money supply. On this point, the original Hines' study specified a causal link from price changes to unionisation and finally to wages: such a model is not inconsistent with a demand explanation of inflation.[36] This illustrates a major problem in empirical work, namely the clear identification and testing of the *alternative* predictions of competing theories. The 'world' seems to be varying shades of grey rather than a distinctive black and white. Other UK evidence, such as the original Phillips curve, does not help. An inflation-unemployment trade off could be consistent with cost or demand explanations of inflation, the former being reflected in a relatively steeper function. None of this helps a government with the choice of an appropriate policy for achieving price stability. Until the late 1960s, the original Phillips curve seemed to be a useful framework for presenting the policy choice: deflate and accept higher unemployment for price stability, and/or try to reduce the conflicts through regional and incomes policies.

WHATEVER HAPPENED TO THE PHILLIPS CURVE?

With the benefit of hindsight, perhaps the question should be whatever happened to economics? The original curve was very much an empirical creation: a statistical association of observed outcomes satisfying standard statistical criteria for curve fitting but ignoring underlying causal explanations, especially the consistency of the trade off with established macro-models and their micro-foundations. Following Phillips's pioneering study there was a rush to fit curves for every nation in Christendom – and some outsiders![37] Extra variables representing labour reserves, regional unemployment, productivity, profits, price expectations and incomes policies were added on an *ad hoc* basis, the aim being to improve 'fits'. Hardly anyone questioned the economic logic of the observations and the distinctions between movements along, and shifts of, the curve. Admittedly, in the early stages, simple explanations of the curve were offered, mainly of an excess demand type. For example, wages and prices increase at a faster rate with greater excess demand, whilst a rise in unemployment and excess capacity increases competition for jobs and market sales, so slowing any upward pressure of wages and prices. Years later, it seems surprising that, at the time, economists so readily accepted a wage-employment relationship which did not incorporate *real* wages and which made money wages rather than employment the dependent variable. Perhaps the general acceptability of the curve – almost like the flat earth theory of navigation – resulted from its reliability as a forecaster of wage increases in the UK, at least until about 1967, after which the traditional relationship appeared to collapse. In 1972, for example, with unemployment at 3·7 per cent, the curve predicted a rate of wage increase of under 1 per cent: the actual rate exceeded 10 per cent. Clearly, a return to the 'drawing board' was required, as well as new explanations, many of which centred on the possibility that the curve had been shifting and that the shifts were predictable. For taxonomic purposes, the Phillips curve can be regarded as the outcome of two other sets of relationships, namely one between wages and excess demand and the other between excess demand and unemployment as shown in Figure 5.2.[38] Changes in either or both of these relationships can lead to shifts in the curve.

The wages-excess demand function (quadrant I) can be shifted upwards by greater trade union pushfulness. Increased union militancy can reflect accelerating price expectations, reductions in public expenditure, tax increases[39] or the adverse real income effects of pay policies and devaluation, as well as opposition to state legislation on industrial relations: such events occurred in the period 1966–75, when the Phillips curve exploded. The fact that workers raised money wages in response to higher tax rates modifies the conventional view that increased taxation is anti-inflationary. The excess demand-unemployment relationship can also change in response to variations in the regional dispersion of unemployment rates and search be-

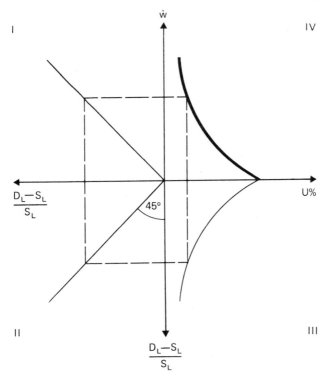

Figure 5.2

haviour in the labour market. Between 1945 and 1966, unemployment dispersion exerted upward pressure on the aggregate rate of
wage change of more than two percentage points.[40] It has also been
asserted that since 1966 redundancy payments plus increased unemployment benefit have reduced the costs of both leisure and job
search, so that there has been a fundamental change in the traditional
relationship between unemployment and vacancies. The result has
been a reduction in the effective supply of labour at any given level
of unemployment and vacancies. There is some tentative support for
this hypothesis, the UK evidence for 1966–71 suggesting that the
effect of the Social Security changes can be estimated by dividing the
recorded unemployment rate by a 'correcting' factor of 1·44.[41] Other
evidence also shows that registered unemployment may not have
been an accurate indicator of excess labour supply. Tests with alternative indicators have confirmed the absence of a Phillips relationship between inflation and registered unemployment during the
1960s but an alternative trade off between inflation and labour

hoarding has been identified.[42] Once again, the taxonomic approach provides only *ad hoc* explanations of shifts in the Phillips curve without any underlying theory, especially at the micro-level. A major attempt at explanation incorporates inflationary expectations and labour market search behaviour to derive a set of short-run Phillips curves but only one long-run curve, which is vertical at the natural unemployment rate. The resulting explanation is remarkably consistent with classical economic theory with its distinction between real and nominal magnitudes,[43] and provides further insights into the Monetarists' model of inflation.

In a conventional model of the labour market, equilibrium employment depends on the demand for labour, as reflected by the 'real' forces of labour's marginal physical product, and the supply of labour resulting from workers' preferences between real income and leisure. Markets tend to be cleared through the real wage rate and at equilibrium there will be no excess demand in the economy as a whole. In such an equilibrium, unemployment due to frictions and imperfections is classified as the natural unemployment rate. Employment depends on real rather than on money forces and real wages can remain constant even though money wages and prices are changing. As long as people completely and correctly anticipate, and fully adjust to, the rate of inflation, it cannot affect real economic activity. Inevitably, *short-run* problems arise because in forming expectations about future price changes, economic units have imperfect information. Knowledge of market prices and opportunities is neither costlessly nor instantly available and transactions costs are required to change behaviour, the inevitable adjustment period being reflected in money illusion. For example, if the inflation has been about 5 per cent for several years, firms and workers will tend to expect it to remain around 5 per cent, with wages and prices expected to rise at a similar rate. Assume now a vote-maximising government aims to reduce unemployment below its natural level by expanding the money supply at a rate which will *eventually* move the economy to an inflation rate of, say, 10 per cent. At first, few people will realise what has happened, given the recent stability of inflation. As long as price expectations remain unchanged and money illusion operates, the monetary expansion will *temporarily* increase output and employment along with prices. There results a short-run Phillips curve for a given set of expectations. Initially, rising nominal wages and prices are interpreted as rising real magnitude by labour and firms, respectively. Workers whose previous search experience in the labour market had led to the choice of voluntary unemployment, now interpret rising money wages as rising real incomes and so re-enter the job market: initially, they do not completely anticipate, and adjust to, the new inflation rate. Similarly, firms initially recognise rising prices and interpret the situation as one of falling real wages, hence their increased demand for labour.[44] Thus, workers perceive the situation as one of rising real wages and so supply the extra labour required for firms who, in the event, regard the change as one of falling real wages. However, the increased output and employment will only be temporary since both workers and firms will 'learn from experience' and revise their price and wage expectations to take account of the new inflation rate. When workers realise what has happened, they will bargain to restore their real wages, and employment will fall to its original and natural level, where the new inflation rate is completely and correctly anticipated. To reduce unemployment again, the government has to re-create money illusion by unexpectedly boosting the inflation rate, so that the authorities are required to operate on successively higher short-run Phillips curves. On this interpretation, there exists not one but a whole series of short-run trade offs, each corresponding to a different set of price expectations, as shown in Figure 5.3. Friedman and Phelps further postulate that in the long run, if the actual rate of inflation is equal

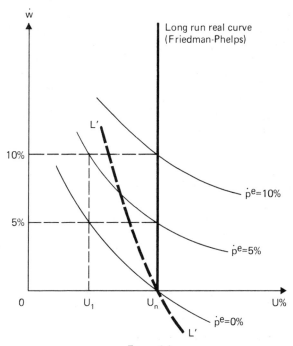

Figure 5.3

to the expected rate, the result will be a vertical line, or no trade off, at the natural unemployment rate (U_n in Figure 5.3). The hypothesis of a long-run vertical Phillips curve rests on the absence of money illusion, with equilibrium occurring at the natural unemployment level on a short-run Phillips curve corresponding to any rate of inflation, so long as it is not unexpected.[45]

The explanation outlined above has major implications for full employment and price stability policies, different from those based on the original Phillips curve. This model predicts that any reduction in unemployment below its natural rate will be associated with an accelerating, and ultimately explosive, inflation. This is an alternative prediction to that derived from the original Phillips trade off and it means that attempts to maintain unemployment at, say, U_1 in Figure 5.3 require the authorities to operate on successively higher short-run Phillips curves. If society requires a *steady* rate of inflation, it will have to operate on the vertical curve at U_n. This is not an irreducible minimum. The natural rate depends on factors affecting real conditions in the labour market, namely labour's marginal productivity, union control of supply and the extent to which markets are cleared. Relevant factors include the existing quantity and quality of information on jobs and workers, trade union barriers to entry, labour immobility, training and imperfections in the human capital market.[46] Interestingly, trade unions can affect U_n, but a given amount of union monopoly power does not produce continuing inflation.[47] Thus, manpower policies which remove imperfections in the labour market can reduce U_n. In comparison, use of the orthodox Keynesian aggregate demand policies will only reduce unemployment at the expense of accelerating inflation. Not surprisingly, the Monetarists conclude that the British inflation beginning in the late 1960s was due to government attempts to reduce unemployment below its natural rate using 'incorrect' macro-policy instruments and that high inflation rates and rising unemployment are explained by shifts in the short-run curves.[48]

The acceptability of this model depends on its empirical verification, the major issue being whether the long-run curve is vertical.[49] The evidence shows that whilst people do adjust to inflation, they apparently fail to adjust completely and remain subject to money illusion even in the long run. In other words, much of the empirical work indicates that a trade off exists at all times, but the long-run curve is steeper than the short-run and resembles curve L' in Figure 5.3. Nevertheless, in view of the history of the Phillips curve, the evidence has to be treated with a degree of scepticism. At the analytical level, we know little about what determines inflationary expectations, why they change and how they influence micro-economic be-

..aviour. Nor do expectations provide conclusive support for demand
or cost explanations of inflation. They could, for example, reflect
either passive or aggressive adjustment by unions. Difficulties arise
in accurately measuring people's expectation of inflation. *Ex post*
data are used to represent an *ex ante* and subjective concept, namely
expectations and the statistical methods of representation tend to be
biased *against* the hypothesis that inflation can be correctly anticipated.[50] It is almost like assuming that people *never* learn from experience and that you can continue fooling all of them all the time: a
proposition which is far from convincing. Moreover, the lack of
support for a vertical Phillips curve would reflect the attempt to fit a
curve to a set of short-run observations, not all of which may be
equilibrium positions. The tendency to capture short-run curves will
be reinforced if the data embrace a period of change in the labour
market, creating variations in U_n.[51] In addition to the estimation
problems, the concept of U_n has been refined. It might be a vertical
band rather than a point and there might be a relationship between
the position of U_n and short-run reductions in unemployment below
U_n. For example, an expansion of aggregate demand will raise
employment and provide more of the labour force with job experience, and such a learning effect will raise labour productivity, so
securing a permanent reduction in U_n.[52]

Regardless of whether the long-run Phillips curve is vertical or
continues to show a trade off, there is general agreement that inflationary expectations are relevant to understanding price and wage
decisions. Policy which aims to reduce the inflation rate has to achieve
a downward revision in expectations about inflation. This can be
achieved by a period of less than expected inflation. One policy
solution will be to allow unemployment to rise above U_n, where
actual inflation will be less than expected and the economy will
eventually adjust to a lower inflation rate by operating on successively
lower short-run Phillips curves. Regrettably, evidence is lacking on
the magnitude and duration of the requisite unemployment. If such
a policy is believed to be too costly and 'undesirable', society could
decide to adapt and adjust to changing rates of inflation by general
indexation of all factor incomes. Automatic cost-of-living or escala-
tor clauses could be used to maintain real incomes and reduce the
transaction costs of adjusting to changing inflation rates.[53] An alternative policy could involve government intervention to directly promote the downward revision of price expectations through the
introduction of wage and price controls. This is a persuasive policy
option, by which governments can apparently legislate and 'talk-
down' the inflation rate without massive unemployment. Are prices
and incomes policies costless?

PRICES AND INCOMES POLICIES: AN EXAMPLE OF
KING CANUTE ECONOMICS?

From time to time since 1945, the UK has operated various voluntary
and statutory prices and incomes policies. There have been freezes,
restraint, ceilings and norms, with some form of policy operating
almost continuously since 1965 and being variously used as an instrument for price stability, balance of payments, growth and income
distribution objectives. Wage and price freezes were used in 1966 and
1972–3, with an earlier variant applying in 1948–50. A voluntary
prices, incomes and productivity policy operated in 1965–6 and
during the 1970s various ceiling and norm policies were used, such as
$n - 1$ per cent in 1971–2, a £1 + 4 per cent norm subject to a
maximum in 1973, threshold payments in 1973–4 and a £6 maximum
for 1975–6. Using models of inflation, the different policies can be
classified according to the extent to which they have 'acted' on prices,
wages and other factor incomes, including the distribution of income,
as well as on inflationary expectations, on efforts to raise productivity
and reduce union militancy and on changing the traditional relationships in wage-bargaining and price-setting.[54] Whilst the variety is
bewildering, the evidence on the effectiveness of incomes policy is less
so. With the exception of 1948–50, '. . . incomes policy apparently
has little effect either on the wage determination process or on the
average rate of wage inflation . . .' and '. . . no identifiable effect on
the price equation'.[55] Nor does it seem that for 1961–73, wage–price
guideposts or the political party in power had anything other than a
trivial or totally insignificant effect on inflationary expectations. In
comparison, the 1967 sterling devaluation had a once-and-for-all
upward effect, raising the expected rate of inflation by about six
percentage points.[56]

Using the most favourable UK evidence, it has been estimated that
with the 1948–50 restraint, the rate of increase of weekly wage rates
was over two percentage points below the rate expected in the absence of an incomes policy. Similarly, with the prices and incomes
policies operated in the UK between 1965 and 1967, the increase in
earnings was slowed by between 1 per cent and 4 per cent. But in
1968–9, as soon as the prices and incomes policies were relaxed,
earnings tried to 'catch up' and they rose by up to 4 per cent faster
than they would have done if there had never been a policy. For
1965–9 as a whole, the total impact of the policy was nil! As for the
effect on prices, the three periods of an incomes policy operated
between 1961 and 1966 showed no significant reduction in the rate of
price increases, with the possible exception of a slight restraining
effect in 1965–6. Similar results have been obtained from studies of

the US ninety-day 'freeze' and Phase II of 1971–2. American controls reduced the rate of price increases by more than one percentage point but the wage effect was ambiguous. One model indicated a reduction of 1·5 percentage points whilst others showed *greater* wage increases of up to 1·6 percentage points![57] A more controversial British study concluded that incomes policy reduced UK inflation at low unemployment levels and increased it at high levels, the pivoting of the Phillips curve occurring at an unemployment rate of about 1·8 per cent.[58] This and other evidence has not been universally accepted. Major statistical problems arise. All the relevant determinants of aggregate prices and wages have to be correctly identified and measured (for example, SET, REP, RPM, etc.), otherwise the results will give a distorted estimate of the effectiveness of incomes policy. At the same time, a satisfactory model is also required to accurately predict what would have happened to inflation in the absence of an incomes policy: an exacting requirement in view of the controversy over the causes of inflation, the 'collapse' of the Phillips curve and the generally inexact nature of applied economics. Even identifying periods when incomes policy operated is not a simple task. Did, for example, a policy operate in 1970–1, when the Conservative administration publicly rejected controls and yet expressed views on the desirable level of wage settlements, especially in the public sector? Moreover, are incomes policies homogeneous? Most empirical studies have assumed so and given equal 'weighting' to statutory freezes and voluntary norms. Others have criticised the statistical studies because of their concentration on inflation and the neglect of other objectives of incomes policy, such as securing improvements in income distribution, in payments systems and in bargaining processes.[59] Even if such variables could be measured, it has to be recognised that policy-makers, as distinct from researchers, have traditionally placed most emphasis on the direct and short-run anti-inflationary aspects of incomes policy: hence the valid concern of statistical studies with the effects of policy on wages and prices.

To the Monetarists, the lack of evidence showing that incomes policy has permanently reduced inflation is not surprising. Monetarists regard inflation as always and everywhere a monetary malady curable only by the therapy of monetary discipline. Interestingly, some prices and incomes policy advocates have used the Quantity Theory to argue that price controls will be successful if they induce economic units to hold larger money balances. Such advocates also believe that with controls, velocity will fall continuously in response to the growth of the money stock, so ensuring price stability. There is evidence to show that price controls can *temporarily* reduce velocity, thereby postponing some of the inflationary impact of excessive monetary growth. However, the hypothesis of continuously falling velocity is not supported. For the UK, the price controls which existed between 1940 and 1950 eventually reduced velocity below its long-run trend relationship with real income. But, after 1946 with price controls still operating, velocity rose continuously and had returned to trend by 1950.[60] Casual empiricism reinforces the doubts about the effects of price controls on velocity. If people expect controls to cause shortages, spending and velocity might initially increase. Eventually, the disruption of previously free markets will create uncertainty and increase the demand for money, resulting in a once-and-for-all fall in velocity. In the circumstances, continued monetary expansion will cause upward pressure on official and black market prices and will undermine the controls. Finally, if people expect controls to be lifted, money balances are likely to be increased and velocity reduced in anticipation of future spending opportunities. The abolition of controls will lead to a spending 'spree' and a rise in velocity until it eventually returns to where it would have been in the absence of controls. On this basis, the Monetarists conclude that price controls are not the answer to inflation. Whilst they might temporarily reduce inflation by reducing velocity, they cannot do so in the long run.

In addition to the evidence of their ineffectiveness, prices and incomes policies are not costless. State intervention in the determination of factor and product prices interferes with the allocative function of markets and leads to shortages and surpluses. For example, any reduction of pay differentials reduces the incentive to train and acquire skills, possibly leading to shortages of skilled labour for future economic growth.[61] Examples of the effects of price and wage controls are examined in Chapter 8. Further costs arise if the unions respond by becoming more militant and increasing work stoppages, as seemed to happen in the late 1960s and early 1970s. And there are the transactions costs of negotiating, bargaining, searching for information, administering and policing some form of prices and incomes policy. Past UK incomes policies illustrate the problems and costs involved. At the outset, proponents of incomes policy 'solutions' are required to specify the form of their proposed policy and its relationship with the economy's central policy objectives. Is 'the policy' designed to reduce inflation, to re-distribute incomes (from whom to whom?) or to increase productivity? Is it to be temporary or permanent, voluntary or statutory, a partial or total freeze on all factor incomes and product prices? If a wage 'ceiling' is specified, will this be based on past or expected productivity, and how is it proposed to prevent this becoming an automatic minimum? The use of a productivity criterion also raises measurement problems for employees in service occupations and in the public sector such as lawyers, doctors, nurses, refuse collectors, policemen and military personnel. What is the productivity of a fighter pilot, a marine and a nuclear-submarine captain? Further difficulties arise in identifying labour's contribution to any increase in productivity. Theory suggests that the appropriate concept is labour's net marginal productivity. In fact, productivity is usually measured as an average relationship between labour input and output, neglecting the contribution of other factor inputs.

An obvious reaction to many of these problems is to see whether economic analysis offers any 'rules' for a prices and incomes policy. If, for example, society wishes to achieve an optimum allocation of resources, a Prices and Pay Board could be required to implement marginal cost pricing in product markets and ensure payments based on marginal value products in factor markets. In other words, the agency could use price and income controls based on the standard marginal rules to simulate a competitive market solution, intervening wherever it identifies market failure. However, given the complex interdependencies between various product and factor markets and the lack of complete demand and cost information, it is most unlikely that a policing agency will successfully choose a set of product and factor prices which will simultaneously clear all markets in every time period! Second-best problems also exist, since there are always product and factor markets which form constraining sectors. In the circumstances, policing agencies for UK incomes policies have been more pragmatic, sometimes using economic analysis to offer 'guidelines' and then modifying the results for considerations of equity, the 'national interest' and their subjective judgement of 'other relevant factors'. Certainly, economic analysis has not been totally ignored. For example, the Prices and Incomes Board in its 1970 review of the armed forces recommended a pay structure based on civilian pay for comparable jobs, plus an additional X factor to reflect the danger, military discipline and constraints on job mobility in the services.[62] In other words, the PIB used standard economic concepts of relative scarcity and the principle of net advantages. More controversial issues were raised by the 1972 Wilberforce Report on coal miners' pay. This concluded that miners had a 'just case for special treatment' because of the dangers and disadvantages of underground work, their past co-operation in raising productivity, the absence of shift pay and the low pay of certain groups.[63] In addition, the Report stressed the decline which had occurred in the relative position of miners in the national pay structure. Mention was made of '... the national interest, which requires the survival of a viable coal industry in competitive conditions, with a contented and efficient labour force'.[64]

The Report was also clear that if its proposed pay increases could not be met from the NCB's revenue account '. . . we think that the public, through the Government, should accept the charge'.[65] In total, these points reflected standard notions of net disadvantages adjusted for the Wilberforce Court of Inquiry's subjective interpretation of equity, relativities, the national interest and the obligations of the taxpayer. Certainly there is nothing in economics which specifies the appropriate relative position of miners in the national pay structure. Should they always be at the top of the pay league; should they always receive, say, twice as much as civil servants or the same as doctors or judges? Economics simply suggests that relative pay requires adjusting for relative scarcities so as to attract or retain more labour in an industry. But the Wilberforce Report went further and committed itself to a specific size of labour force for coal-mining, using its own valuations to conclude that it would be 'desirable' to achieve this regardless of cost in terms of foregone alternatives. Once an output figure and employment constraint is selected and accepted, the requisite price has to be paid without further debate about the price of alternative combinations of output and employment. There are other instances where the apparent neglect of economic analysis has produced predictable but perverse results which frequently seem to surprise policy-makers. For example, price and profit controls are a politically attractive part of any incomes policy, but there are costs. There are likely to be adverse effects on private investment, which

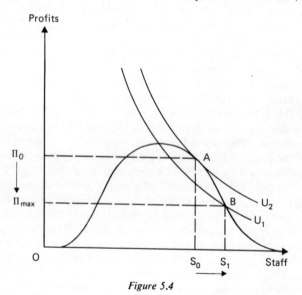

Figure 5.4

might then lead some politicians to criticise the capital market for its 'failure' to solve Britain's lack of investment. Some companies might incur losses, so requiring the state to formulate a policy towards 'lame ducks' (see Chapters 12 and 13). Others might no longer have an incentive to raise profits and will substitute inefficiency, on-the-job leisure and other management expenditures for profits. An example, is shown in Figure 5.4 in which managers are utility maximisers where utility (U) is dependent on profits (Π) and staff expenditures (S) (for example, the number of pretty secretaries and subordinates). The hump-shaped curve is a profit 'frontier' showing the profit levels associated with different staff expenditures. In the absence of profit restrictions, utility will be maximised at point A, with Π_0 profit and S_0 staff. The introduction of a government limit on profits will restrict the firm to point B, where increased staff expenditures are substituted for profits.[66]

CONCLUSION: WHAT CAN ECONOMISTS CONTRIBUTE TO THE POLICY DEBATE ON INFLATION?

'Now it is a singularly pleasing thought that, although ordinary people are wrong occasionally, experts and intellectuals are wrong practically all the time.' (H. Hobson)

Our survey of theory and evidence has revealed controversies about the explanatory value and predictive accuracy of alternative models and the effectiveness of different policies. A substantial research agenda has been identified! In fact, at least one economist in answer to the question: Why have money wages risen since 1945? has concluded: 'We do not know. Unions seem to have some effect . . . so do the tightness of the labour market and price expectations . . . But we only have tentative corroboration of these propositions.'[67] Once again, the uncertainty does not help governments who have to choose between policy targets and instruments. Like managers, policy-makers have to use judgement in interpreting the evidence and their eventual choice will partly reflect their established beliefs about the appropriateness of alternative policies. Given the uncertainties and the vote-consequences of mistakes, governments are likely to choose risk-minimising policies which if 'wrong' will not be too costly in terms of sacrificing other policy objectives and the associated vote-losses. Not surprisingly, governments frequently choose elements of each policy solution without committing themselves to any one. However, within the available range of policies, incomes policy solutions have obvious attractions to political parties and to budget-maximising bureaucracies. Compared with the Monetarist solution with its adverse effects on unemployment, incomes policy is a potential vote-winner since it can be 'sold' to the electorate as an apparently costless solution to inflation. Political parties frequently resemble firms in the fashion and car industries: always searching for, and offering, new and alternative 'models' in an effort to attract the median voter. Various forms of prices and incomes policy were in 'fashion' in the period 1965–76, the inevitable failures being quickly discarded and replaced with new 'models'. The failures are not too difficult to explain. An effective prices and incomes policy will, by definition, produce outcomes different from those of private interests. This will inevitably create frictions and conflicts with established interest groups, both labour and capital, and in the Downs model, vote-maximising governments tend to be influenced by such pressures. At the same time, the model would also predict that since there are more workers than capitalists, vote-maximising governments will tend to favour labour in any incomes policy. Within this framework, budget-maximising government Departments are likely to support incomes policies because of the opportunities they provide for extending state intervention of a market-displacing type. The economics of politics offers a further, and perhaps fundamental, insight which explains why governments might regard inflation as a preferred solution. Inflation results in forced savings, allowing vote-maximising governments to raise public expenditure without raising taxes to reduce private consumption. Short-run reductions in unemployment are also likely. In addition, societies eventually adjust to inflation and minimise its costs to fixed income groups with the result that more and more people become aware that they seem to profit from inflation. In the circumstances, inflation can become a 'desirable' vote-winning element in the political constituency: hence both major political parties in a two-party system will tend to adopt similar policies which favour the *continuation* of inflation! Certainly, a government with its monopoly of the domestic money supply has a mechanism for contributing to, if not causing, inflation. This is not to deny that inflation has potentially serious social consequences on employment and the distribution of income and wealth. Nor can governments wishing to maintain the exchange rate completely ignore the balance of payments implications of inflation. Nevertheless, successive British governments have permitted inflation. Presumably, a vote-maximising government's perception of the expected costs and benefits of inflation compared with its regulation explains an inflationary-biased economic policy. But does the balance of payments provide any checks on inflationary policy? Much depends on whether a country has fixed or floating rates. The former ensure that in the long run, a country can only inflate at a rate similar to that in the rest of the world.[68]

Chapter 6

The Balance of Payments

INTRODUCTION: WHEN IS THE BALANCE OF
PAYMENTS A PROBLEM?

International trade is a large-scale example of the standard gains
from voluntary exchange which are central to market transactions.
The exchange and trade pattern between nations results from differences in their comparative advantages as reflected in costs, prices and
qualities of goods and services. Trade takes place at a set of prices and
the resulting payments and receipts for the purchase and sale of
goods and services in world markets is reflected in the current account
of Britain's balance of payments. In addition, the private and public
sectors in the UK and overseas buy and sell short- and long-term real
and financial assets and whether the UK is a net creditor or debtor
on such transactions is shown in the capital account of the balance
of payments. *Ex ante*, a nation's planned expenditures and receipts
will not necessarily balance. If Britain's foreign expenditures on
goods, services and assets exceeds its receipts, there will be a deficit
or net outflow of payments to foreigners. This will be financed by a
reduction in the UK's foreign exchange reserves and by short-term
borrowing so that, *ex post*, the balance of payments as an accounting
identity will always balance. For simplicity, this chapter will concentrate on the current account.

Britain is substantially dependent on foreign trade. Exports and
imports each amounted to some 25 per cent and over of GNP between
1965 and 1975. Exports have consisted mainly of manufactured goods
with engineering products, especially mechanical and electrical
machinery, typically accounting for some 40 per cent of the total.
There has also been a change in the geographical composition of
exports. Since the mid-1950s, UK exports to the Sterling Area have
declined in relative importance whilst markets in the industrial
nations, especially the EEC and North America, now account for a
larger share. With UK imports, the most striking feature has been the
rising share of manufactures, particularly from the EEC and a corresponding decline in the share of primary commodities from the
Sterling Area.[1] Together, exports and imports form the visible or
trade balance which is usually in deficit. In addition, there are

invisibles consisting of government overseas payments (defence), interest, dividends and private services. Despite a deficit on government services, Britain typically earns a net surplus on invisibles.

Since 1945, the UK has repeatedly experienced balance of payments 'crises'. This immediately raises a policy-relevant question: when is the balance of payments a 'problem'? For the UK it might be argued that a deficit on current account is a necessary condition, even though consumers of domestic and imported goods might disagree. But a persistent surplus, similar to the position of Germany in the 1960s and early 1970s might also constitute a 'problem'! This suggests that the balance of payments might become a problem whenever there are persistent surpluses or deficits. Such a disequilibrium will mean that at the ruling prices, planned overseas expenditures and receipts are not equal. Since the exchange rate is the relevant 'ruling price', a balance of payments problem is initially defined by the foreign exchange market. An explanation of the link between the two is required. Britain's balance of payments is the outcome of a set of international market transactions in which sterling and foreign currencies are exchanged to finance overseas payments (for example, imports) and to provide income from abroad (for example, exports). In the absence of state intervention, the rate of exchange between pounds and foreign currencies will be determined by the forces of demand and supply in the market for foreign exchange. Price, or the exchange rate, will adjust to clear the market. In principle, the foreign exchange market is no different from any other market such as those for bananas, fish or shares. So long as prices can vary to clear these markets, no problems in the form of surpluses or shortages occur, the difficulties arising whenever prices are not allowed to clear markets (see Chapter 8). Similarly with the foreign exchange market, where problems arise when exchange rates are not allowed to adjust to clear the market. If, for example, the government fixes the exchange rate for sterling 'too high' (over-valued), there will be an excess supply of pounds and an excess demand for foreign currency. As a result, the current account of the balance of payments will tend to show overseas expenditure exceeding foreign earnings. In these circumstances, an external payments 'problem' is associated with the fixing of a non-equilibrium exchange rate. International capital movements can modify the analysis by making it possible for a trade deficit to be offset by a net inflow of foreign capital. An example is shown in Figure 6.1[2] which combines domestic employment, private investment demand (I), international trade in goods and services (B), and foreign capital inflows (K). In the foreign exchange market, net capital inflows will favourably affect the demand for sterling.

At full employment (Y_f) and with a fixed exchange rate (e_0), there is

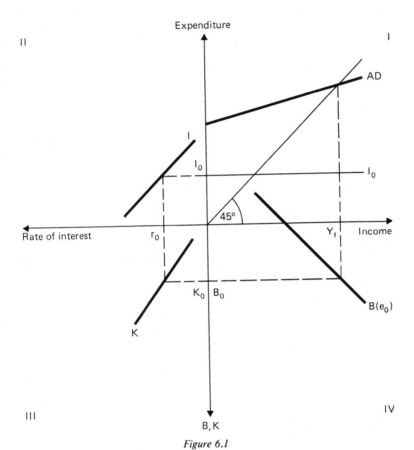

Figure 6.1

a trade deficit (B_0). The flow of capital into the UK is determined by its interest rates in relation to those in the rest of the world. In Figure 6.1, the UK monetary authorities have determined an interest rate (r_0) at which the capital inflow (K_0) exactly equals the trade deficit without sacrificing full employment. However, relatively high domestic interest rates involve costs through adverse effects on investment and hence growth and on the politically sensitive housing market. If policy-makers accept an upper limit on domestic interest rates, they will be constrained in the use of this instrument to attract foreign capital to offset the trade deficit. Thus, whether a balance of payments situation resulting from a disequilibrium exchange rate constitutes a problem will ultimately depend upon the objectives of policy-makers. In short, Britain's balance of payments becomes a problem when it is 'too costly' for policy-makers to maintain an existing fixed exchange rate. The price becomes 'unacceptable' in terms of the sacrifice of other preferred policy objectives such as full employment, domestic price stability, growth and overseas aid. In this situation, where exchange rates are fixed, policy-makers are simultaneously attempting to pursue a variety of conflicting policy objectives with an insufficient range of instruments. Britain's abandonment of fixed parities in 1972 meant that the balance of payments acquired the status of a deposed objective.

To eliminate an international payments deficit, a government has three policy alternatives, two of which involve acting on prices. First, it can vary the external price level, namely the exchange rate, so reducing the size and/or the duration of any domestic deflation required to obtain a given improvement in the balance of payments. However, where the existing exchange rate is regarded as a prior objective of policy – as was the case in the UK between 1955 and 1967 – a constraint is imposed on the choice of policy solutions to eliminate the deficit. With such a constraint, it becomes necessary to resort to an alternative possibility of changing the internal income and price levels (that is, rate of increase of prices). The income reduction will act directly on imports and exports and a lower inflation rate will further assist by bringing the UK's costs and prices into line with those of its major foreign competitors. Traditionally, and in the short-run, such a result has been achieved by reducing the pressure of domestic demand in the economy. Deflation is not costless: it tends to achieve external balance at the expense of the domestic economy and the associated internal policy objectives in the form of higher unemployment and the possibility of adverse effects on economic growth.[3] As a third possibility, governments might use discretionary policies to improve the current account. These consist of direct controls in the form of import quotas and licences, the rationing of foreign exchange, and subsidies to UK import-saving projects.

THE CAUSES OF THE PROBLEM: WHAT DETERMINES BRITAIN'S BALANCE OF PAYMENTS PERFORMANCE?

Criticisms of Britain's balance of payments performance are frequently summarised in terms of the record of imports, exports and market shares. Total imports have frequently risen faster than GDP. Within the total, rising imports of finished manufactures have been a major concern, especially since they are frequently substitutes for domestic production. Imports of Italian scooters, Japanese motor cycles, cars, ships, radios and TVs and East European shoes have adversely affected domestic industries' share of the UK home market.

Further criticisms of Britain's payments performances have concentrated on exports and our share of world trade in manufactures. Except for a short period after 1967, the UK's share of world exports in manufactures has shown a long-run decline – from 20 per cent in 1955 to some 9 per cent in 1973. Whilst there is nothing sacrosanct about a particular share figure, the relevant point is that given the importance of exports in the balance of payments, the decline in the UK's share has occurred during a period when world trade was expanding: 'the opportunities to sell more in the world market have been there, but British manufacturers have not taken them up'.[4]

A variety of reasons have been proposed to explain the decline in the UK's share in world trade and its balance of payments performance. These include hypotheses relating to overseas military expenditure, the export of capital, foreign aid, the Sterling Area and the geographical and commodity composition of British exports. A number of further hypotheses can be included under the general heading of competitiveness. In this context, competitiveness is an all-embracing term incorporating price and non-price factors: for example, the term includes managerial attitudes, innovation, marketing, product quality and style, advertising and delivery dates, service, credit facilities and public relations. Such factors contribute to a nation's competitive advantage so that Britain's balance of payments performance is apparently explained in terms of a relative lack of competitiveness. Costs and prices are obviously a major determinant of competitive advantage. With a fixed exchange rate, Britain's balance of payments will be adversely affected if its costs and prices rise more rapidly than those of its major competitors. This occurred during the 1950s and up to the mid-1960s and the trend reappeared in the early 1970s. Evidence from industrial countries for 1956–63 suggested that 43 per cent of the variation in a nation's export performance was attributable to relative export prices and that, other things being equal, a reduction of 1 per cent in price competitiveness will be associated with a decline in exports of about 3 per cent.[5] Another study of Britain's declining share of world trade between 1959 and 1966 – prior to the 1967 devaluation – estimated that a loss of export price competitiveness 'explained' over half of the reduction in share, with the UK's relatively low growth rate accounting for much of the remainder.[6] As with all statistical work, the empirical estimates of price competitiveness and the elasticities of exports and imports should be treated as approximations rather than as precise magnitudes. Estimates are frequently based on statistical aggregations of commodity groups such as 'manufactures' for which average unit values are used to represent 'prices', the outcome being only remotely related to the standard economic concept of product demand curves.

Disaggregated studies are preferable but even within a product group, such as motor cycles, there are various sub-markets, namely, those for mopeds, scooters, mini-motor cycles and medium-large machines. Moreover, estimates of price competitiveness frequently encounter difficulties in incorporating the influence of all relevant non-price factors, especially those central to monopolistically competitive markets. To neglect such factors is likely to lead to incorrect estimates of the rôle of price competitiveness in international trade. Despite these limitations, the evidence shows that relative costs and prices are important determinants of the UK's balance of payments performance. But what are the underlying causes of changes in Britain's costs and prices?

Answers to this question involve a maze of hypotheses, some of them ill-specified, others untested and a number non-testable! A starting point is the internal pressure of demand. If the UK has generally maintained a relatively higher pressure of domestic demand (for example, for employment objectives), the results will have been a greater rate of inflation, higher imports and a diversion of British exports to the home market. There is some empirical support for the pressure hypothesis. A second group of hypotheses maintain that investment, technical progress and productivity have been lower in the UK than amongst our major foreign competitors. For example, productivity is felt to have been adversely affected by restrictive practices amongst labour and management. A further set of hypotheses explain Britain's international trade performance in terms of deficiencies in the structure of industry. In some cases it is argued that British industries contain too many relatively small firms, each producing a slightly differentiated product, with enterprises failing to obtain all the worthwhile economies of scale (monopolistic competition, large group case).[7] Others suggest that the UK's problem is one of structural adjustment. The hypothesis – for which there is some tentative support – is that on the supply side, the UK has adjusted less well to the changing patterns of both domestic and world demand.[8] Clearly the various hypotheses are not necessarily independent and a model can be formulated which would provide causal links between government demand management (stop-go), investment, productivity, restrictive practices and market structures. Indeed, the Labour Government's Industry Act 1975 (see Chapters 7, 9 and 13) can be regarded as a policy framework for improving the long-run competitive performance of the economy. The National Enterprise Board, Planning Agreements and industrial democracy are the policy instruments which will be used to raise investment, re-structure industries and raise productivity.[9] However, these are long-run structural policies. Governments also have available a set of policy instruments which can directly affect a nation's payments position. Three such instruments are exchange rates, the pressure of domestic demand and tariffs. In choosing between these alternatives, policy-makers have to be able to compare their predicted effects on the balance of payments. For simplicity, we shall concentrate on the contribution of the alternative instruments to 'solving' a British payments deficit.

EXCHANGE RATE POLICY: DEVALUATION

Between 1945 and 1972 sterling was subject to a fixed exchange rate system. The result was a fixed price of pounds in terms of foreign currency, with changes occurring in the form of the devaluations of 1949 and 1967. Fixed exchange rates are not unique and can be analysed in the same way as any competitive market which is subject to price controls (see Chapter 8). Assume that there are only two currencies, sterling and dollars, with the rate of exchange or price of pounds fixed in terms of dollars. Figure 6.2 shows the UK with a balance of payments current account deficit. With a fixed dollar price for sterling (P_f), the supply of pounds (S_0) exceeds the demand for pounds (D_0).

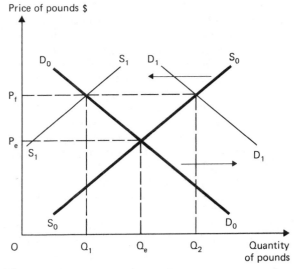

Figure 6.2

The demand function for pounds reflects Britain's overseas earnings. For example, foreigners require sterling to buy British goods (exports), so that they will exchange dollars for pounds. Similarly, the supply of pounds results from the overseas expenditure of UK citizens. UK importers of foreign cars have to exchange pounds for dollars. Figure 6.2 shows that the price is fixed 'too high' in relation to the market equilibrium and consequently the pound is over-valued. In other words, at the ruling price (P_f), there is an excess supply of pounds ($Q_2 > Q_1$) with overseas expenditure exceeding foreign income, the result being a payments deficit.[10] This situation occurred in the UK in the period after 1964 and prior to the 1967 devaluation.

If a government wishes to maintain an over-valued exchange rate (P_f), it has to introduce policies to shift the demand (D_1) and/or the supply (S_1) curves for sterling. To maintain an over-valued exchange rate, a government can use its gold and dollar reserves to 'buy-up' surplus pounds and so support the existing price.[11] Of course, such a policy is constrained by the size of Britain's currency reserves. These can be temporarily supplemented by international borrowing from the IMF and central banks, although such loans are not costless. The demand for pounds can be further increased by policy measures which raise exports. Examples include the export rebate scheme of 1964–7 which was a means of subsidising exports, as well as state support for advanced technology projects with export potential (for example, British civil aircraft). To decrease the supply of pounds, the Labour Government of the 1960s reduced overseas military expenditure, supported import-saving projects (for example, aluminium smelting plants), used an import surcharge to make imports more expensive and attempted to further reduce overseas expenditure by rationing foreign currency for travel. A deflation of domestic demand can also be used to maintain the exchange rate: such a policy (to be explained below) directly reduces imports and 'shocks' firms into searching for additional export markets. However, like all other policies for maintaining an over-valued exchange rate, deflation involves costs – there are short-run losses of output and employment and long-run adverse effects on growth and the economy's competitiveness. Once policy-makers decide that it is too costly to maintain an over-valued exchange rate, they are obliged to change the price (devalue) to its market-clearing position.

Devaluation operates on a payments deficit in a number of ways, depending on the reaction of firms. For example, if the exchange rate were changed from \$4 = £1 to \$2 = £1, British firms could respond by reducing the dollar price of their products by the full extent of the devaluation, or by maintaining the dollar price (so raising the sterling price by the full amount of the devaluation) or by a combination of both (that is, partly reducing the dollar price and partly raising the sterling price). Take the case of British cars which prior to devaluation are sold in New York at a price of \$12,000 (£3,000). If the dollar price is reduced by the full amount of the devaluation, the new price will be $6,000. As a result, more cars will be bought at the lower price, the quantity demanded of exports will increase and if, over the relevant price range, demand curves are elastic, total *dollar* expenditure on British cars will rise. Alternatively, British firms could maintain the dollar price of cars at $12,000, so that after devaluation, exports and dollar expenditures will initially remain unchanged, but sterling receipts will rise. Exports will become relatively more profitable, so that at the margin, British firms will have an incentive to substitute exports for domestic sales with favourable effects on overseas earnings. Economic theory can be used to offer predictions about the effects of devaluation on British firms in various market structures. As an example, a profit-maximising British firm exporting the whole of its output under monopoly conditions is shown in Figure 6.3.[12]

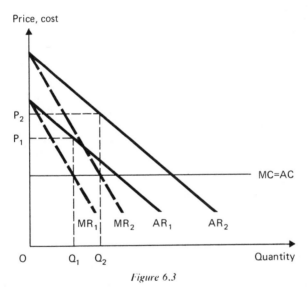

Figure 6.3

Figure 6.3 shows a profit-maximising monopolist in initial equilibrium, exporting Q_1 at a sterling price of P_1. Following devaluation, the firm will move to a higher profit position involving greater exports (Q_2), a rise in sterling prices (P_2), and an associated partial reduction in dollar prices. A similar analysis can be applied to the import effects of devaluation. At the extremes, the dollar price of, say, $120,000 for US machine tools can remain unchanged but the sterling price will rise from £30,000 to £60,000. The result will be a fall in both the quantity demanded and dollar expenditure on imports into the UK. The extent of the fall in dollar expenditure will depend on the price elasticity of demand for imports in response to a rise in sterling prices: an elastic demand curve will reduce sterling expenditure (supply curve in Figure 6.2), whilst inelasticity will raise it. Alternatively, the US machine tool firms could reduce dollar prices to $60,000 and so maintain their sterling prices. This will leave imports unchanged but reduce dollar expenditures and also reduce the relative profitability of exporting to Britain. The net effect of a sterling devaluation on the British payments position will depend on the price elasticity of demand for exports and imports. If the dollar prices of British exports fall and demand curves are elastic, foreign currency earnings will rise, so contributing to an improvement in the trade balance. Similarly, devaluation will usually reduce dollar expenditure on imports.[13] As a result, a devaluation will improve Britain's payments position when the sum of the elasticities of demand for exports and imports is greater than one. The next question is whether these predictions are consistent with the facts. The 1967 devaluation (14·4 per cent against the dollar) is the obvious starting point.

At first glance, the 1967 sterling devaluation appears to have been successful. Britain's current account deficit in 1967 was about − £300m.; by 1969 there was a surplus of some + £450m. reaching a peak of over + £1,000m. in 1971. In estimating the contribution of devaluation to this improvement, allowances have to be made for changes in other variables, such as the deflation of domestic demand, the prices and incomes policy and the import deposit scheme which accompanied the 1967 devaluation, together with variations in world demand. The NIESR has estimated that by 1970, devaluation had improved the current account by about + £425m.,[14] with other influences such as domestic deflation and world demand accounting for the remaining change of almost £600m. (that is, the difference between the 1967 deficit and the 1970 surplus). The price elasticities of demand for UK exports and imports were found to be − 1·4 and − 0·25, respectively. Both figures are lower than the estimates used at the time of the devaluation, but nevertheless indicate that trade responds to relative price changes. With combined elasticities greater than one,[15] the predicted improvement in the payments position is consistent with the facts. Even so, there was a two-year lag before devaluation was seen to be working. In addition, a successful devaluation requires additional resources in the export and import-saving sectors of the economy. If devaluation occurs when there is substantial domestic unemployment, resources will be available to satisfy the increased demand for UK output. The rise in exports will, in fact, result in a foreign trade multiplier effect which will raise the domestic income level by a multiple of the increase in overseas sales.[16] If, however, devaluation occurs when there is full employ-ment, a domestic deflation is required to release resources for the export and import-saving industries (see below).

Evidence exists on the micro-economic foundations of devaluation. A set of interview-case studies was undertaken on the export pricing behaviour of nineteen British manufacturing firms following the 1967 devaluation.[17] Only three firms appeared to be profit-maxi-misers, the majority being satisficers. Following devaluation, six firms maintained foreign currency prices, seven cut them across the board by the maximum amount, whilst the remainder made differen-tial price cuts to different markets. Surprisingly, it was discovered that firms were reluctant to attribute increased export sales or profits in 1968–9 to devaluation. Yet the study concluded that ten firms, or about half the 'sample', obtained a clear benefit from devaluation. However, the results of the interview-questionnaire method of re-search, or any other method, have to be treated with some caution. With interview-questionnaires, there are problems of holding other things constant, of relying upon beliefs rather than statistical evidence and difficulties arise of bias, prompting, and of identifying the rele-vant decision-maker in the firm. There is, for example, a difference between simply asking a manager for his views on exporting (and the state of the world!) and asking him a set of specific questions on the determinants of the firm's exports using an underlying economic model. There is also a difference between asking a businessman whether prices, domestic or world demand affect his exports and asking him to estimate and quantify the relative importance of each factor. In other words, a carefully structured questionnaire which attempts to test unambiguous hypotheses can provide a useful source of evidence on the predictive accuracy of economic theories. Where data are unavailable, a questionnaire might be the only method of testing hypotheses. Also, the method has the considerable merit of being able to explore the individual decision-making process, so providing insights into the micro-economic foundations of macro-economics.

Devaluation is a policy response where a government operates a fixed exchange rate which has become considerably over-valued. It is not the only exchange rate policy. The alternatives to fixed rates are freely floating rates or the intermediate cases involving varying pro-posals for greater exchange rate flexibility between the extremes of completely fixed and free market prices (for example, crawling pegs). In June 1972, British Government exchange rate policy changed and sterling was allowed to float. The case for floating rates is that they can adjust automatically to changed conditions in international trade and so establish a set of prices which will always clear the foreign exchange market (see Figure 6.2 where P_e is the market-clearing price). With floating, exchange rates are determined by market forces and will reflect the inevitable changes in comparative advantages, domestic inflation rates and relative costs and profitability. Floating also allows a nation greater independence in domestic economic policy, especially the pursuit of full employment objectives. In one form, the argument is that with floating rates, the UK could have avoided most of the policy dilemmas of the 1960s. This, perhaps, gives a misleading impression of utopia – a vision of an illusory economy in which floating rates will completely eliminate conflicts and 'solve' all problems, presumably at zero cost! A more accurate and realistic interpretation would be that floating rates provide the government with a further policy instrument for the pursuit of its objectives in a situation where there has been a 'shortage' of policy instruments (see Chapter 1).

The opponents of freely floating rates raise a variety of criticisms, some of which are analytically dubious. Major controversy surrounds the role of private speculation and whether it will have a stabilising or de-stabilising effect on floating rates.[18] Large fluctuations in rates are claimed to be a source of uncertainty with adverse effects on international trade, so reducing economic welfare by restricting opportunities for mutually advantageous exchange. Such criticisms raise both analytical and empirical problems. If the proposition about private speculation is one of markets failing due to imperfections or externalities, it is not at all obvious that fixed rates are the only, most appropriate and least-cost solution. All economic systems involve risks and uncertainty and state intervention to maintain the exchange rate simply ensures that the community as a whole bears the costs of this particular solution to reducing uncertainty – for example, through higher unemployment, the maintenance of large reserves of foreign exchange, and resource mis-allocation associated with a disequilibrium price. As for the evidence on the stability or instability of floating rates, there is an awkward cause and effect issue. In a number of cases, countries faced with financial and economic instability due, say, to mismanagement of domestic demand, have resorted to flexible exchange rates. Thus, floating rates have frequently been *associated* with crises and instability, so that many observers have confused correlation with causation and have mistakenly concluded that floating produces instability!

Floating rates are also criticised for their likely effects on domestic inflation in an open economy. Using British experience after mid-1972 it is argued that exchange depreciation raised sterling import prices, increased domestic costs and prices and stimulated demands for higher wages. This criticism once again confuses cause and effect.

It is not disputed that downward movements in the exchange rate lead to higher import prices. For example, evidence from the 1967 devaluation indicates that import prices rose by 1·5 per cent in 1967 and 8·2 per cent in 1968:[19] both figures show that whilst import prices rose, they did not immediately rise by the full amount of the devaluation. The dispute arises about the casual relationship between the domestic inflation and the exchange rate. If, for example, the Monetarist analysis of inflation is correct, and vote-maximising governments in the UK have been operating the economy at less than the natural unemployment rate, the result will be permanently accelerating inflation. If the UK's inflation is greater than abroad, there will be a continuous deterioration in its international price competitiveness which will be reflected in the foreign exchange market in the form of currency depreciation. Some commentators even criticise floating rates for relieving pressure on the foreign exchange market and so giving a false sense of security with regard to the state of the economy.[20] This is a strange criticism since, on the one hand, it condemns floating rates for clearing the foreign exchange market (which is the aim of floating) and then proceeds to 'blame' the instrument because it frees governments from the 'discipline' (vote-losses?) of fixed rates. This is not to argue that floating rates – or any other exchange rate policies – are completely costless: there are no *free lunches*. All policies involve costs, which will be borne by taxpayers or consumers or equity owners. The task for the policy-maker is to choose the policy which minimises costs in terms of foregone alternatives. In this context, depreciation or devaluation are no panaceas for a trend of increasing 'uncompetitiveness' and, at best, will only buy time while more fundamental corrective policies are implemented. Floating rates can 'buy' more time for resource re-allocation. Associated with exchange rate policy is domestic demand management. Will deflation 'solve' a balance of payments problem?

THE PRESSURE OF DOMESTIC DEMAND AND THE
BALANCE OF PAYMENTS: A DOMESTIC DEFLATION

With a fixed exchange rate, a payments deficit can generally be eliminated by a deflation of domestic demand. This policy has three effects on the balance of payments, relating to relative prices, imports and exports. First, a deflation will reduce the relative rate of increase of costs and prices for British goods and services. The magnitude and length of the domestic deflation will depend upon the time required for the costs and prices of foreign goods to rise and restore Britain's competitive position by re-establishing relative equality between domestic and world prices.[21] Secondly, through its effects on the level of domestic income, a deflation will reduce imports. During the 1960s, evidence suggested that for every £2·50 to £5 reduction in domestic income, imports would decline by £1.[22] For example, to reduce imports by £100m. required a deflation of between £250m. and £500m. Thirdly, a deflation will release goods and resources from supplying the domestic market and so permit a short-run expansion of UK exports. The export effect requires some explanation.

The argument is that in a period of peak domestic demand, goods and resources which would otherwise be used to supply export markets will be diverted to domestic sales. In these circumstances, it is argued that government domestic deflationary measures (for example, credit squeezes, tax increases, cuts in public spending) will release goods and resources from supplying the home market so allowing firms to increase their exports. At the same time, it is maintained that a domestic deflation will encourage firms to seek overseas outlets for the products which can no longer be sold at home. In other words, the export effect contains both push and pull elements. It predicts an inverse or negative relationship between the pressure of domestic demand, on the one hand, and short-run variations in export performance, on the other: high pressures of domestic demand will reduce exports below their trend value and vice versa. Micro-economics provides an analytical framework for a more formal statement of the export effect.

Consider Figure 6.4, which shows a market with a domestic supply

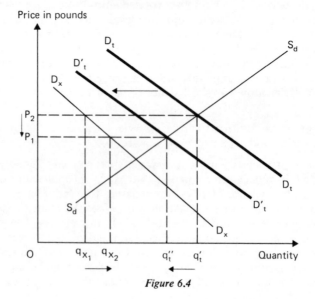

Figure 6.4

curve S_d, a demand curve for exports D_x and a 'total' (home and export) demand D_t, together with an equilibrium price (P_2). Initially, exports are oq'_{x_1} and total output is oq'_t. A deflation of domestic demand will change the total demand curve to D'_t and lead to a lower price (P_1). Total output and domestic sales will fall, but with a lower price, exports will rise to oq_{x_2}.

The export effect can be more appropriately analysed in terms of a discriminating monopoly. Consider a profit-maximiser, producing a single product and faced with two markets, home and overseas. In the home market, the firm is a price-maker. In the export market, the firm is a price-taker. The allocation of the firm's output between the two markets and the resulting prices in the short run are shown in Figure 6.5(a). Profits are maximised where the firm's combined marginal revenue curve from both markets (MR_w) equals its marginal cost (SMC) curve. In Figure 6.5(a), AR_d and AR_w show the firm's demand curves in the domestic and world markets, respectively. Total output will be oq_t, with oq_d sold in the home market and exports of $q_d q_t$. The domestic price (P_d) of the product will exceed its export price (P_w) and profits per unit of domestic sales will exceed the unit profitability of exports. A deflation of domestic demand, shown in Figure 6.5(b), will reduce home sales and increase exports, so that the model predicts an inverse relationship between changes in domestic demand and export sales. The model can be expanded to include the discriminating monopolist as a price-maker in both home and overseas markets and subject to increasing, decreasing and constant cost conditions. It can be shown that the inverse relationship between a firm's exports and domestic demand depends upon increasing marginal costs.[23]

In providing a framework for analysing the relationship between internal demand and short-run export performance, micro-economic theory specifies the conditions required for an increase in overseas sales. In particular, it shows that the crude statement of the export effect is a supply-side hypothesis. Even if a deflation releases goods and resources (depending on factor mobility?) from supplying the home market, the products still have to be sold in the export market. In other words, overseas demand, as well as domestic supply, is a determinant of exports.[24]

The available evidence suggests that the pressure of domestic demand is a major factor explaining both the level and the share of UK exports in world trade. A study of UK manufacturing exports for 1954–64 found that a high pressure of domestic demand adversely affected the UK's short-run export performance.[25] For example, it was estimated that in the boom of 1964, when the unemployment rate fell below $2\frac{1}{2}$ per cent, the UK economy probably 'lost' some £180m. of

(a)

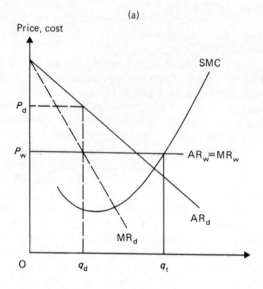

(b)

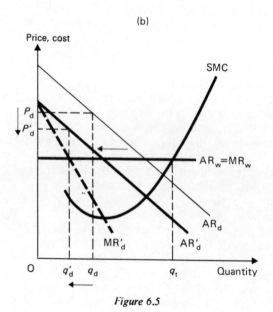

Figure 6.5

exports. Further evidence based on a study of individual firms and industries tends to support these findings, although it is recognised that any generalisations conceal a wide variety of experience.[26] The UK results show that the export effect of demand pressure varies not only between industries but also between different markets for the same industry: such a variety of experience can be predicted from a simple model of discriminating monopoly under different market and cost conditions. For policy-makers, deflation achieves an improvement in exports and in the balance of payments at the 'expense' of higher unemployment for longer periods, 'lost' output and adverse effects on investment incentives. In the circumstances, some commentators have advocated increased tariff protection for British industry as an alternative policy solution.

TARIFFS AND THE BALANCE OF PAYMENTS: THE CASE FOR PROTECTION

Compared with deflationary policies, increased tariff protection *appears* to be an attractive policy. It is argued that tariffs will improve the balance of payments by reducing imports and, at the same time, will raise domestic employment levels. The argument can be analysed by using a standard demand and supply framework.

Consider the market shown in Figure 6.6, which initially has no foreign trade and is represented by domestic demand and supply schedules D_d and S_d, respectively, and domestic equilibrium price P_d. Total output (oq_d) is supplied by the domestic industry. Assume that foreign trade now takes place and that there are no tariff barriers. If there are lower-cost foreign firms, the supply in the domestic market will increase to S_{d+f}, as shown in Figure 6.6. The result of free trade will be lower prices in the home market (P_f), a fall in domestic output and employment (to oq'_d) and the emergence of imports ($q'_d q_t$). At the new equilibrium price of P_f, the total amount supplied is oq_t, of which oq'_d is from the domestic industry.

Not surprisingly, the import and associated domestic employment effects of free trade encounter opposition from producer interest groups. Such groups might be supported by a budget-maximising Department of Industry which has every incentive to retain and protect rather than eliminate sectors in which it has a major budgetary involvement. In view of the lower prices resulting from free trade it might be thought that consumers would form an interest group to oppose the producer–Ministry protection lobby. However, the groups with a special interest in protection are the concentrated producer groups (management and unions) to whom the issue makes a great deal of difference. Consumers are widely dispersed and the

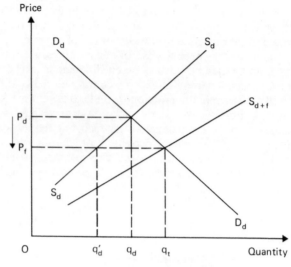

Figure 6.6

free trade product might account for a relatively small proportion of their total expenditure. As a result, in the absence of any general legislation favouring consumers, democratic governments will inevitably be influenced by producer groups. If a tariff is introduced on imports, the supply curve will shift upwards to $S_{d+(f+t)}$, as shown in Figure 6.7. The market price will rise to P_t and total consumption will fall. Within the smaller total, imports will be reduced to $q_d''q_t'$ and the higher price will stimulate domestic output and hence employment. The results of imposing a tariff, or raising a tariff, compared with free trade are shown in Figure 6.7.

The prediction is that tariffs will reduce imports and raise domestic employment. Evidence supports these predictions. The imports surcharge (tariff) which the UK imposed on imports of manufactures between 1964 and 1966 was estimated to have reduced the 1965 import bill by some £130m. (at 1964 prices) and the 1966 import bill by £80m. compared with what it would otherwise have been.[27] Similarly, it has been estimated that for the British aircraft industry, protection in the early 1970s enabled it to support an extra 50,000–100,000 employees out of a total employment of some 200,000.[28] And yet tariffs are not the attractive policy option they appear to be. As with other policies they involve costs. In the world economy, a general, rather than a partial, equilibrium approach suggests that the introduction of a tariff might have 'feedback effects'. Foreign countries will suffer an initial fall in exports. Through a multiplier process this will eventually reduce their domestic income and em-

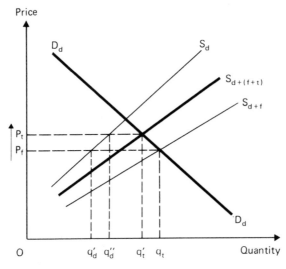

Figure 6.7

ployment levels as well as their imports. If both rising unemployment and balance of payment deficits are unacceptable, foreign
countries will introduce 'corrective' policies. Where these involve
import restrictions, the original tariff-imposing nation is likely to find
its exports adversely affected! Tariffs also adversely affect opportunities for mutually advantageous trade (real-income raising)
according to a nation's current comparative cost position.[29] The
evidence, however, suggests that whilst there are gains from removing tariffs, these are relatively modest. For the elimination of 20
per cent tariffs, the gains from extra trade might be no more than
1 per cent of national income.[30] Such estimates greatly depend on the
assumption that firms in protected industries are operating efficiently
and minimising costs. If this assumption is not valid, and protected
firms are technically inefficient, the 'shock effect' of foreign competition would be a *further* source of real income gain following the
elimination of tariffs (see Chapter 10).

CONCLUSION: WHAT ARE THE LIKELY TRADE OFFS?

The choice between alternative instruments will depend upon the
objectives of the policy-maker. Positive economics can make a contribution by analysing, predicting and measuring the implications of
alternative courses of action for the achievement of some specified
goal. In the case of the balance of payments, empirical evidence is
required on the magnitude of the trade offs between alternative

policies. A study of Britain's balance of payments performance in the mid-1960s estimated some of the trade offs for a set of alternative policies which could be used to achieve a £100m. improvement in the balance of payments.[31] First, the target unemployment rate could be raised by 0·34 percentage points. Secondly, a 4 per cent import surcharge could be imposed. Thirdly, overseas military expenditure could be reduced by £143m. Fourthly, foreign aid could be cut by £159m. The final possibility was a 1·4 per cent devaluation. Additional evidence is available on the effects of devaluation. On the basis of the period 1967–71, it has been estimated that a 10 per cent devaluation for the UK will lead to a 2·7 per cent increase in Britain's retail prices and a 1·2 per cent decrease in domestic real wages. As a result, less than 70 per cent of the initial price advantage achieved by devaluation will be retained. More significantly, the wage-price experience of 1967–71 compared with that of 1954–71, 'implies a larger domestic price adjustment to exchange rate changes and, hence, a relatively less effective role for devaluation in improving the UK's competitive position'.[32] The causes of domestic inflation cannot be ignored. However, during the early 1970s, a new explanation for Britain's balance of payments deficit was formulated.

The New Cambridge School hypothesised that there is a relationship between the public sector financial deficit and the current account of the balance of payments: the larger the former, the larger the payments deficit. The hypothesis depends on the basic identity that the net acquisition of financial assets by the public, private and overseas sectors must sum to zero. It also assumes that the private sector will accumulate small and predictable financial surpluses. For example, if the private sector is expected to run a £750m. financial surplus (income minus expenditure) and the target current account surplus is £500m., it follows that the public sector deficit should be around £250m. On this basis, any change in the budget deficit must be reflected in the balance of payments so that the government is to blame for a balance of payments deficit. If valid, the hypothesis suggests a complete reversal of the orthodox approach to targets and instruments. The budget becomes the appropriate instrument for balance of payments policy and the exchange rate is the instrument for employment policy. Indeed, in 1976 the National Institute estimated that for the UK a 5 per cent devaluation together with a 6 per cent rise in earnings would create an extra 200,000 jobs.

Simple explanations of the economy are always attractive but frequently wrong. There are problems of two-way causation. Changes in the budget deficit through variations in aggregate demand can change the current account of the balance of payments. But changes in the balance of payments can also affect the budget deficit.

If world demand increases and British exports rise, the balance of payments will improve and the resulting rise in national income will increase tax revenues and so reduce the public sector deficit. Moreover, when used for forecasting, the New Cambridge equation appeared to break down massively in 1973–4.[33]

Chapter 7

Economic Growth

By international standards, Britain's growth performance in the 1950s and 1960s was relatively poor. Between 1955 and 1972, industrial output grew at an annual rate of 2·5 per cent compared with almost 6 per cent in the EEC. International comparisons of income levels raise numerous problems relating to the definition and valuation of items, the differences in leisure, externalities, the mix of consumption and investment goods, employment levels and the distribution of income.[1] Nevertheless, whichever indicator of growth is used, be it GDP, or GDP per head or per man hour, the UK remains at the bottom of the international league table.

Successive British governments have aimed to increase the economy's growth rate and so raise living standards and *per capita* incomes. Various policies have been tried. In the early 1960s, the 'dash of planning' resulted in the formation of the National Economic Development Council (NEDC) and the Department of Economic Affairs (DEA). Planning involved greater state intervention to achieve growth targets. The state became more involved in promoting research, improving efficiency, identifying 'bottlenecks' in the economy (for example, shortages of skilled labour) and correcting regional imbalances. The DEA's National Plan aimed to raise the annual growth rate of GDP to 3·8 per cent between 1964 and 1970, but the Plan was officially abandoned in mid-1966. Major difficulties arose because the target growth rate was chosen as an assumption without properly examining the means of achieving it. The target was substantially in excess of past UK experience and, without any justification for the chosen rate, it looked like mere wishful thinking in which the act of planning was regarded by some as sufficient to modify long-established trends. In other words, growth and planning lack an adequate theoretical foundation. For example, 'if an army is told that it must march at four miles an hour and is then asked how many paces a minute must be taken on that assumption, it is not surprising if the discovery is finally made that the army will march at four miles an hour. So with the Plan.'[2] It is generally believed that the failure of the

National Plan was due to the deflationary policies introduced to correct the balance of payments situation in the second half of the 1960s. This is a misleading explanation since it neglects the fundamental issue of whether the Plan's targets could have been achieved even with a balance of payments surplus: 'there is nothing in the past experience of the UK economy to suggest that this could have happened'.[3] Plans also involve costs. The National Plan took a year to prepare. More significantly, the target growth rate is likely to be the basis for wage claims and for the planned growth of public expenditure, despite the fact that the target might not be achieved!

Greater investment has always been a popular candidate for policy-makers wishing to raise the growth rate. Policies have ranged from lower interest rates, tax changes and incentives, together with expansions of aggregate demand to selective intervention in 'key' sectors of the economy. By the mid-1970s, policy was emphasising the need to raise investment in manufacturing industry and to regulate the growth of public expenditure. According to the de-industrialisation hypothesis, the really striking development in 1965 to 1975 was the great growth in non-industrial investment, namely public investment in central and local government services, and private investment in housing, office building and service industries.[4] This was achieved at the expense of investment in manufacturing industry and a relative decline in the UK manufacturing sector. Evidence suggests that for the UK, a 5 per cent rise in the share of public expenditure (excluding transfers) in national income eventually implies a 1 per cent reduction in the growth rate. Apparently, increased state consumption takes place at the expense of investment, with a 1 per cent rise in the former being associated with almost a 1 per cent drop in the share of investment in national income.[5] On this basis, increased manufacturing investment is believed to be the solution to raising our growth rate. Moreover, Britain's growth rate, or the lack of it, is regarded as a central causal factor in explaining our balance of payments and inflation problems. De-industrialisation has meant that as a boom develops, UK industrial capacity has been 'insufficient', so resulting in rising imports and balance of payments crises. It has also been argued that the UK economy has failed to 'produce the increase in material living standards that might have done something to satisfy the aspirations of workers, and so reduce their militancy and the perpetual need for prices and incomes policies'.[6] Such explanations appear convincing but lack an analytical framework which clearly specifies the causal relationships linking growth, the balance of payments and inflation.

Before policies can be formulated to raise the growth rate, the *causes* of growth have to be identified. Here, it must be admitted that economic theories of growth have not been very satisfactory. They have been unsatisfactory in explaining the observed facts of different growth rates between countries and they have been unsatisfactory in providing accurate predictions about future growth rates. Nevertheless, a knowledge of production functions can improve our understanding of the growth process. Such an approach indicates some of the major determinants of growth and associated policy issues.

A MODEL OF GROWTH: THE PRODUCTION FUNCTION APPROACH[7]

Growth can be regarded as an outward shift in the economy's production possibility frontier. It differs from short-run variations in the utilisation of the economy's resources. Since growth increases the economy's productive capacity, some understanding is required of the determinants of output. The simple proposition that output in the economy depends upon the inputs of labour and capital results in a general production function of the form

$$Q = f(L, K)$$

where Q is output in the economy, L is labour inputs and K is capital inputs.

A specific form is the Cobb-Douglas production function

$$Q = AL^{\alpha}K^{1-\alpha}$$

where A is a constant reflecting the state of technical knowledge, and α and $1-\alpha$ show the extent to which a given percentage increase in both L and K will increase total product. Evidence from a number of countries suggests a value for α of about 0·75.

The Cobb-Douglas production function shows that, with given K, a 1 per cent increase in L will add α or 0·75 per cent to output. Similarly, with given L, a 1 per cent rise in K will add $1-\alpha$ or 0·25 per cent to output: these are both examples of diminishing returns with one fixed factor. If *both* L and K are increased by 1 per cent, output will expand by 1 per cent: this is the case of constant returns to scale. Finally, in this production function, the coefficients α and $1-\alpha$ measure the shares of L and K, respectively, in the total product. For example, if $\alpha = 0·75$, labour in the economy will receive pay equal to 75 per cent of the total product, capital the remaining 25 per cent.

Using the general production function relating output and factor inputs, questions arise about the meaning of factor inputs. The contribution of a factor to total output will depend upon its *quantity* and its *quality* or factor productivity. Each will be considered separately, beginning with factor quantities. If the economy's growth rate depends upon the available *quantities* of L and K, we need to identify their determinants.

FACTOR QUANTITIES: LABOUR AND CAPITAL

What determines the quantity or supply of labour in the British economy? Analysis suggests that the quantity of labour supplied will depend upon such variables as: the size of the population, which will depend upon birth and death rates and international migration; the age and sex distribution of the population; the hours of work and wage rates. In the UK, many of these variables have been *partly* influenced by government policy. For example, the resources allocated to the National Health Service and to transport improvements affect life and death in the economy. Immigration policy affects the size of the population. Legislation on retirement age affects the population of working age. Finally, the state has affected wage rates through minimum wage legislation in specific industries and successive pay policies.

What about the quantity of capital in the economy? Capital is a *stock* and additions to this stock result from the *flow* of new investment. The general belief is that investment in Britain has been 'too low': '... for years now, the level of productive investment in this country has been low by comparison with that of our major trade competitors. For example, in 1970, Japan invested no less than 28 per cent of her national income. The average figure for the Six was 19 per cent. In this country it was 15 per cent.'[8] Some politicians argue that the '... primary factors which determine the level of productive investment are two-fold: business confidence in a sustained growth of demand and profitability'.[9] These determinants have some analytical foundation.

Theory suggests two models of gross investment. The Keynesian model stresses the role of interest rates and the marginal efficiency schedule. The latter reflects businessmen's expectations, which depend upon such factors as beliefs about future consumption demands and future profitability. According to the accelerator model, investment depends on changes in the level of aggregate demand and output.[10] In total, the models stress the relevance of interest rates, expectations, profitability and output levels. The evidence shows that '... demand factors as represented by the Accelerator are more important than relative prices in determining investment'.[11] Nevertheless, successive governments have tried to stimulate investment by various types of incentives, including initial allowances, investment allowances and cash grants. Investment incentives have also been used to discriminate between industries, type of asset and regions. The economic basis of such discrimination is far from obvious. Intervention in the investment decisions of 'key' sectors raises questions about the definition of a 'key' industry and its potential significance for growth. Where increased investment is required to expand industrial capacity, the presumption seems to be that capacity is in some sense 'inadequate'. What is 'adequate' and how are we supposed to define and measure industrial capacity? Is it physical capacity somehow defined, or does it include human capital and the skills and mobility of the labour force? Doubts also arise about the benefit of subsidising capital in regions of high unemployment. Finally, the evidence indicates that investment incentives in their various forms have not been very effective in stimulating UK investment, especially in relation to the investment records of the industrial nations. Nor does investment completely 'explain' growth. For a set of industrial nations between 1961 and 1972, the share of investment in national income only explained some 50 per cent of variations in the growth of real GDP.[12]

So far we have a simple model in which the growth of output depends on the available *quantities* of labour and capital. The evidence shows that increases in factor quantities do not by themselves explain the whole of the increases in output. There is a substantial unexplained residual sometimes called the *residual factor* or the *coefficient of ignorance*.[13] The existence of the residual factor has led economists to consider the contribution of factor quality or productivity to growth. Investment in human capital in the form of education, together with research and development and technical progress provide possible explanations of the 'residual'.

FACTOR QUALITY OR PRODUCTIVITY

Factor productivity depends on:

(1) The extent of any productivity-raising investments in labour and capital – for example, education and training are productivity-raising investments in human beings; technical progress and associated new investment are methods of increasing the productivity of capital.

(2) The allocation of labour and capital which depends on:
   (a) The allocation of resources between agriculture, manufacturing and services. For each sector, there will be different productivities and opportunities for scale economies.

(b) The mobility of factors, both labour and capital, between regions and industries. Factor mobility is important for any *re*-allocation of resources from the low to the high productivity sectors in the economy.

HUMAN CAPITAL AND LABOUR PRODUCTIVITY

The productivity of both labour and management can be improved through learning-by-doing:[14] this simply means that labour and management will become more productive as they acquire more experience of production. The basic idea is that the more frequently labour and management perform a specific task, the more efficient they will become at that task. In other words, with learning-by-doing, labour productivity rises with cumulative output (that is, aggregate output over time rather than output per time period). Learning is not the only source of increases in labour productivity. Education and training are also relevant.

The quality of labour can be improved through investment in human beings: by creating human capital through the education system together with on-and-off-the-job industrial training. In other words, education and training can be regarded as productivity-raising investments in human beings, the result being the creation of human capital.[15] This view of formal education as an investment process has directed attention towards efforts at measuring the rate of return to specific forms of education.

The rate of return on, say, university education is calculated by expressing the extra earnings from university education as a rate of return on the costs of university education. In other words, we compare differences in education costs and lifetime earnings between a person with a degree and one without. The costs of university education will consist of both public and private costs, including any income 'sacrificed' or 'foregone' because a student is not working. Difficulties arise with such rate of return exercises. For example, it is necessary to 'standardise' for all other influences such as intelligence, sex and social class which can affect lifetime earnings. Problems arise if monopoly exists in the labour market and there is also the task of estimating lifetime earnings. At the end of all this, two calculations emerge, namely private and social rates of return. The *private* rate of return is based on the costs borne by the individual (for example, foregone income plus out-of-pocket tuition expenses) and the resulting *post-tax* earnings. For example, in Britain in 1963 the private rate of return on three years of higher education was about 14 per cent,[16] making higher education a worthwhile investment. Following university expansion in the 1960s, the private rate of return to a first degree had fallen to under 10 per cent by 1972. The *social* rate of return is based on the costs borne by society (that is, total resource costs both public and private) and the resulting pre-tax earnings. In 1971 it was estimated that for scientists and engineers the social rate of return for first degrees was about 8 per cent per year. This compares with the 10 per cent target rate of return for the nationalised industries and, on this basis, there might be no 'shortage' of scientists and engineers in Britain. PhDs in science and engineering yielded a social rate of return of about 4 per cent![17]

THE PRODUCTIVITY OF CAPITAL

This section is concerned with the productivity of physical as distinct from human capital. The quality of physical capital will be affected by research and development, technical progress and the organisational attitudes of management. Research and development will result in new machinery and new methods of production such as computers, and these will be incorporated into firms through new investment. As a result, technical progress will be *embodied* in new plant and equipment, some of which will be labour-saving.[18] In this way, new investment will raise productivity and so contribute to growth. Thus, the vintage, or age structure of the capital stock is relevant for growth. New factories are likely to embody best practice technology. However, an Australian study of labour productivity in new factories compared with all factories concluded that the vintage effect was quantitatively insignificant as an explanation of cross-section variations in productivity.[19]

Expenditure on research and development (R&D) appears to be an obvious source of growth and one which has been the focus of various policies, culminating in the formation of the Ministry of Technology (1964–70). In this area, the UK's record compares favourably with other countries. For example, in 1971 total UK expenditure on R&D was 2·3 per cent of GNP compared with 2·1 per cent for Germany and 1·5 per cent for Japan. Similarly, in 1969 government expenditure on R&D as a proportion of GNP was 1·2 per cent in the UK, 0·7 per cent in Germany and 0·2 per cent in Japan.[20] And yet, the UK's growth record remains poor by international standards. This suggests that if there is a relationship between growth and R&D, Britain and its governments have been relatively poor at project selection or relatively inefficient in the use of scientific resources. Criticisms have been made of state support for a narrow range of advanced technology industries, especially aerospace. For example, government support for UK civil aircraft projects is believed to have resulted in a net loss of national welfare.[21] Alternatively, the British evidence might be used to create doubts about the relationship between R&D and growth. One survey has concluded that '. . . the enormous growth of R&D expenditures appears to have had little impact on the aggregate growth rate for countries.'[22]

THE EVIDENCE ON UK GROWTH: WHY GROWTH RATES DIFFER

An attempt to explain Britain's comparative growth performance was undertaken by Edward Denison[23] (other nations included the USA, France, Germany, Italy and Belgium). Although the study was based on 1950–62 and is now dated, it provides insights into the growth process. One of its major contributions was to emphasise that there are various determinants of growth: growth is a complex process which cannot be explained by one simple variable (for example, investment). The Denison study used the analytical framework outlined above and attempted to quantify the contribution of different variables in explaining Britain's comparative growth performance. It was found that our relative performance was explained by:

(1) Smaller factor inputs of labour and capital. Other countries had grown at a faster rate than Britain because they had greater increases in the quantities of labour and capital inputs.
(2) A smaller growth of factor productivity and this was the major source of differences in growth rates. In general, other countries had experienced larger increases in factor productivity. There were two sources of productivity gains in other nations. First, other countries had experienced greater gains from economies of scale. Secondly, other countries had gained from a decline of self-employment and a re-allocation of labour and other resources from agriculture to manufacturing. In contrast, Britain had a relatively small amount of labour allocated to relatively inefficient agriculture and self-employment and hence fewer opportunities for raising productivity from these sources. The Selective Employment Tax (SET) was originally designed to solve this specific British problem. Although the SET was abolished in 1973, its logic provides fascinating insights into the underlying growth model.

GROWTH AND EMPLOYMENT IN MANUFACTURING AND SERVICES

In the mid-1960s, and on the basis of an international study, Professor Kaldor argued that the potential growth of industrial or manufacturing productivity was limited by the supply of labour. He claimed that when industry suffers from a shortage of labour, it is unable to exploit economies of scale, with adverse effects on productivity. Put simply, Kaldor's hypothesis or 'law' was that a faster growth of productivity requires a faster growth of manufacturing employment. It was argued that Britain's relatively slow growth of industrial productivity was caused by a chronic shortage of labour in the manufacturing sector.[24] Unlike its rivals, Britain did not possess a large surplus of agricultural labour available for industrial employment. Thus, to obtain the scale economies available in manufacturing, labour had to be found elsewhere, with the services sector as a potential source: hence the Selective Employment Tax (SET 1966–73). In its original form the SET was a poll tax-subsidy designed to increase labour costs in services and reduce them in manufacturing. The result was expected to be a re-allocation of labour from services to manufacturing, with favourable effects on Britain's growth rate.[25]

The evidence on Kaldor's law remains controversial, with some results supporting the hypothesis, others rejecting it. One study of productivity and employment growth in thirty-nine nations for 1958–68 found absolutely no relationship between the two variables. Elsewhere, support for the hypothesis depends on the inclusion of Japan in the sample: without Japan there is no real evidence of any correlation between productivity growth and employment growth in the period 1951–65.[26] Nor are correlations proof of causation, especially in a single variable model of growth. Inevitably, such controversy creates difficulties in erecting impartial criteria for the 'satisfactory' test of a hypothesis! In the circumstances, economics resembles religion with its various scientific interest groups of believers, atheists and agnostics. Interestingly, Professor Kaldor has now admitted that he was wrong in 1966 in thinking that the UK's 'comparatively poor performance was to be explained by inability to recruit sufficient labour to manufacturing industry rather than by poor market performance due to lack of international competitiveness'.[27] By 1975, Kaldor was emphasising that growth is demand-induced and not resource-constrained, particular stress being placed on the role of exports as a determinant of growth.[28] Given such changes in thinking, as well as uncertainty about the underlying causes of growth, what can policy-makers do? Both analysis and evidence show that there is no single cause which completely 'explains' Britain's comparative growth performance. This finding contrasts with popular beliefs that there is a single, simple solution, with more investment being the favourite.

SHOULD THE STATE INTERFERE IN THE
GROWTH PROCESS?

Competitive markets might be expected to produce the growth rate
required by society. A government wishing to achieve Pareto-optimal
growth will formulate policies for correcting market 'failure' and
allowing individuals to choose between present and future consumption. Imperfections and externalities are sources of 'failure', with
information as a specific example. Opportunities exist for expanding
the range of sources providing information about current and future
prices.[29] However, second-best arguments might be used to oppose
such piece-meal policy recommendations. Moreover, individuals
might not be regarded as the best judges of their welfare and that of
future generations, so that state intervention might be required to
achieve a growth rate which governments regard as desirable and
which will differ from the market rate. The policies of the Labour
Government in the mid-1970s illustrate some of the controversies
and show how economists can approach policy problems. In this
period, emphasis was placed on the need for increased growth
through the regeneration of British industry.[30] The National Enterprise Board (NEB), Planning Agreements and industrial democracy
were seen as the appropriate policy instruments. From government
statements, the underlying growth model can be deduced which
suggests a case for state intervention based on beliefs about market
failure. A second set of propositions explains the choice of policy
instruments.

State intervention appears to have been based on the following
propositions:

(1) Free markets have 'failed' to improve and to solve Britain's
    relatively poor economic performance. It is maintained that:
    'Since the war, we have not as a nation been able . . . fully to
    harness the resources of skill and ability we should be able to
    command. We have been falling . . . further behind our com-
    petitors.'[31]
(2) Industrial problems are believed to be the major source of the
    economy's poor performance.
(3) Britain's industrial problems are characterised by:
    (a) A lack of emphasis on jobs, especially in the Development
        Areas (that is, regional inequality).
    (b) A failure to exploit the opportunities for increasing exports
        and reducing 'undue' dependence on imports.
    (c) Too little domestic investment.
    (d) Industrial inefficiency, including inefficient industrial struc-

tures, restrictive labour practices and private monopoly. When it comes to making effective use of our manufacturing equipment, we are less successful than most of our competitors.[32] Similarly, it is believed that the traditional lack of government emphasis on job-security and the general absence of worker participation in industry has contributed to restrictive practices. Private monopolies have been criticised, especially the aggregate concentration of output in the top 100 companies.

Thus, the policy model suggests that markets have failed to provide the investment, the regional distribution of jobs, the efficiency in the allocation of resources and the balance of payments performance required to 'solve' Britain's economic problems. Both imperfections and externalities seem to be the general sources of market failure. Whilst the failure embraces product and factor markets throughout the economy, the failure of the private capital market is central to the policy model. It was believed that Britain's private capital market had 'failed' to provide 'sufficient' funds for new investment and had not promoted the restructuring of industry required to improve the economy's competitive position. Nor had it created sufficient jobs in areas of high unemployment. All too often, decisions affecting companies and jobs have been made by shareholders (for example, asset 'strippers') and have failed to reflect the preferences of workers. Because workers are not shareholders in the firms in which they work, they have been excluded from exercising the right to shape and plan their work and to obtain job security. Also, the market has failed to '... assist sound companies which are in short-term financial or management difficulties'.[33] In other words, the market in company shares is believed to fail because it reflects commercial profit motives (the unacceptable face of capitalism) which are likely to conflict with the 'public interest' (never defined).

Some of the criticisms reflect a misunderstanding of the role of profits in the economy and the allocative function of the private capital market. The existence of scarcity means that there will never be 'sufficient' funds for all activities (needs) in the economy. The capital market allocates funds by the potential profitability of the competing demands. If the development of, say, *Concorde* cannot attract sufficient private funds, it does not follow that the market has 'failed'. Rather, it reflects the judgement of the private capital market that *Concorde* is a relatively less profitable user of its funds. Of course, actual capital markets might fail. But the critics rarely inquire about the causes of market failure. For example, is the capital market's apparent failure due to government profit controls and plans for public ownership, which are likely to adversely affect investment opportunities?

The case for the NEB, Planning Agreements and industrial democracy as the most appropriate policy solutions follows from the alleged causes of market failure. Also, Labour administrations are likely to prefer market-displacing policies. The choice of instruments appears to have been based on a number of propositions:

(1) The solution of industrial problems and the decisions that matter cannot be left to random forces in the form of private markets. For example, one view is that public enterprise is required to ensure that the state is 'institutionally equipped to make the decisions that matter for the British economy rather than leave it to random forces to make them'.[34]

(2) The decisions that matter and which require state involvement include:
   (a) Investment;
   (b) Regional employment;
   (c) Industrial efficiency, embracing productivity, industrial structure and prices policy;
   (d) Raising exports and reducing 'undue dependence' on imports;
   (e) Unacceptable foreign control of a company;
   (f) The regulation of private monopoly;
   (g) Industrial democracy, the aim being 'full involvement' of employees in decision-making at all levels.

(3) The NEB and Planning Agreements provide the state with the policy instruments for making the decisions that matter. These instruments were seen as the basis for creating a 'new partnership' between government and industry. The NEB was designed to offset the effects of the short-term pull of market forces and so 'correct' the alleged failure of the capital market. Planning Agreements aimed to create a 'closer understanding between companies – work force as well as management – and the Government on the aims to be followed and the plans to be adopted in pursuit of them. They will not only help to ensure that the plans of companies are in harmony with national needs and objectives, they will also provide a . . . basis . . . for ensuring that government financial assistance is deployed where it will be most effectively used.'[35] By involving employees, Planning Agreements were regarded as an important advance in industrial democracy.

(4) Workers must also be involved in the decisions that matter. A policy on industrial democracy was regarded as a means

of achieving a major shift in economic 'power' from capital to labour and so correcting some of the existing inequalities in the economy. It has also been claimed that industrial democracy will raise productivity by reducing those industrial relations disputes and restrictive labour practices which result from the conflict between labour and capital. The view seemed to be that it is right that those who invest their lives in industry should be participating in decisions.

The mixture of normative and positive statements in the above policy model offers a wealth of material for critical appraisal. There are propositions about the desirability of re-distribution and of extending state intervention of a market-displacing type. Policy-makers seem to be using a growth model which stresses the importance of investment and factor productivity as determined by industrial structure, monopoly and restrictive labour practices and which recognises the role of the balance of payments. Investments in human beings, including the geographical and occupational mobility of labour, are noticeable absentees. Indeed, the emphasis on job security is a potential source of conflict with the resource re-allocation which is inevitably required in any growing economy. Elsewhere there are hypotheses about industrial inefficiency and the relationship between industrial democracy and productivity. Some of these will be assessed in subsequent chapters. For present purposes it is sufficient to have shown how a policy model can be constructed from ministerial statements and White Papers and how the specification of such a model is an essential preliminary in any critical exercise. Opportunities also exist for applying alternative models of behaviour to predict some of the consequences of proposed policy changes. For example, if the state is to be involved in 'decisions that matter', including Planning Agreements, will there be any 'checks' on the state's performance in resource-use and decision-making or will the costs of mistakes be borne by the taxpayer? Will decisions reflect the desire of the political constituency to maximise votes and budgets rather than efficiency in the use of scarce resources?

CONCLUSION: IS IT WORTH IT?

The debate on Britain's growth performance raises the more fundamental question of whether society as a whole wants growth. Growth is not a costless process. It involves present sacrifices of consumption for future benefits, many of which will be reaped by future generations. Other policy objectives such as full employment, price stability and the balance of payments might have to be sacrificed. Growth also involves certain adverse 'spillover effects' called social costs or external diseconomies.[36] Examples include traffic congestion, noise, the pollution of oceans, inland waterways and the atmosphere and the destruction of the countryside. These effects arise because in any transaction, buyers and sellers only consider the benefits and costs which they have to bear: their decisions ignore any possible costs which might be imposed on the rest of the community as a result of their actions. In many cases such as pollution of the air and sea, noise and the destruction of countryside views, the problem of social costs arises because these 'commodities' are common property. No one owns such amenities as clean air, peace and quiet and countryside views; no individual nation owns the high seas. Once it is accepted that growth is not costless, it might be that society is unwilling to accept the costs of change which would be required for Britain to achieve a higher growth rate.[37] If this is the case, part of Britain's comparative growth performance might reflect the preferences of society.

Part III

Micro-Economic Policy

Part III

Macro-Economic Policy

Chapter 8

Price Controls, Markets and Income Distribution

The state frequently intervenes in the market price-setting process. In the UK in recent years, various prices and incomes policies have been used to control the prices of goods and services and of factor incomes. The state also fixes prices in such markets as agriculture, air travel, health, housing, foreign exchange, North Sea oil and gas, roads, university admission and sectors of the labour market (for example, minimum wages and equal pay).[1] Each illustrates the application of both positive and normative economics. The former is used to offer predictions about the likely effects of, and the available evidence on, price controls. The latter considers the 'desirability' of such controls. Thus, economists might agree about the predicted effects of rent control and minimum wage legislation but disagree about whether such controls should be retained or abolished. This chapter considers why governments attempt to control prices and shows how the basic demand and supply framework can be used to analyse regulation. The analysis is straightforward but the frequency with which governments attempt to set prices and incomes and subsequently express concern about the perverse effects of controls suggests that the message cannot be repeated too often. Examples are taken from rent control and the housing market, minimum wage legislation, equal pay and air travel.

WHY DO GOVERNMENTS CONTROL MARKET PRICES?

A government might use price controls to 'correct' market failure. Such controls can be introduced as a means of regulating private monopoly power (for example, NHS drugs). In addition, state control of monopoly prices in product and labour markets has formed the microeconomic foundations of pay policies. Elsewhere, prices might be controlled because of externalities as in the case of the domestic agricultural and defence equipment sectors. Here it is believed that, if left to themselves, private markets will provide 'too little' of the desired commodity, namely, *home* supplies of food and weapons. In each instance, a two-stage exercise is involved which distinguishes the technical and policy aspects of the problem. First, significant market failure and its causes have to be identified. Secondly, from the range of possible alternative policies, it has to be recognised that the choice of price controls to 'correct' a market deficiency represents the policy-maker's preference for market-displacing measures. However, an additional argument is frequently used to justify state control of prices, namely, inequalities in income distribution. It is often claimed that with free market prices, those on relatively low incomes will experience hardship and be unable to purchase the 'basic essentials of life', such as food, clothing and accommodation. Markets are criti-cised because the 'wrong people get the goods': the rich can buy second homes and fresh meat and clothing for their pets, whilst the poor are homeless and unable to feed and clothe their children. Not surprisingly, it has been concluded that these are the 'faults' of mar-kets and that price ceilings and wage floors will 'solve' the problem by redistributing income from rich to poor. Economists can contri-bute to this policy debate by clarifying the issues and, in particular, by separating the technical from the policy aspects of the problem. For example, it can be pointed out that market prices are *one* mechanism for allocating scarce commodities and resources. In their absence, alternative allocative mechanisms are required. The alter-natives include allocation by voting, bureaucracy, dictatorship, bargaining, queuing, force, fraud and deceit, as well as by gifts, in-heritance and chance. Certainly, the allocation problem is not auto-matically solved by preventing market prices from reflecting relative scarcities: there are no costless solutions. At the same time, market prices have never been presented as devices for ensuring that the 'right' people (for example, not the rich?) receive the goods. Such an interpretation misunderstands the essential allocative function of markets. This is not to deny the existence of a poverty problem of concern to policy-makers but rather to suggest that the cause is the existing distribution of income and wealth and not the operation of markets. On this basis, income inequality is regarded as a separate and distinct policy problem and not as an *additional* source of market failure.

Once the policy problem has been defined, economists can assess alternative solutions. Analysis can predict the costs and consequences of alternative measures which can then be related to the stated aims of policy. If poverty is the main problem, policy solutions can include maximum price controls on 'key' commodities (defined by whom?), raising wages for the lower paid, cash transfers or payments in kind, such as education, training and 'free' clothing. The resource costs of alternative policies have to be considered, in particular the extent to which a measure contributes to its stated aims. For example, do the poor benefit and are there any perverse effects such that some poorer members of the community are actually worse off? A demand and supply framework can be used as a general starting point for considering some of these questions and offering predictions about the effects of price controls.

WHAT HAPPENS WHEN A GOVERNMENT INTRODUCES MAXIMUM PRICE CONTROLS?

Consider the market for petrol: it could equally well be bank loans, clothing, eggs, football or theatre tickets, houses, meat, sugar, refrigerators or TVs. Suppose that the government decides to introduce maximum price controls which legally restrict the price of petrol below its market-clearing level. If the price control is effective, the result will be excess demand at the regulated price ($\bar{p}_c$). The initial excess demand in the market period will be q_2q_m in Figure 8.1, but this will rise as suppliers make short- and long-run adjustments reducing the quantity offered in the market to q_S and q_L, respectively.[2]

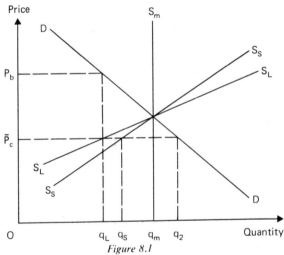

Figure 8.1

Excess demand raises a fundamental problem. If the price mechanism is not allowed to allocate the available quantity of petrol, other methods of allocation must be found. The excess demand will reveal itself in the formation of queues at petrol stations. In the absence of state intervention, garages may decide to allocate the available quantity (oq_m) amongst those requiring oq_2 on the basis of 'first come, first served' or, say, three gallons per customer. Other forms of informal seller rationing might include allocation on the basis of the pump attendant's personal feelings towards his customers or on the basis of his customers' past purchases and behaviour. However, in the case of petrol and commodities such as meat, eggs and butter, it might be deemed socially undesirable to leave the choice of rationing method to the seller. Considerations of equity, need and income distribution will probably dictate a state rationing scheme in which the government would issue ration coupons to each household. Even so, government officials have to ensure that the number of ration tickets issued exactly equals the available quantity of the commodity: an exercise which is not without its costs!

'Black markets' are likely to emerge with maximum price controls. The development of a black market simply means that the price system re-emerges illegally and takes over part of the allocation function outside of the law. For example, petrol might be sold outside the legal market and ration coupons are likely to be traded for cash. Figure 8.1 shows that the black market price for oq_L is P_b. To prevent black markets, the state might have to impose severe penalties, such as heavy fines, imprisonment and even firing squads for those who undertake transactions outside the legal market: this will involve substantial 'policing' costs.

Over time, the market will adjust to the price regulation. Smaller quantities of petrol will be forthcoming. Refining companies will have every incentive to transfer supplies to any unregulated markets, such as domestic central heating. Garages will not be maintained and repaired and some will be converted into units not subject to price controls, such as shops, restaurants and car repairs.

The analysis of maximum price controls shows that in a world of scarcity, the basic forces of demand and supply cannot be eliminated by passing a law. A price ceiling simply transfers the allocative task to some other channel. Whether the allocation is performed by official state rationing, informal seller rationing or by black markets, someone or something has to decide who is to obtain the available quantity of a commodity when a price ceiling is imposed below the market equilibrium. In the case of statutory maximum wage policies, the excess demand will be reflected in unfilled vacancies at employment agencies, with labour being allocated more on non-wage criteria. Black market pressure will be created in the form of illegal payments above the statutory limits ('backhanders') or through legal substitutes, such as the provision of cars, holidays, promotion or second jobs. Whether such price and wage controls are desirable is a normative issue and one which can be assessed using welfare economics as a starting point.

WHAT ARE THE EFFECTS OF CONTROLS ON
ECONOMIC WELFARE?

The total economic welfare of the community consists of the aggregate of consumers' and producers' surpluses.[3] The former is the
difference between the price consumers are willing to pay for a
specific amount of a commodity and the price actually paid: it is the
triangle PBC below the demand curve and above price in Figure 8.2.
Producers' surplus or economic rent accrues to the owners of factors
of production and it is the difference between the minimum supply
price and the price received (the area PCA in Figure 8.2). In the
absence of price controls, total welfare for the community is shown
by aggregating consumers' and producers' surpluses (the triangle
ABC in Figure 8.2, which is also a maximum).

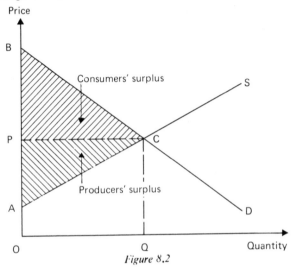

Figure 8.2

What happens to total welfare and to its distribution when a
maximum price control (P_c in Figure 8.3) is introduced into the
market? Who gains and who loses? The controls immediately result
in a net or deadweight loss of welfare to the community, consisting of
losses in both consumers' and producers' surpluses: society is worse
off by the sum represented by triangle *DEC* in Figure 8.3. Within the
smaller total (area *ABED*), there is a redistribution of welfare from
producers to consumers, shown by area P_cPFD. Since some groups
are made better off and others worse off, the desirability of the change
cannot be assessed using the strong Pareto criterion that at least one
person should gain and no one else lose. Indeed, the analysis suggests

that if society wishes to maximise welfare, the abolition of price controls is desirable since the potential gainers can *overcompensate* the potential losers.

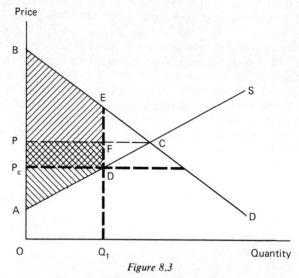

Figure 8.3

The concept of economic surplus has its critics. Problems arise in measuring surplus or utility and in aggregating it for commodities across different individuals. Further distributional difficulties occur where implicit equal 'weightings' are introduced for, say, consumers and producers. Should, for example, the same 'weight' be given to benefits received by consumers and producers (for example, 'wicked' monopolists)? These are some of the questions which confront both economist and policy-maker when assessing the desirability of price controls. However, the fact that economic surplus raises questions is not sufficient to invalidate the use of the concept as a *point of departure* for analysing the welfare effects of policies. Do we have any alternatives?

THE UK HOUSING MARKET AND RENT CONTROL

Rent control is an example of government maximum price controls. Its analysis requires some consideration of the housing problem as seen by policy-makers, the features of the housing market and, ultimately, whether the demand and supply framework yields accurate predictions. The exercise is especially useful in showing how basic demand and supply can be applied to a particular market and how the neglect of such elementary analysis has contributed to the housing problem.

What is the Housing Problem?
Whenever housing policy is debated by politicians, they inevitably refer to such problems as homelessness, overcrowding, slum clearance and urban renewal, the position of low-income families, the level of rents and house prices, mortgages and the issue of subsidies for council tenants and owner-occupiers. Housing 'need' is also a popular phrase, although its meaning is not at all clear. For example, when someone talks about society's housing 'needs', is he imposing his own value-judgements on what is desirable for the community or is he reflecting the majority opinion of the electorate, or is he simply observing that with rent control there are 'shortages'? To economists, it is not at all clear whether houses are 'needed' regardless of cost in terms of the sacrifice of alternatives such as hospitals, schools, roads and private consumer goods.

One political view of the housing market maintains that it is a major aim of policy to ensure that the nation is 'decently' housed.

'We have seen ... that a free market in housing does not work. Rising prices do not stimulate new supplies, on the contrary they intensify the shortage because potential sellers hold off. There could be no solution to the house price problem until we had a government prepared to abandon the free market mechanism and to regard houses not as a commodity to be bought and sold like other resources but as a social service with allocation decided by need. The property market has ceased to be a mechanism for meeting need. Those with the greatest need for housing did not have the income to pay for accommodation. ... The problem of homelessness was growing. A major element in its solution must be the provision of far more publicly owned houses to let.'[4]

Such a quotation is typical of the general methodological approach to housing policy. A single preferred policy recommendation (more publicly owned houses to let) is somehow derived from a proposition that free markets have 'failed' due to two causes. First, the effects of rising prices on supply is believed to be perverse. Such an interpretation is incorrect. If prices in the future are expected to be higher than in the present, then, not surprisingly, income-maximising agents will tend to transfer supply from current to future periods. In other words, supply responds to higher *relative* prices and the observed behaviour is consistent with an upward-sloping supply curve and does not, by itself, constitute a market deficiency. At the same time, the fact that house prices are rising suggests that the market is working properly and attempting to perform its clearing function by eliminating excess demand. Secondly, markets are believed to have failed because housing is regarded not as a commodity but as a social service to be allocated in some unspecified way, by an undefined concept of need (whose?) and presumably by a state housing agency required to act in the 'public interest' (undefined).

Features of the Market for Accommodation

The housing market is basically a market for accommodation in which the major problem is the allocation of the existing *stock*. New constructions can make only a marginal contribution towards increasing the stock of accommodation. To understand the market, it is necessary to outline some of its major features, especially the absence of a single market, the importance of owner-occupied and council housing and the influence of public policy.

There is no single market for houses. Instead, there are a series of related markets in both the private and public sectors. There are markets for owner-occupiers and for rented accommodation. These markets can be further subdivided into private and public sector accommodation, houses and flats, freehold and leasehold, furnished and unfurnished. First impressions might suggest that housing is not a perfect market. Observers might point to imperfections due to product differentiation associated with differences in the location and in the quality of houses, as well as in different prices for physically identical accommodation in various regions. Appearances can be misleading. Competitive markets are characterised by large numbers of buyers and sellers, each acting as price-takers with free entry and exit. With the competitive model, different localities can be viewed as separate 'products', between which there are possibilities of substitution (for example, people can, and do, move). Each area offers different 'product characteristics', such as proximity to a workplace or to clean air, views, peace and quiet. Within each locality, say a city, there will be different accommodation sub-markets, each related through opportunities for substitution. For example, within the private sector, semi-detached houses in different suburbs of a city are likely to be fairly close substitutes so that price movements between areas will be related. So too will relative prices between such substitutes as flats, terraced houses, semi-detached and detached property. In each sector of the private market, there are, in general, sufficiently large numbers of buyers and sellers for their behaviour to *approximate* that of price-takers. Admittedly, information about prices and quality is not instantly available to everyone at *zero* cost.[5] Since resources are scarce, the acquisition of information and knowledge

involves costs for buyers and sellers in the form of direct money outlays and the allocation of time to bargaining and 'searching the market'. However, both buyers and sellers of accommodation are likely
to devote some resources to collecting more information about
exchange possibilities to assist them in making better transactions.
Not surprisingly, since information is a commodity which has
market value, firms are likely to enter the market to exploit any
potential opportunities for profit. In the case of accommodation,
estate agents act as information exchanges, together with local and
national press and TV advertisements. Information in the accommodation market (and in any other market) is certainly not complete
and freely available but this simply reflects the fact that after a point,
it is no longer worthwhile for buyers and sellers to reduce ignorance.
In other words, the accommodation market has a set of specialist
arrangements which lower the costs of acquiring information and so
promote market transactions. In the circumstances, it seems plausible
to suggest that the imperfections in this market are not substantial
so that the market approximates a competitive situation. Ultimately,
of course, the applicability of the competitive model to the housing
market will depend on the accuracy of its predictions rather than on
the detailed realism of the underlying assumptions. Does the model
'explain' the observed facts and are its predictions about the effects
of price controls consistent with the evidence?

Table 8.1   The Total British Housing Stock, 1914–72

Type	1914 %	1947 %	1972 %
Private-rented	88	55	14
Owner-occupied	10	26	52
Local authority	1	12	31

Source: Alex Henney, 'The Housing Situation in the
UK', in *Moorgate and Wall Street* (Autumn
1974); also NIESR, 'The Price of Accommodation', in *Economic Review* (August 1964).

Note: Figures are approximations. 'Others' account for
residuals.

One 'fact' has been the contraction of the private rented sector and
the corresponding growth of local authority and owner-occupied
housing. The evidence is shown in Table 8.1. Demand theory would
partly explain these trends in terms of rising real incomes and changes
in the relative prices of homes, but such an explanation would be

incomplete without reference to the further fact that the market has been influenced by public policy.

Public policy has influenced prices, supply and standards. On prices, one of the facts is that the capital cost of a dwelling greatly exceeds the average workers' annual income. Because of insufficient income and savings, many families are unable to buy a house and must resort to rented accommodation. In the private sector, unfurnished rented accommodation has traditionally been subject to government rent control, first introduced in 1915 (Table 8.1). The 1974 Rent Act extended rent control to furnished accommodation. In addition, local authority house rents have usually been set *below* the free market level, in some cases as part of the state's prices and incomes policy. The relative prices of accommodation have been further influenced by the state subsidisation of owner-occupied housing. Policy has offered tax relief on mortgage repayments and has regulated interest rates. For example, estimates show that between 1949 and 1970 the *real* rate of interest for mortgages was relatively low and even negative in some years.[6] Predictably, with cheap finance and with house ownership an attractive asset offering an estimated return of 15 per cent to 20 per cent,[7] demand has been stimulated and prices have risen.

On the supply side, new rented houses have been almost exclusively provided in the public sector by local authorities. With the contraction of the private rented sector and for those unable to buy and wishing to rent, the only alternative is a council house. For rented accommodation, the private sector has been substantially replaced by local authorities. The explanation for this change is not unrelated to the state regulation of private sector rents. The fallacy is to advocate public-sector housing on the grounds that the private-rented stock has contracted, whilst completely ignoring the contribution of rent control to the housing problem. Clearly, where rents are controlled at too low a level, private firms will *always* 'fail' to supply sufficient housing to eliminate the excess demand (the housing 'problem'). If the state wishes to remove the excess demand whilst operating within a constraint of private-sector rent control, then government intervention to supply public-sector houses is one possibility for public policy. The 'logic' is impeccable: if you do not let markets work they will be seen to fail and hence have to be displaced! Governments have also intervened in the housing market to maintain minimum standards for public health reasons. Such intervention might be justified on externality grounds. Private markets will otherwise tend to neglect the costs which 'unhealthy' sanitation might impose on the rest of the community through infectious diseases. Once the state controls rents, further intervention is required to ensure that minimum housing standards are observed, the belief being that this will provide low-income families with socially acceptable conditions of accommodation.

The Effects of Rent Control

If the general model of price controls is valid, it should be revealed in evidence of excess demand for rent-controlled property, black market pressures and landlords transferring their property and new investments to the unregulated and more profitable activities. These predictions are consistent with the facts.[8]

Excess demand for rent-controlled accommodation in both the private and public sectors has been reflected in 'waiting lists'. Indeed, the length of waiting lists measures the extent to which the controlled rent is *below* the market rent. Waiting lists for council houses are a well-known fact, with allocation frequently based on a points system determined by such factors as size of family, number of years on the list, age, health and current accommodation. Size of waiting lists has also been used as an indicator of society's 'need' for housing (for example, homeless, shortages). When accommodation becomes available in the rent-controlled private sector, it is not unknown for rent collectors to require 'key money'[9] from the prospective tenant. The excess demand in the private sector results in the re-emergence of the price mechanism in such black market forms as key money. Further evidence of excess demand and black markets was provided in the Francis Report which examined the operation of the 1965 Rent Act.[10] Evidence was found of harassment and illegal eviction in the private sector. Whilst the law provides penalties for these offences, the Francis Report felt that, at the time, these were inadequate. Clearly, offences such as illegal eviction are not really surprising in a market situation where there were possibilities of cash gains to landlords if they could change their tenants and obtain higher rents for their property.

The existence of waiting lists and queues in the controlled sectors means that some of the unsatisfied demand 'spills over' into the remaining substitutes, especially the market for house purchase. This spillover effect together with rising real incomes and the availability of cheap mortgage finance have resulted in an increasing demand for house purchase. Theory predicts rising house prices in a situation of increasing demand: a prediction which is supported by the evidence. The average purchase price of both new and used houses has generally followed an upward trend throughout the post-war period.

Rent control results in a reduction in the rate of return on private investment in rent-controlled property compared with the return on an investment in similar markets which are not subject to price regulation. As a result, it must be expected that rent control will reduce the long-run supply of *new* buildings for the rent-controlled private sector. One UK survey has concluded that 'private building for rent has virtually disappeared due partly to rent control, partly to competition from local authorities and partly to increased and more attractive opportunities for investment in industrial and commercial undertakings'.[11] Table 8.1 provides the supporting evidence.

But rent control also provides every incentive for landlords to transfer their *existing* property and any new investments from the regulated to the uncontrolled sectors, such as shops, offices and luxury flats. Until 1974, regulation was restricted to unfurnished accommodation. Many landlords responded by transferring their property to the furnished sector of the market. The 1974 extension of regulation and security of tenure to furnished accommodation predictably led to an immediate and substantial diminution in the supply of this type of rented property.[12] Finally, landlords have also adjusted by selling their rent-controlled property to tenants so contributing to an increase in the stock of owner-occupied dwellings and a further decline in privately rented houses.

Rent control adversely affects the quality of privately rented houses and this is seen in the existing stock of dwellings. Controls reduce the relative rate of return on rented property. Landlords receive lower incomes which might be expected to reduce both their *ability* and the *incentives* to maintain and repair accommodation. This has happened on a substantial scale, with obvious implications for slums. The eventual demolition of these slums will further reduce the stock of privately rented houses! A government White Paper succinctly described the problem when it stated that rent control had accelerated '. . . the deterioration of Britain's older houses. A landlord who receives only a controlled rent cannot be expected to maintain, let alone improve, his house. If the present system [of rent control] is continued, slum clearance will be neutralised by the drift into "slum-dom" of controlled houses.'[13]

A Conclusion on Rent Control

Is rent control desirable? The answer to this normative question depends upon the aims of public policy and on the valuation placed by society on the effects of regulation. Some of its advocates suggest that rent control results in a 'desirable' re-distribution of income. Presumably, this re-distribution takes place from supposedly rich landlords to apparently poor tenants. Certainly, where the tenant pays a controlled rent which is less than the market rent, there is a re-distribution of income from landlord to tenant (see Figure 8.3). If, however, the aim of policy is to re-distribute income from rich to poor then the advocates of rent control are required to show that in general landlords are 'rich' and tenants are 'poor' (with unambiguous definitions of rich and poor). On this empirical question, one government White Paper has stated that 'Rent control was introduced to protect the tenant but most controlled rents . . . barely cover the cost of proper maintenance. Tenants are being subsidised by their landlords. Many landlords are poorer than the tenants who enjoy a very low rent at their expense.'[14]

If rent control is retained for distributional objectives, its advocates are also required to show that it is a more efficient policy instrument than such alternatives as minimum wage legislation, industrial training and cash payments to the poor, such as negative income taxes. Analysis and the evidence have shown that the policy is by no means the attractive and costless option it appears to be. Its long-run effects have been perverse, in that there has been a reduction in the supply of houses for people it was designed to protect. Nor are there any incentives for the efficient use of controlled accommodation, and its tenants are unlikely to be mobile. Even the apparent cheapness of controlled accommodation is illusory. Queuing is not costless. New entrants will be required to bear such costs in the form of waiting, searching, negotiating and perhaps making black market payments. In the circumstances, the continued government retention of rent control might be more appropriately explained by the economics of politics. There are more voters amongst tenants than landlords. Controls are also consistent with substantial budgets for central and local authority bureaucrats who are required to provide public-sector housing to replace private slums and to remove 'shortages'. And yet, with other products such as cars, TVs and refrigerators, we have achieved relative affluence. Had any or all of them been subsidised by the state and their prices kept artificially low, it is certain that similar shortages would exist.

WHAT HAPPENS WHEN A GOVERNMENT INTRODUCES MINIMUM PRICE CONTROLS?

Minimum price controls in product and labour markets are the opposite of maximum prices. The state establishes a price or wage *above* the market-clearing level. In the case of, say, the British agricultural and aircraft industries, such a policy aims to support a larger domestic industry than would otherwise exist. Support might be justified for balance of payments, technology or defence reasons. Similarly, in the labour market the state might pursue distributional objectives and try to raise the incomes of the lower paid by increasing wages above the equilibrium level. Minimum prices create excess supply which will be revealed in stocks and surpluses in goods markets and unemployment in labour markets. Excess supply situations lead to downward pressures on prices which might be reflected in illegal price-cutting or in state intervention to support the controlled price level. Once again, 'successful' state intervention in markets is not costless. Who bears the costs and are there any perverse effects of minimum price and wage controls? The International Air Transport Association (IATA) price-fixing cartel provides an example of excess capacity, price-cutting pressures and competition from substitutes. Minimum wage legislation and equal pay show some of the perverse effects of policy.

The IATA Cartel

International air transport is a regulated market, with IATA acting as a price-fixing and regulatory agency for the scheduled airlines. Fares are fixed at a level acceptable to all members, namely the costs of the least efficient airline. The result is a price above the market equilibrium. This producers' cartel is supported by governments who, with their ultimate sanction of 'property rights' (sovereignty) over airspace and landing, have exerted a major influence on the structure of the world airline market. Thus, IATA is basically a state-supported monopoly whose existence constitutes a substantial imperfection and hence a source of market failure. Why has state intervention been 'market-displacing' rather than 'market-improving'?

Airlines as producer interest groups regarded price regulation as a solution to the 'chaos of rate wars' and the alleged adverse effects of price competition on the safety of air travel. It has also been suggested that a free market in air transport would result in bewildered, uninformed consumers swamped with conflicting information.[15] These arguments have to be critically assessed. Apparent 'chaos' is a major characteristic of any competitive market in which firms are competing in prices and responding to uncertainty and associated changes in consumer preferences and in technology. In such markets, the impression of 'chaos' will be reinforced by bankruptcies as the resources employed by inefficient firms and those which make mistakes are re-allocated to more profitable alternative uses. The safety argument is dubious since the fixing of fares does not automatically eliminate the incentives for airlines to cut costs. In principle, safety in air travel is no different from public safety in other forms of transport or in food consumption, housing or in the workplace. If the state wishes to 'protect the consumer' whilst allowing opportunities for choice, it can do so by introducing and enforcing minimum standards rather than by fixing prices and controlling entry. For example, the state imposes minimum road safety standards in the form of tests for both drivers and vehicles, without regulating car prices and entry into the industry. Also, in the case of air transport, a poor airline safety record will be reflected in no business (bankruptcy?) and in pilots unwilling to fly. As for the allegation that a free market in air transport will lead to 'bewildered and uninformed consumers', it is not at all clear that such 'characteristics' are completely absent from the current confusing 'mix' of scheduled and charter fares and flights. Moreover, consumers are the judges of the product. The evidence shows that where markets operate, say, for insurance, house purchase, new and used cars, clothing and jobs, consumers are far from 'bewildered and uninformed' and use the available sources of information (for example, insurance brokers; newspapers) to exercise their choices. As for the airline market, one study has predicted that the removal of price controls will not cause any significant instability in the industry.[16]

A producer's cartel might be expected to operate like a monopolist but IATA differs somewhat in that there are no entry restrictions and new airlines are encouraged to join. The result has been a fare fixed above the market equilibrium (otherwise why operate a cartel?) with excess supply taking the form of empty airliners. Unable to compete in price, the scheduled airlines have resorted to non-price competition to differentiate their products. Airlines have required aircraft which can fly faster within the existing price structure. Thus, non-price competition has resulted in the frequent re-equipment of airlines with new aircraft types, with price restrictions preventing the emergence of a fare structure reflecting marginal costs. Aircraft manufacturers have readily supplied faster airliners since they acquire the relevant technology from state-financed military aircraft projects. Understandably, the manufacturers have applied such 'free goods' to their civil aircraft activities. At the same time, where there are state-owned airlines such as British Airways concerned with non-commercial objectives, some of the costs of operating technically advanced aircraft such as *Concorde* will be borne by the taxpayer.[17] In other words, IATA imposes extra costs on consumers in the form of higher prices, as well as on taxpayers, and results in a re-distribution of income to producer groups in the airline and aircraft manufacturing industries.

IATA has attempted to regulate some forms of non-price competition. In addition to the regulation of schedules and landing rights, there are restrictions on meals, seats, free drinks and film shows on airliners. Once there are constraints on behaviour, airlines will respond by choosing alternative, and less efficient, methods of competition which would not otherwise be chosen. They have competed through advertising expenditures, by offering subsidised car rentals to travellers, sight-seeing tours and 'generous' commission to travel agents. Within IATA, downward pressure on prices has resulted in the introduction of various promotional and excursion fares. The scheduled airlines have also been subject to competition from a substitute market, namely charter flights. In fact, substitutes are one of the major pressures on any cartel, even a government-supported one like IATA.[18] Package holidays and nominal (black market) membership of clubs and societies enable the charter airlines to offer international flights at cut-price fares. Ironically, the non-price competition amongst the scheduled airlines has led to the frequent sale of modern, used jets at relatively low prices to the rival charter companies. In this way, the non-scheduled operators are a means by which the benefits of technical progress in aviation are passed on to the consumer in the form of lower fares! Some scheduled operators have responded to the competition by entering the charter market through subsidiary companies, so providing an outlet for their surplus capacity. Others have demanded restrictions on the flights of their non-scheduled rivals, such as Laker Skytrains, and the introduction of minimum charter fares. The result is a market in which there are major constraints on the ability of the ultimate consumer to express his preferences for combinations of price, speed, route and service. Instead, the regulatory arrangements appear to be aimed at satisfying the interests of both producer groups and bureaucracies. Regulation has been substantial, much of it being a logical extension of the initial decision to fix fares. Thus, British and foreign governments have been involved in the subsidisation of airlines, the regulation of flights in an attempt to restrict supply (compare agricultural policy) and the 'policing' of the non-scheduled competitive sector. Certainly, governments have discovered that price fixing has consequences which extend beyond the initial, *apparently* simple, decision to regulate airline fares!

Minimum Wage Legislation

Minimum wage legislation *appears* to be an attractive solution to the problem of poverty due to low pay. Where the low paid are concentrated in specific industries, politicians frequently argue that workers' incomes can be raised simply by introducing a (higher) legal minimum wage. Demand and supply analysis shows the fallacy of this argument and that the policy leads to perverse results: some of those who are supposed to benefit find themselves without jobs!

An effective legal minimum wage will raise wage rates above the market equilibrium level. Using the competitive model, it can be predicted that there will be a reduction in the quantity of labour demanded or less employment and a rise in the amount supplied, the net effect being unemployment at the new legal minimum price. Those who remain employed receive higher wages, which was the original policy objective. However, others who are supposed to benefit from the policy actually lose their jobs, an outcome which is clearly inconsistent with the aim of poverty-reduction! The market is likely to react in a variety of ways. Some of the unemployed will be willing to undercut the legal minimum or encourage other members of the household to seek work. Others will enter unregulated markets so further reducing relative wages in such occupations. Employers will respond by substituting machines for men, by changing working conditions and, where possible, by re-defining jobs so as to be exempt from the legislation. Whether the introduction of a legal minimum will cause the industry's total wage bill to rise or fall depends on the elasticity of demand for labour. An inelastic demand over the relevant range will result in an increase in the industry's total wage bill. In addition, for the employed, there is a re-distribution of economic surplus from producers to labour, although *total* welfare is reduced (see Figure 8.3).

The competitive model predicts unemployment following the imposition of a legal minimum wage. There are two possible exceptions to this prediction, each depending on the existence of monopoly, and neither of which has much empirical support. First, there is the shock-effect hypothesis. This asserts that firms are technically inefficient and that minimum wage legislation will 'shock' them into increased efficiency without any reduction in employment. Such inefficiency generally arises when competitive pressures are weak or absent, as in private- or public-sector monopolies. Here, the available British and American evidence shows that many of the low-paying private industries are in fact amongst the most competitive and are presumably receiving sufficient shocks from rival firms.[19] Secondly, there is the monopsony (exploitation) hypothesis. A monopsony labour market is dominated by one buyer and to raise employment, the firm has to offer higher wages for new and existing employees so that marginal labour cost exceeds average labour cost. In this market situation, there is a limited range over which it is possible to introduce a higher legal minimum wage without causing unemployment. The range will vary between monopsonists, so that a single minimum wage will not be sufficiently discriminatory. However, the fact that many of the low-paying industries tend to be competitive suggests that monopsony is absent from these sectors. Other economists have been even more sceptical. Some have asserted that 'over a longer period, the flow of workers from other employers and areas makes this case of little significance'.[20]

What is the evidence on the predictive accuracy of the competitive model? In Britain there are wages councils and boards which determine statutory minimum wages. These bodies aim to protect the low-paid in such industries as agriculture, catering, retail distribution, hairdressing and other sectors where collective bargaining is weak. Unfortunately there is little evidence on the income and employment effects of wages councils. Whilst they are most likely to have raised wage rates above their market levels, one report has concluded that they generally afford inadequate protection to the low-paid and their existence inhibits the development of more effective voluntary arrangements.[21] If 'more effective voluntary arrangements' means trade unions, evidence is required on their relative wage effects. It has been tentatively estimated that for British male manual workers in the early 1960s, unions raised the hourly earnings of their members by an average of 0–10 per cent, with the union differential probably increasing to about 25 per cent for 1968–73.[22]

American evidence on the effects of minimum wage legislation is more extensive and persuasive and confirms the predictive accuracy of the competitive model. American studies have found that the average unemployment rate in the States with minimum wage laws has been higher than in areas without such laws. Similarly, it has been shown that in the low-wage industries, increases in Federal minimum wages have generally been followed by employment reductions. Since the minimum wage legislation directly affects the relatively low paid, studies have identified increases in unemployment amongst the unskilled, women, non-whites and teenagers, especially non-white teenagers. Other US studies have confirmed that the firms most affected by minimum wage laws have been induced to substitute capital for labour.[23] Admittedly, empirical work in this area requires all other relevant variables to be held constant. The demand for labour can vary due to technical progress and changes in consumer preferences, whilst shifts in labour supply can occur because of population changes, mobility, education and training. Nevertheless, the available evidence from a variety of sources and using different empirical tests is impressive in its general agreement on the unemployment effects of minimum wage laws.

If society wishes to reduce poverty, legal minimum wages do not appear to be the most appropriate policy instrument: they penalise some of the people they are designed to help! Nor are the poor restricted to low-paid individual wage-earners. They embrace large and one-parent families, pensioners and the unemployed, including the disabled and older workers. Moreover, some further US evidence is equally disturbing. It indicates that legal minimum wages create pressures to re-establish traditional income differentials so that legislation does not appear to have secured permanent, long-run improvements in the relative earnings of low-paid workers. In view of the evidence, a UK report on low pay predicted that the introduction of a *national* minimum wage for Britain would create some unemployment and, through labour market pressures to restore differentials, it would be a source of cost inflation.[24] The report concluded that since there is no single cause of low pay, there is no single remedy. It did, however, express a preference for improved state manpower policies (for example, information, training) and, more especially, for the continued use of redistributive measures through the taxation and social security systems.[25]

Equal Pay

A major feature of labour markets in Britain is that women have traditionally earned less than men. Earnings differentials have existed between men and women within an occupation and women have been disproportionately represented in the low-paying jobs. In competitive markets, such wage differentials reflect relative scarcities. These depend on differences in the productivity of labour, personal abilities and talents, the costs of training and variations in the non-monetary aspects of jobs. Interestingly, some US studies show that when some of these factors, together with differences in hours worked, are taken into account, the earnings differential between men and women is usually much less than is shown by a simple, un-adjusted comparison.[26] However, it has often been argued that discrimination against women is the main cause of wage differentials. Discrimination is rarely defined. Two interpretations are plausible. First, monopsonistic exploitation might be classed as discrimination. If so, it is implied that monopsony markets are confined to, and only discriminate against, women: a proposition which lacks both analytical and empirical support. Secondly, discrimination might be defined as employers having preferences for men rather than for women, even though the situation is remarkably similar to employees, consumers and voters possessing different tastes and preferences! A firm's recruiting patterns will reflect income-maximising behaviour and employers might have concluded that it is too costly to obtain additional information on the productivity of women compared with men at the same wage rate.[27] It does, however, become profitable to employ women at a relatively lower wage. Competitive markets provide a 'check' on the accuracy of these 'discriminatory beliefs' since, if one firm believes that, on average, women are more productive than men *at a given wage rate*, it will have every incentive to recruit women. If its profits rise, rivals will 'copy' the innovating firm and the market will revise its preferences or recruiting rules. Once sexual discrimination is believed to exist (what is the UK evidence?)

laws requiring equal pay for men and women doing the same jobs *appear* to be an attractive solution to the achievement of greater social justice.[28] An alternative interpretation regards such laws as a clever male plot (hence their higher productivity?) to perpetuate the predominance of men in society! Economic analysis is required.

The UK Equal Pay Act of 1970 aimed, within a five-year period, to eliminate any discrimination between men and women's wages and conditions of employment. The intention was to raise female wage rates to the same level as those for men for 'identical' work: what is identical or equal work? The effects of the Act are readily predictable using demand and supply analysis and are similar to those of minimum wage legislation. If the law is effective, women's wage rates will be raised above their market level so resulting in a decline in female employment and the creation of unemployment. Profit-maximising firms will have every incentive to substitute relatively cheaper for more expensive factors of production. A rise in female wage rates will change the price of women in relation to other, non-female inputs. Thus, in so far as factors are partial (but not perfect) substitutes, firms will at the margin respond to the introduction of equal pay by replacing women with men and/or machines.[29] Equal pay will mean that some women will lose their jobs whilst there will be an increase in the demand for *male* substitutes, and this will create upward pressure on *men's* wage rates! The evidence on the effects of minimum wage legislation tends to support these predictions. Of course, many women will retain their jobs and will benefit from the higher wage rates due to the legislation. The possibility that more are likely to gain than lose from equal pay laws explains their attractiveness to vote-maximising, male politicians. Indeed, equal pay laws are attractive to the male interest group in the political constituency. They protect the jobs of men by reducing the opportunities for women to replace men by accepting a lower wage.

CONCLUSION: CAN WELFARE ECONOMICS HELP?

In many cases, price controls are regarded as a policy instrument for tackling the problem of poverty and improving the distribution of income in society. This is the case with rent control and minimum wage legislation, although policy tends to have perverse effects and results in net losses of economic welfare. If society wishes to reduce poverty, alternative policies are available, some of which are more direct and likely to have more favourable effects on economic welfare. Consider, for example, the problem of choosing between general price subsidy policies and cash payments as alternative methods of relieving poverty. The policy-makers' choice will depend on the likely effects of the alternatives in relation to the aims of public policy. The

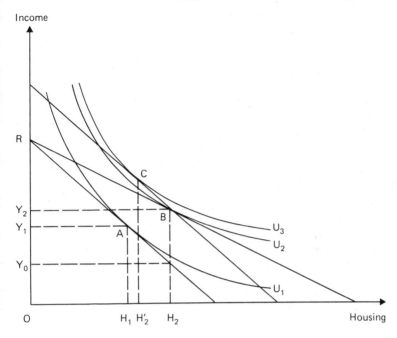

Figure 8.4 Price Subsidies vs Cash Payments

effects of the policies on consumer behaviour and on individual utilities are shown in Figure 8.4.

Price subsidies can be given to low-income groups for the purchase of 'socially desirable' commodities, such as food, clothing and housing (see rent control). If, say, housing is subsidised, there will be a change in the relative prices of goods with consumers buying more of the subsidised and hence relatively cheaper commodity. There will be both income and substitution effects as consumers move to a higher level of utility, namely U_2 at point B in Figure 8.4, point A being the initial equilibrium. The state could adopt the alternative method of reducing poverty by offering lump-sum cash payments to the poor via negative income taxes or cash family allowances. The state expenditure on the housing subsidy for the individual is $Y_2 Y_0$.[30] If this amount is offered to the individual as a lump-sum cash payment, the resulting income effect will move the consumer to position C. Utility is higher than with price subsidies but less housing is bought and more is spent on other commodities. Thus, if policy aims to maximise individual utility, lump-sum cash payments are preferable. If, however, individuals are deemed not to be the best judges of their welfare, society might prefer the policy which maximises housing consumption for a given state expenditure.[31] Once again, the analysis is only a starting point and further complications are possible. For example, the traditional assumption is made that transfer payments are costless. However, in a democracy, the possibility of a redistributory transfer leads income-maximising individuals and interest groups to invest resources in either obtaining a transfer or in preventing its abolition. British examples have occurred with poverty relief, especially for large families and pensioners, as well as with regional aid, tariff protection, the allocation of government contracts and state aid to firms. In the circumstances, transfers are likely to involve costs in forming a pressure group to acquire and present information and to lobby MPs.[32] Further costs have to be considered. For price subsidies, there are substantial administration costs in ensuring that only the poor benefit and not the rich. Cash payments appear attractive, especially since they can be designed to help *all* categories of people rather than specific industrial, occupational, age or wage rate groups. Nevertheless, they involve costs in the form of possible adverse effects on the supply of effort. Cash transfers can take the form of a variant of the negative income tax or social security payments. Their effects on the individual's supply of effort are shown in Figure 8.5, where they are also compared with a higher minimum wage.

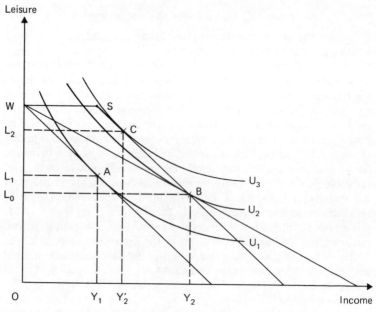

Figure 8.5 Cash Payments and Higher Minimum Wages

Assume that the state wishes to raise the income levels of the low-paid. This can be done either by raising the minimum wage or by offering a cash payment. Before state assistance, the individual works WL_1 hours and receives an income of Y_1 (position A). With an increase in the minimum wage, the worker moves to position B where he supplies more effort (WL_0) and receives a higher income (Y_2). However, if a cash subsidy of WS is offered such that income Y_2 could be earned with the same effort, the individual would choose position C. His level of satisfaction would be higher than with the increased minimum wage, but the supply of effort (WL_2) and the level of income (Y_2') would both be lower. In some cases, the individual's preference might be such that with a cash subsidy he chooses not to work at all. Thus, if society wishes to encourage work and to achieve higher income levels for the poor, increased minimum wages appear attractive – at least for those who retain their jobs! On the other hand, if society is concerned with the satisfaction of individuals, cash subsidies are preferable. Of course, much depends on the individual's preference function, especially the relative magnitudes of the income and substitution effects. Clearly, individual preferences and wage rates are not identical. Even so, the results of UK and US sample surveys and econometric studies of the incentive effects of taxation provide some relevant insights. In general, the studies show that taxation does not have a large and significant effect on the total supply of work effort.[33] Preliminary results from US income maintenance experiments show that negative income tax schemes do not produce substantial reductions in the supply of work effort.[34] A UK survey of the effects of income tax on overtime found that over 70 per cent of the men and more than 90 per cent of the women interviewed claimed no effect from taxation.[35] For this 'no effect' group, it seems that the income and subtitution effects roughly cancelled out each other. At the margin, though, the evidence suggested that taxation makes employees work *longer* rather than shorter hours, but the net effect for men is a relatively small *increase* of about half an hour a week. For this group, the income effect dominates the substitution effect. In total, these results (together with those from other studies) suggest that both increased minimum wages and cash transfers are likely to have disincentive effects on the supply of effort.[36] Whilst the relative magnitudes of such disincentives will differ between the two policies, in both cases they are unlikely to be substantial.

Chapter 9

Large Firms, Mergers and Public Policy

INTRODUCTION

UK manufacturing industry is dominated by a small number of large firms.[1] Not only are the dominant firms large but the trend has been towards larger units. Firms with over 10,000 workers accounted for 14 per cent of total manufacturing employment in 1935 and almost 40 per cent in 1968. At the same time, the reduction in the number of manufacturing firms from 140,000 in 1935 to under 60,000 in 1972 was almost entirely due to the fall in the number of small firms. Even so, small enterprises remain numerically important within the total population of firms. What determines the size of firms?

Recent British industrial policy has been concerned with the size of firms and with the operation of the capital market. State agencies, such as the Industrial Reorganisation Corporation (IRC, 1966–71) and the National Enterprise Board (NEB, 1975), have promoted mergers to create larger units and so re-structure British industry. How do policy-makers view mergers and large firms? What are the economic arguments for bigness and are these arguments supported by the evidence, especially on the performance of large firms? Moreover, since there are no costless policies, what are the likely costs of a policy favouring large units?

POLICY AND THE SIZE OF FIRMS: THE CASE FOR MERGERS AND BIGNESS

Policy-makers have frequently claimed that in a number of industries the average British firm is too small to achieve most of the worthwhile economies of scale and to undertake research and development (R&D). This is a view which resembles Chamberlin's model of monopolistic competition with a large number of relatively small firms, each of less than optimum size and each producing a slightly differentiated product.[2] Not surprisingly, policy-makers have usually concluded that mergers and rationalisation are required to create larger enterprises capable of operating at a greater scale and undertaking more R&D. These are the conventional arguments for 'bigness' which were reflected in the IRC, 1966–71, and in its successor, the NEB. Both agencies were based on the belief that: 'There is no evidence that we can rely on market forces alone to produce the necessary structural change at the pace required.'[3] A 'gap' was believed to exist in the institutional framework of the capital market. It was claimed that no organisation existed with the specific function of searching for opportunities to promote rationalisation schemes which could yield substantial benefits to the national economy. Thus, the IRC and NEB can be regarded as state agencies for 'correcting' an alleged failure in the private capital market. Indeed, in the context of the IRC, it was asserted that there is

'no theoretical or empirical justification for believing that the market in company shares will do the reorganisation job that needs to be done; will do it at all or quickly enough or will achieve the optimum pattern of partnership, or with due regard to domestic economic interests as distinct from overseas commercial ones. The IRC Board was, of course, human and fallible; it could not, and did not, claim to "know best" in every situation; but at least it was able to start from the right place and to look at situations as a whole.'[4]

This is a fascinating mixture of positive and normative, analytical and empirical propositions which at least provide insights into the underlying policy model for the IRC and NEB. For the economist, the task in analysing policy is to distinguish between the *technical issues* concerned with the potential sources of market failure and the *policy issues*, relating to the alternatives and the selection of the most appropriate solution.

If there is a capital market failure, the policy model implies that this could be due to externalities: the market is failing to consider the 'national interest' and, furthermore, it under-invests in information about the range of profitable opportunities in domestic and export markets. Whilst buyers and sellers are willing to pay for information, private competitive markets are unlikely to provide as much of the commodity as consumers require. Under-provision arises because of the difficulty of establishing property rights in information. If a firm sells information to an individual, how can it prevent such information being given to others who might otherwise be willing to pay for the service?[5] However, the existence of market failure does not indicate the most appropriate policy solution. A variety of alternatives are feasible, including the state subsidisation of private information agencies in the capital market, changes in company legislation requiring firms to provide more information, or public ownership. Additional criteria are required for the choice of state agencies, such as the NEB, with discretionary powers to pursue their own interpretation of the 'problem'. The policy case for 'bigness' can also be assessed on empirical grounds. What is the evidence on scale economies and R&D in British industry?

WHAT DETERMINES THE SIZE OF FIRMS?

Theory explains firm size in terms of its objective function and the underlying cost and demand conditions. For example, a firm which aims to maximise sales revenue will produce a greater output, and hence operate at a larger scale, than a profit-maximiser. Once a firm decides that a larger output will contribute to its preferred objective its choice between internal expansion or merger as a means of growth will partly depend on the expected relative costs of each alternative. Given a firm's objective, size will depend on demand and cost conditions. Under competition, a profit-maximiser's size will be limited not by the market but by cost conditions, usually represented by a U-shaped long-run average cost curve (LAC). This is a planning schedule showing the lowest cost of operations when all factors can be varied and the firm is unconstrained by a 'fixed' size of plant. Scale economies lead to lower unit costs as output and the scale of operations is increased, with the optimum size of firm defined by the minimum point on a U-shaped LAC. In a competitive market, firms will tend to be of optimal size so that there are no unexploited scale economies.[6] Also, optimal size is relatively small so that the market will support a large number of firms. Under monopolistic competition, free entry and demand conditions restrict large numbers of firms to less than optimal size: the so-called long-run tangency solution. However, this model raises problems. For example, what is the meaning of an industry and its demand curve with product differentiation – how do we aggregate differentiated products such as Minis and Rolls-Royce cars? In the absence of legal restrictions, why do not income-maximising firms combine and produce the industry's output in a smaller number of plants operating at optimal scale? If prices remain unchanged and unit costs fall, abnormal profits will be available for sharing between members of the combination, so that each firm will gain by joint profit-maximisation. Finally, observations of the tangency solution using accounting cost data can be misleading. If an optimal size firm earning abnormal profits is sold, its market price will be based on the capitalised value of the foregone profits.[7] This acquisition price, including rent or profit, will enter the firm's accounting data as expenditures which, if mistakenly interpreted as costs, will give a tangency solution!

EVIDENCE ON SCALE ECONOMIES

The evidence on LAC curves shows that they are typically L-shaped, sloping downwards at first and then tending to be horizontal. The point at which the curve becomes horizontal defines the minimum optimum or efficient scale. Although the evidence conflicts with the traditional U-shaped LAC, its acceptance depends on the validity of the empirical work. Confusion can arise if accounting concepts of 'cost' are used to measure what is basically an *ex ante*, subjective planning schedule existing in the mind of an entrepreneur. Estimating LAC curves requires that variations in technical efficiency, factor prices and technical change, including learning effects (see Chapter 7), be isolated and held constant. Two examples of the estimating problems are shown in Figure 9.1, where each dotted curve shows an estimated LAC (LÂC) curve of the observed L-shape. Since only one point on each short-run cost (SAC) curve is a long-run equilibrium, there is a danger that the estimated LÂC curve might be based on unit costs which are not 'true' long-run positions, as shown in Figure 9.1(a). Even if points on the true LAC curves are identified, if technical change is not correctly allowed for, the estimated LÂC curve might once again appear, incorrectly, to be L-shaped, as shown in Figure 9.1(b).[8] Presumably policy-makers have no such doubts about the validity of the evidence and its significance for their preference for large firms!

A policy favouring large firms requires evidence on the output where scale economies are exhausted and on the cost implications of lower outputs. Evidence of L-shaped LAC curves exists for such

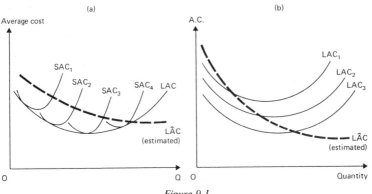

Figure 9.1

British industries as aircraft, books, cars, chemicals, footwear, news-papers, steel and oil tanker operations.[9] In the case of cars, minimum efficient scale (*mes*) in the 1960s required an annual output of 500,000 units of one model. Car firms operating at only 50 per cent of *mes* were likely to experience a cost disadvantage of some 6 per cent. For aircraft, books, bricks and newspapers, there are substantial cost disadvantages of 20 per cent or more when output is only 50 per cent of *mes*. A major policy question is how many plants of *mes* can the market support? If it can support only a small number of *mes* plants there will be a conflict between efficient scale and competition. The price of efficient scale might be monopoly or oligopoly. For example, in a study of thirty-five UK industries, there were eight where *mes* was 100 per cent or more of the UK market, including exports; and the sample was biased towards products with substantial scale economies. Not surprisingly, the list included aircraft, computers, diesel engines, machine tools and newspapers.[10] In contrast, there were some twenty products where the UK market would support four or more firms: a number consistent with the Government's definition of competition. These included plants in beer, bricks, footwear and textiles. In other words, if policy-makers rely solely on the criterion of *mes*, there are substantial parts of the UK economy where a re-structuring of in-dustry would allow scale economies to be fully exploited without creating monopoly.

TECHNICAL PROGRESS

Supporters of large firms also maintain that they promote technical progress, the benefits of which will be passed on to consumers in the form of lower prices. The hypothesis is that only firms which are of large absolute size can afford the costly R&D necessary for technical progressiveness. A further distinction is usually made between ab-solute size and industrial structure, the argument being that market power is also required for technical progress. Thus, Galbraith has argued that:

'The competition of the competitive model . . . almost completely precludes technical development. Because development is costly . . . it can be carried on only by a firm that has the resources which are associated with considerable size. Moreover, unless a firm has a substantial share of the market it has no strong incentive to under-take a large expenditure on development.'[11]

Central to the debate is the difficulty or costs of establishing property rights in new ideas. Consider an individual who discovers a new product or process which has market value. If the inventor cannot establish property rights or ownership in his ideas, he is unable to prevent copying and imitation. Rivals who have not borne any development costs will capture some of the pioneer's profits. More formally, the copying or 'theft' of ideas creates a spillover or external economy since rival firms acquire valuable knowledge at zero price (a free good). So, if an inventor cannot establish property rights in his ideas, there will be an adverse effect on their profitability which will reduce the incentive to invest. On this basis, it is argued that competitive markets will tend to under-invest in invention and research: an innovating competitive firm will find its new ideas promptly copied. The analysis is not without its critics.[12] Property rights depend on legal arrangements and their enforcement by private or public means. Inventors can be 'protected' by patents, by higher penalties for illegal copying and by private policing arrangements, all of which involve costs. But information is not unique and resembles any valuable asset such as antiques, cars or jewels, in that its 'theft' cannot be eliminated at reasonable cost. As a result of scarcity, there will be an optimal amount of 'theft' in an economy. Consequently, it is possible for a free enterprise system to achieve the 'correct' adjustment to risk and theft once it is recognised that such adjustments are not costless. Although these reservations are non-trivial, they do not accurately reflect the extent of the debate about 'bigness'. This can be most appropriately presented by considering the case for large firms in oligopoly markets.

In an industry consisting of a few large firms, price competition will be non-existent. Each oligopolist will be faced with a kinky demand curve reflecting his beliefs or expectations about his rival's reactions to a price change. A kinky demand curve in Figure 9.2 shows that, if the oligopolist reduces price below *OP*, he expects that his rivals will follow, so that his demand curve is believed to be relatively inelastic for price-cutting. Similarly, if price rises above *OP*, he expects that his rivals will not follow, resulting in a relatively elastic demand curve for price increases. Owing to the oligopolists' beliefs about his rival's reactions to price changes, price is supposed to stabilise at *OP*.[13]

The absence of price competition under oligopoly creates *pressures* for non-price competition in such forms as technical innovation. Also, the large absolute size of firms means that they have the *capacity* for costly R&D. Moreover, the existence of small numbers means that each oligopolist possesses market power which provides an *opportunity* for innovation. Without price competition, the returns from costly R&D will accrue to the innovator and a few rivals who might imitate, but the benefits will not be immediately passed on to

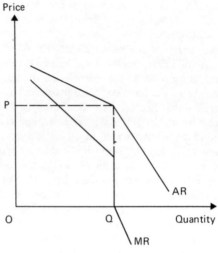

Figure 9.2

consumers through lower prices. Casual empiricism supports the advocates of large, oligopolistic firms. For example, in 1960 over 90 per cent of all UK industrial R&D was spent by large firms of over 2,000 employees. Similarly, in both the UK and USA the highly research-intensive industries, such as aircraft, chemicals, electronics and vehicles, are oligopolistic. Appearances, however, can be deceptive. R&D expenditures are inputs and not measures of output. Nor does it follow that *all* large, oligopolistic firms will innovate: some might prefer a 'quiet life'. Indeed, one study of some sixty recent inventions found that only twelve came from the laboratories of large firms whilst over half were the work of independent inventors and small firms.[14] For policy purposes, it is also necessary to know whether R&D continues rising with greater size or whether there is some minimum threshold level. A survey of available empirical work has concluded: 'The hypothesis that sheer size and a monopolistic-type market structure are sufficient prerequisites of a greater volume of research rests on shaky empirical foundations. It is true that R&D effort is concentrated in large firms but research intensity appears not to increase significantly with size or the degree of concentration of the market.'[15] If this is the case, doubts attach to some of the dynamic arguments for bigness.

THE PERFORMANCE OF LARGE FIRMS:
ARE THEY SUCCESSFUL?

Scale and technology are standard arguments for bigness but policy-makers require additional information on the actual performance of large firms. Are they relatively more profitable and 'good' for growth? A major British study found no systematic relationship between the size of firm and *average* growth and profit rates.[16] Indeed, the independence of profitability and size supports the modern managerial theories of the firm which deny the existence of an optimum size to which all profit-maximising firms should tend. It was, however, found that the *variability* of both growth and profit rates decrease as size increases. Comparing large and small units, the former have more predictable growth and profit rates but not, on average, higher ones. Since it is not obvious that larger firms result in above-average profit and growth rates, there is scope for a more critical policy approach to bigness. British evidence also shows that profits are a major influence on the growth of firms. A strong positive relationship was identified between the growth of firms and profitability, with profitability 'explaining' about 50 per cent of the variability in growth rates.[17] Thus, if society wishes to raise the growth rate, policy-makers cannot ignore the role of profits in the economy. This raises questions about the allocative function of the capital market and, for our purposes, the role of take-overs. Is there any support for the IRC assertion of capital market failure?

TAKE-OVERS AND THE CAPITAL MARKET:
DO TAKE-OVERS IMPROVE EFFICIENCY?

Take-overs or mergers are a means by which firms can grow. In theory, they are a possible mechanism by which the capital market promotes a more efficient use of the existing assets of firms. This is likely to arise through either the threat or actuality of take-overs. It is believed that the *threat* of take-overs acts as a 'policing and disciplinary' mechanism forcing managers to maximise profits, otherwise they would not survive. Actual take-overs are likely to raise profitability if scale economies are obtained or if superior management is injected into the acquired unit. The accuracy of such predictions will have further implications for policy towards mergers and bigness as well as contributing to the debate about whether firms are profit-maximisers.

Acquisition explains why most firms disappear. Between 1955 and 1973, company 'deaths' were mostly due to take-overs, whereas before 1955 the main cause was liquidation.[18] The change could reflect the post-war stability in the level of economic activity, the greater ease of acquisition due to widely dispersed share-holding, together with the 1960s government policy which favoured large units. During the 1960s, the number of mergers varied between a minimum of some 630 in 1961 and a maximum of about 1,000 in 1965. Thus, a substantial amount of structural change occurred before the formation of the IRC in 1966. In other words, private markets were adjusting so that the case for an IRC-type agency had to be based on the market failing to provide the 'correct' structural change in the sense of 'too little of the desirable type'.

WHAT ARE THE CHARACTERISTICS OF THE ACQUIRING, SURVIVING AND TAKEN-OVER FIRMS?

Between 1955 and 1970 the UK firms which were taken over were, on average, smaller, less profitable and slower growing, with possibly lower valuation and higher retention ratios, than the companies not taken over.[19] However, whilst the acquired companies usually had worse records than those not taken over, there was an extremely large degree of overlap between the characteristics of the two groups of firms, so that none of the variables could be deemed a 'good' discriminator. For example, between 1967 and 1970, almost 60 per cent of the taken-over companies were below the median profitability for their industry; but this means that some 40 per cent of the 'victims' were in the top half of the profitability league and were nevertheless taken over. Thus, whilst there is selection for survival on the basis of profitability, especially against firms with very low profitability, the take-over mechanism cannot be relied upon to distinguish among the large number of firms whose profitability is neither extremely high nor extremely low. Indeed, the evidence shows that for a firm wishing to survive, it is likely to be a superior strategy to increase its relative size rather than its relative profits. Above some minimum relative size of firm, the probability of acquisition declines markedly with further expansion. Clearer distinctions existed between the acquiring and taken-over firms. Between 1967 and 1970, the acquiring companies were generally bigger, more profitable, faster growing and showed greater improvements in profitability and retained more of them compared with the units they acquired.

The evidence appears to indicate that, in the sphere of take-overs, the British capital market is a potential source of market failure. It seems to be an imperfect disciplinarian, especially for larger units. For medium-size and large firms with low profitability, the best way to avoid being taken over might well be to increase their size rather than their rate of profit. Such behaviour provides tentative support for the managerial theories of the firm in which managers prefer greater size to larger profits: 'the take-over mechanism, rather than being a constraint on managerial discretion, may encourage them in the same direction'.[20] The tendency is reinforced by the managerial payments system. In the UK, company size was usually the major determinant of chief executive's pay, with profitability being relatively unimportant.[21]

Nor is there much support for the hypothesis that take-overs result in improved efficiency and hence a more profitable use of the total resources of the firms which amalgamate. One study found that in at least half the cases, there was a decline in relative profitability after take-over; another showed that the profitability of merged units was less than that of internal growth firms.[22] In an interview survey, some 60 per cent or more of firms claimed that there had been zero or negligible plant closure or redundancy after merger and 70 per cent or more reported that their sales and exports increased by 1 per cent or less as a result of a merger.[23]

CONCLUSION: IS THERE A CASE FOR BIGNESS?

The general conclusion must be one of considerable scepticism about the advantages of mergers and large firms and, where market power is increased, concern for the wider issue of social welfare. The use of evidence on take-overs to conclude that the capital market is imperfect has also to be treated with some caution. Reservations arise from the *ex post* nature of the evidence. The behaviour of firms is based on *ex ante*, subjective assessments which are quite likely to differ from *ex post* outcomes. Firms will assess the *expected* profitability of mergers with alternative investments. All this makes empirical work difficult and is likely to lead to a 'failure' of the researcher rather than the capital market! In addition, a comparison of before and after profitability is subject to all the difficulties of completely specifying the determinants of a firm's profits (that is, of holding other things constant and comparing like with like). Even the use of profits as a performance indicator is dubious. Profits can be raised by restricting competition. Finally, in concluding that the capital market is imperfect, there is a danger of the *nirvana* approach: a model of a 'perfect' capital market is erected, where the costs of achieving 'perfection' are completely ignored. For example, where there are costs of obtaining information on, say, the performance of potential candidates for take-over, actual capital markets are likely to be characterised by an optimal amount of ignorance which is too costly to eliminate completely. On this basis, it is not surprising that the UK capital market through its take-over mechanism does not discriminate 'perfectly' between companies with varying profit rates. Except at the profit extremes, it might be too costly for transactors to discriminate on the basis of profitability so that other subjective, and less costly, criteria are likely to be used.

Two points are relevant for policy. First, if the private capital market in the UK is relatively inefficient (relative to what?), what 'improved' decision-making criteria will be used by such state agencies as the NEB? Will such bodies possess 'superior' skills, information and knowledge likely to 'improve' market efficiency? At the most, the evidence on take-overs suggests that state intervention *might* be required to 'correct' imperfections in the capital market. The 'appropriate' form of intervention requires a choice between such alternatives as the state subsidisation of information, changes in the system of executive pay and removing any entry barriers on the stock exchange. Secondly, the evidence on profitability *after* take-overs might be partly explained by the lack of competitive pressures in product markets. Firms might become X-inefficient and pursue objectives other than maximum profits. An obvious solution would be a greater policy emphasis on promoting competition and regulating monopoly in product markets.[24] How extensive is monopoly in Britain? Do large firms and mergers involve costs in the form of increased monopoly power in the economy?

Chapter 10

Monopoly, Mergers and Public Policy

INTRODUCTION

Since 1945 legislation has been concerned with single-firm mono-polies, mergers and restrictive practices in product markets. The 1948 Monopolies and Restrictive Practices Act established the Mono-polies Commission which had to decide whether particular mono-polies operated against the 'public interest'. There was no general ruling that all monopolies were 'undesirable' and the approach was pragmatic with the emphasis on inquiry rather than control. Initially, the Monopolies Commission also dealt with restrictive practices. This changed with the 1956 Restrictive Practices Act which estab-lished the Restrictive Practices Court. The Act established a general presumption that restrictive agreements between firms were against the public interest unless the parties could prove otherwise by using one of the standard exemptions or 'gateways'. These included agree-ments which could be shown to confer benefits on consumers or avoid local unemployment or promote exports. Where the parties to a restrictive agreement successfully used one of the gateways, the Court still had to be satisfied that the benefits to the public out-weighed the detriments. In 1964 a similar procedure involving the Restrictive Practices Court, gateways and a balancing of benefits and detriments was applied to resale price maintenance. The 1964 Resale Prices Act established a general presumption that resale price main-tenance was against the public interest. There followed the 1965 Monopolies and Mergers Act. This was concerned with the control of mergers and whether *proposed* mergers are likely to create a monopoly. Merger inquiries were undertaken by the Monopolies Commission and where there was an unfavourable report, the Act allowed the government to prohibit proposed mergers, to impose conditions on a merger and to dissolve completed mergers. Finally, the 1973 Fair Trading Act established a Director-General of Fair Trading responsible for the regulation of monopolies, mergers and restrictive practices, and a new emphasis was placed on consumer protection. The public interest was re-defined to include as *one* of its elements the desirability of maintaining and promoting competition. However, the re-named Monopolies and Mergers Commission retained considerable discretion in interpreting the public interest since it was required to consider 'all matters which appear to ... be relevant'.

Against this legislative background and regulatory system, concentration has been increasing at all levels of aggregation. Worries have been expressed that UK economic activity is highly concentrated in a small number of firms, that concentration will continue to increase and that mergers have contributed to the rising concentration. This means that major decisions on employment, investment, prices, exports, regional jobs and plant closures are more likely to be concentrated than before, and these are decisions which affect consumers, employees and the community as a whole. They are also issues on which theory might be expected to offer guidance. Questions arise about the economic logic of existing policy.

DOES THEORY OFFER ANY GUIDELINES FOR A PUBLIC POLICY TOWARDS MONOPOLY AND MERGERS?

The competitive model provides a useful benchmark for assessing actual market structures. It is like '. . . a Euclidean line or point. No one has ever seen a Euclidean line – which has zero width and depth – yet we all find it useful to regard many a Euclidean volume – such as a surveyor's string – as a Euclidean line.'[1] Under competition, market power is completely absent. As the number of firms in a market decreases, as their market share rises and as entry barriers are created, competition will decline and market power will increase. Markets will become increasingly imperfect until the limiting case of monopoly. Theory shows that under profit-maximisation, monopoly, imperfect competition and restrictive practices result in a higher price and lower output than competition. Moreover, since monopoly prices exceed marginal costs, standard Paretian welfare economics concludes that there will be a mis-allocation of resources and hence a market failure: monopoly is condemned as 'undesirable'. The neoclassical case against monopoly has been reinforced by recent theoretical developments which suggest that many people associated with a firm will not attempt to minimise costs unless there are strong pressures for them to do so: such behaviour results in X-inefficiency[2] which is likely to exist in monopoly markets where competitive pressures are absent. There is certainly evidence of organisational slack or X-inefficiency amongst British firms. It was estimated by the Ministry of Labour that in 1966 British industry was over-manned to the extent of 10–15 per cent. Unfortunately, there are no systematic international studies of comparative X-inefficiency: we do not know whether X-inefficiency is relatively greater in Britain than amongst our major foreign competitors.[3] Nevertheless, the concept of X-inefficiency has implications for a critical assessment of UK public policy towards mergers, monopolies and profit controls. Prospective mergers are frequently justified on grounds of scale economies and *expected* cost savings. But if a merger results in a decline in competitive pressures in an industry, there is the possibility that X-inefficiency might increase! As a result, any cost-benefit analysis of a proposed merger has to recognise that the *expected* gains from scale economies might be reduced by possible increases in X-inefficiency. The evidence on post-merger performance might be explained by this hypothesis. Similarly, a concern with a monopolist's profit performance might be distorted by X-inefficiency. As for state regulation of monopoly profits, a likely result is that firms will have a further incentive *not* to minimise costs but to maximise managerial utility rather than profits.[4]

The standard welfare economics framework which leads to the conclusion that competition is 'desirable' cannot explain the existence of monopoly. Quite simply, if competition results in a welfare maximum why do not the potential gainers bribe or compensate monopolists to induce them to produce at the competitive equilibrium? Monopolists would be no worse off and consumers would be better off and this result would apply under any set of cost conditions, including technical monopoly. Within the framework of the model, the continued existence of monopoly results from relatively high transactions costs. Consumers would pay enough to eliminate monopoly but do not because of the substantial costs involved in the search, information, negotiation, exclusion, revenue collection and legal transactions required to form the requisite consumer interest group. Public policy can 'solve' the problem by lowering the transactions costs for consumers or by establishing regulatory rules which raise the costs to business of purchasing monopoly rights.

Whilst theory appears to establish a general presumption in favour of competition, British anti-trust policy has not condemned monopolies and mergers as undesirable. Each case has been examined on its merits, resulting in a discretionary cost-benefit approach. Policy seems to accept that single-firm monopolies and mergers involve not only costs through reduced competition but possible benefits in such forms as economies of scale and technical progress. Opportunities for X-inefficiency raise doubts about whether such benefits will be realised. Moreover, the economies of scale 'benefit' is suspect since it can be shown that, at the new larger scale, the competitive equilibrium where price equals marginal cost is superior on welfare grounds.

Nevertheless, existing British regulatory policy might be partly defended using second-best arguments. The standard welfare economics rules on monopoly regulation have to be modified where governments regard the continued existence of specific monopolies in product, factor and public-sector markets as policy-created constraints. Examples include the nationalised industries, the trade unions and monopoly state agencies. In such second-best situations, the standard policy rules of Paretian welfare economics are no longer appropriate. However, rather than retreat into the agnosticism of second-best, questions can be raised about the rationale of policy-created constraints and their implication for the underlying behaviour of governments. The economics of politics can explain British monopoly legislation with its vague public interest criteria, inconsistencies in policy and a general reluctance to act against monopolies.

The Downs model suggests that democratic governments will favour producers more than consumers. The model predicts that any pro-competition or vigorous anti-monopoly policy is unlikely to be introduced and enforced simply because of opposition from producer interest groups. In addition, in formulating anti-monopoly policy, vote-maximising governments find it difficult to assess the preferences of the median voter who is likely to be undecided between the benefits of large firms and the 'unacceptable face of capitalism'. Since anti-monopoly policy has never been a major election issue, politicians are unlikely to be well-informed on voter preferences. A possible outcome is that a vote-maximising government which wishes to avoid risks will introduce inconsistent legislation.[5] Examples occur where a government accepts a recommendation of the Monopolies Commission and then fails to implement it. A further example occurred in the late 1960s when the Government simultaneously pursued policies for controlling monopolies and mergers (1965 Act) and policies for promoting mergers in the economy (IRC, 1966). It could be argued that the policies of the Monopolies Commission and the IRC were not inconsistent since British policy allows state agencies some scope in defining and valuing both costs and benefits. On this basis, it might be deduced that for all mergers supported by the IRC, benefits exceeded costs whereas mergers condemned by the Monopolies Commission would be those where costs exceeded benefits. This is a far from satisfactory rationalisation of apparent inconsistencies in policy. With a discretionary policy, two regulatory agencies are unlikely to have identical preference functions, so that differences can arise in the specification and, more especially, in the valuation of costs and benefits. Also, there is a presumption that choices are inconsistent when decision-makers choose policy set A (for example, control of monopolies and mergers) to set B (for example, pro-merger policy) and then subsequently select set B when A is available!

MARKET CONCENTRATION IN UK MANUFACTURING
INDUSTRY: HOW PREVALENT IS MONOPOLY?

Theory defines a monopolist as a single seller of a product with no close substitutes. No ambiguities exist about the number of sellers but problems arise with close substitutes. Substitutability between two products can be measured by cross elasticity of demand. This measures the effect of a change in the *price* of one product, say rail fares, on the *quantity* demanded of another good, such as bus journeys. The goods will be substitutes if the sign of the cross elasticity is positive. Now assume that for any firm's product, all the cross elasticities have been calculated. A major difficulty remains. What value of cross elasticity separates close from distant substitutes? Similarly, the definition of a monopoly concentrates on a single seller, whilst theory recognises the range of imperfections between the limiting cases of monopoly and competition. But how many firms constitute the large numbers required for competition and how few constitute a substantial imperfection? Theory provides no quantitative guidance on these issues, so that policy-makers have to use the available evidence and their judgement. The results are expressed in monopoly policy.

British policy defines a monopoly as a situation where one-quarter of a given category of goods or services is supplied by a single seller or subject to a collective agreement or is likely to result from a proposed merger.[6] The presumption is that substantial imperfections occur where a firm's market share is 25 per cent or more, which embraces both oligopoly and monopoly. It also implies that as the number of similar-sized firms declines from five to four, a market changes from competition to monopoly. Concentration ratios are one of the standard methods of measuring monopoly power in a market. The ratio shows the percentage of an industry's sales or employment accounted for by a small number of the largest firms, usually three, four or five. The ratios are subject to limitations. Why three, four or five firms and not one? With a five-firm ratio we cannot know the distribution of output between each of the top five. Also a high level of concentration might be associated with little *domestic* market power due to foreign trade (for example, imports of cars, paper, washing machines and TVs), anti-monopoly policy or countervailing power (for example, government defence contracts, nationalised industries). Problems arise because of local monopoly, foreign ownership and restrictive agreements. Much also depends on the definition of a market or industry. The British Standard Industrial Classification which is the basis for concentration ratios is not necessarily an accurate indicator of the degree of substitutability or cross elasticity between products.[7] Quite different products may be close substitutes without being allocated to the same industry grouping. Finally, statistical difficulties result from changes in definitions and coverage as well as delays in the publication of data. Nevertheless, some indicators of general trends can be obtained.

The average level of five-firm concentration ratios increased from 52 per cent in 1935 to 69 per cent in 1968.[8] Since 1951 there has been a steadily rising level of concentration with more industries showing increasing than static or declining concentration. One study of sixty-three comparable industries between 1951 and 1958 found that concentration rose in thirty-six and decreased in sixteen.[9] After 1958 the trend towards greater concentration continued and was especially marked between 1963 and 1968. By 1968, almost 25 per cent of product groups in British manufacturing industry had five-firm concentration ratios of 90 per cent and over. Some of the highly concentrated sectors were vehicles, metal manufacture, bricks, pottery, food and chemicals. Competition is not completely absent and low concentration ratios exist in timber, clothing, footwear, leather and textiles.

There is a general presumption that highly concentrated product groups such as those with concentration ratios of 90 per cent and over are industries where there might be a monopoly situation. However, evidence on the 'critical' level of concentration remains controversial. Different concentration measures can lead to different conclusions! Some studies suggest a positive but weak relationship between the level of concentration and the level of profits.[10] For the USA it was found that the critical level of concentration occurred at 55 per cent at the four-firm level and 70 per cent at the eight-firm level and that increased concentration beyond the critical levels did not appear to raise the level of profitability.[11] In comparison, one of the few British studies in this area found no evidence of a correlation between high profits and high concentration![12] Similar controversy surrounds the evidence on the relationship between concentration and advertising. A classic US study by Telser found an unimpressive correlation between the two.[13] Some British studies have reached a similar conclusion, whilst others have found that advertising intensity is greatest at moderate levels of concentration (five-firm concentration ratios of 60–65 per cent) and lower in both unconcentrated and highly concentrated sectors.[14] Inevitably, there are analytical and empirical problems of two-way causation, of completely specifying the determinants of advertising and of obtaining accurate data. Yet again, empirical work raises more questions than answers for policy-makers. Additional questions arise about the causes of the long-run trend towards increased concentration, especially the contribution of mergers.

HAVE MERGERS INCREASED MARKET CONCENTRATION?

Public policy suggests that a merger is likely to lead to a monopoly situation where it involves one-quarter of the share of a market or where the value of the assets acquired exceeds £5 million. Although the £5m. figure is arbitrary, the inclusion of an absolute size of firm criterion allows vertical and conglomerate mergers to be investigated. This criterion has been criticised because of the confusion between absolute size and market power. Some economists have argued that absolute size is absolutely irrelevant. Economic theory suggests that market power is associated with the relative size of a firm in a specific market and not absolute size. However, the Downs model provides some analytical support for the argument that large firms, including conglomerates, might be undesirable. In the Downs model, large size can result in dominant producer interest groups which are capable of influencing the spending and regulatory policies of vote-maximising governments and political parties. On this basis, large firms might be undesirable.

A study by the Monopolies Commission found that a 1958 sample of 2,024 companies had been reduced as a result of mergers to 1,253 by 1968[15] – almost a 40 per cent reduction. During this period, the average five-firm concentration ratio rose from almost 57 per cent to over 65 per cent and the increase was especially great in the merger-intensive period of 1963–8. It has been estimated that mergers probably contributed up to 50 per cent of the increase in concentration in UK manufacturing industry between 1954 and 1965. In such industries as chemicals, food, drink, metal manufacture and vehicles, the proportion was much higher.[16] Between 1965 and 1973, diversified or conglomerate mergers became more important but nonetheless only accounted for under 20 per cent of sizeable mergers within this period. Over 70 per cent of sizeable mergers were of the horizontal type with potentially adverse effects on competition.[17] In addition to their effects on market concentration, mergers have implications for aggregate concentration and the creation of giant companies.

AGGREGATE CONCENTRATION IN THE UK

In recent years, some politicians and economists have criticised the increasing concentration of decision-making in a small number of large corporations. Examples of giants include ICI, GEC, Unilever,

British Leyland and Distillers. Giants are especially dominant in the retailing, chemicals, food, drink, engineering and transport sectors. The top 100 firms in the UK are frequently mentioned and, as such, they constitute potential producer interest groups. They have been the focus of various government efforts to monitor price and profit controls and are obvious candidates for Planning Agreements.

In 1969, the top 100 UK companies accounted for 65 per cent of net assets compared with 46 per cent in 1948. Mergers were an important influence on this rising concentration. Indeed in 1964–9, the typical giant spent more on take-overs than on net new investment in fixed assets. In this period a typical giant acquired another quoted company once every two-and-half years, whereas other firms acquired a quoted company once every thirty-three years.[18] However, life at the very top is no more secure than life in the rest of the top 100. Between 1948 and 1968, the proportion of firms surviving in the top 12, top 25, top 50 and top 100 was remarkably similar.[19] Also, by 1968 nearly 50 per cent of the 1948 top 100 had disappeared from the top 100 list: 12 firms fell below the rank of 100; 9 companies were nationalised and 27 'died' due to merger or take-over. This suggests that policy which concentrates solely on the 'magic' figure of the top 100 and assumes that this is static is in danger of neglecting some of the substantial changes which are continuously taking place in this group.

Whilst a careful distinction has to be made between aggregate and market concentration, there is the possibility that the two types of concentration might be linked. The largest manufacturing firms might be amongst the largest firms in individual markets. A UK study of a random sample of thirty product groups in 1963 examined this possibility.[20] In half of the sample, at least one of the three largest firms in each market was amongst the largest one hundred firms in manufacturing. In almost 25 per cent of the industries, the leading two or three suppliers were also among the largest firms overall. It was also found that the average level of concentration was much higher (at least 20 percentage points) in industries where one or more of the leading firms were from the top 100. Thus, for UK manufacturing a relatively small number of very large firms not only dominates overall but probably plays an influential part in about half of the industries within the manufacturing sector. Absolute size is not absolutely irrelevant. What have been the achievements of UK regulatory policy?

HAS ANTI-TRUST POLICY BEEN EFFECTIVE?

British anti-trust policy has been confined to product markets and has generally ignored the substantial imperfections in factor markets and in the public sector. Even within product markets, there is considerable scope for investigation. One study indicated that over a quarter of British trades might be priority candidates for official investigation.[21] However, the case study approach of the Monopolies Commission has been slow. Since the Commission was established, a mere forty-plus dominant firm monopolies have been investigated. These have embraced monopolies such as British Oxygen and Pilkington and dominant firm oligopolists such as Unilever and Procter and Gamble together with Imperial Tobacco and Gallaher. Other firms investigated have included ICI (fertilisers), Kodak (colour film), Lucas (electrical equipment), Metal Box (metal containers), Rank (cinema films) and Roche (drugs). In some instances, such as British Oxygen and Rank, the Commission found the position of a dominant firm to be objectionable whilst in other instances it condemned the behaviour of monopolists. The Commission usually condemns excessive profits and anti-competitive behaviour, especially entry restrictions. For example, in the report on household detergents,[22] Unilever and Procter and Gamble were found to be in a monopoly situation, each with over 40 per cent of total sales. The Commission concluded that

'. . . the price policies and the policies on advertising and promotion of Unilever and Procter and Gamble operate, and may be expected to operate, against the public interest, in as much as, while tending to keep new entrants out of the market, they result in over-concentration on advertising and sales promotion to the detriment of effective direct price competition and in unduly high profits with the consequence that the public are charged unnecessarily high prices.'

The quotation suggests a definition of 'public interest' and also some of the indicators used to assess the performance of monopolists. In this case, the Commission interpreted the 'public interest' to include entry conditions, the extent of direct price competition and the level of prices: these are features which characterise the competitive model. The behaviour and performance of the two companies was assessed in terms of the extent of non-price competition (undesirable advertising) and the relative absence of price competition. Also, profits were deemed to be unduly high. In 1963, the rate of return on capital was some 27 per cent for Unilever and about 40 per cent for Procter and Gamble, compared with a national average for manufacturing industry of some 11 per cent. The Commission recommended that both firms should reduce their wholesale selling prices by an average of 20 per cent and should be 'encouraged' to reduce their selling expenses by at least 40 per cent. These recommendations were not accepted by the Government. Instead, after negotiations with the Board of Trade, the companies agreed to provide an alternative range of detergents at 20 per cent lower prices, reflecting less expenditure on sales promotion for the new cheaper products; the higher-priced and more intensely advertised products remained unchanged! This is typical in that some of the Commission's more drastic and controversial recommendations have not been accepted by the Government. Examples have included proposals for price and profit controls for British Oxygen and the recommendation that Imperial Tobacco should divest itself of its holding in Gallaher. Not surprisingly, the economics of politics would predict such an outcome since any vigorous anti-monopoly policy is unlikely to be enforced because of opposition from producer interest groups.

The fact that the Monopolies Commission can interpret the public interest is an obvious source of criticism. For example, in a number of instances such as Pilkington and Cigarette Components, dominant firms were found to have no features contrary to the public interest and no objection was raised to their monopoly positions. Even though the 1973 Fair Trading Act included competition, entry conditions, and consumers in the public interest guidelines, the Commission retained the discretion to consider 'all matters of relevance'. In the circumstances, it is not at all obvious who is maximising what for the benefit of whom! A concern with excessive profits also raises interesting conceptual problems.[23] Past reports have found that profit rates of between 21 per cent and some 58 per cent on capital (historic cost) over five-year periods were excessive, particularly in relation to the average for manufacturing industry. Theory shows that a distinction is required between normal and abnormal profits. Even if such a distinction can be made (how?), abnormal profits can exist in the short run in competitive markets. Once again, theory only suggests some general concepts and judgement is required for a rate of return in a specific market to be interpreted as 'excessive'. Given that rates of return will reflect different degrees of risk and uncertainty, the Commission's judgement that a return is excessive requires it to take a view about the appropriate profit rates on extremely risky projects. Is, say, a 40 per cent return on capital a reflection of monopoly or the temporary success of a high-risk innovation? The relationship between price and *marginal* cost could help to clarify the issue. Whilst the Commission usually examines the linkage of prices to costs, the latter are unlikely to be accurate indicators of marginal costs based on X-efficiency. In the circumstances, it is perhaps not surprising that UK public policy has had little effect in modifying the behaviour and organisation of dominant firms.

Government policy towards mergers accepts that 'many mergers can be beneficial and that in the majority of cases the judgement of the market about them can be accepted'.[24] As a result, over 800 mergers or proposed mergers have been screened since the 1965 Act but, by 1974, only twenty-seven or some 3 per cent had been the subject of a reference to the Commission. In the majority of referred cases, the mergers were eventually allowed, although not all took place. Examples of approved mergers included BMC–Pressed Steel, *The Times–Sunday Times* and British Match–Wilkinson Sword. In a limited number of cases such as Ross–Associated Fisheries, Barclays–Lloyds–Martins, Rank–De La Rue and Beechams or Boots–Glaxo, the Commission found the proposed merger to be against the public interest. Once again, the public interest guidelines are discretionary. The Commission assesses the *expected* costs and benefits of a merger in terms of its effects on competition, efficiency, regional policy, the balance of payments, redundancy and 'other aspects'.[25] The inclusion of regional policy, redundancy and the balance of payments as part of regulatory policy raises further doubts about what the Commission is supposed to be maximising. Inevitably, successful mergers will involve a re-allocation of resources through plant closures and redundancy and to prevent mergers on such grounds requires the Commission to act as a job-creation agency rather than a regulatory body. In addition, the Commission is required to consider the trade-off between competition and increased efficiency due to scale economies and innovation (see Chapter 9). In this context, one economist has argued that the benefits of a merger resulting from lower unit costs reflecting scale economies are likely to outweigh the welfare losses arising from increased market power.[26] If valid, such a conclusion would be a persuasive rationalisation of the UK's pro-merger policy. Doubts arise because it can be shown that even at the *new lower cost* level, the competitive equilibrium with price equal to marginal cost is superior on welfare grounds.[27] Worries about income distribution, X-inefficiency and the evidence on post-merger performance raise further doubts about a policy of uncritically allowing mergers.

With restrictive agreements some 2,500, mainly price agreements, were registered between 1956 and 1968. By 1968 the Registrar reported that virtually no cases of significance remained to be dealt with, the majority having been terminated, others having been varied. One study of the 1956 Act concluded that it resulted in greater competition in 53 per cent of the sample, the remainder responding with anti-competitive devices, especially information agreements.[28] In other words, it is a mistake to view the abandonment of agreements as marking the general onset of competition: the 1956 Act appears to have been subverted on a considerable scale. However, the 1968 Act brought information agreements within the scope of legislation and their subsequent abolition or modification appears to have resulted in greater price competition. Once again, some firms responded to the legislation by searching for alternative anti-competitive devices, including illegal evasion, mergers, cost surveys and unregistered collusion especially under oligopoly. Nevertheless, one study concluded that the 1956 Act 'can be judged to have improved resource allocation, however incompletely, and to have done very little real harm'.[29] Weaknesses remain in British competition policy. Some of the 'gateways' can be criticised, especially the inclusion of exports and employment gateways as part of competition policy. The gateway which allows a restriction to be retained if it confers a specific and substantial benefit on the public is far too vague. Moreover, it has to be recognised that firms will search for new forms of competition and co-operation, so that public policy will need to evolve to reflect the dynamic nature of firm behaviour, industrial organisation and market conduct.

CONCLUSION: WHITHER POLICY?

There is no shortage of candidates for investigation by the Monopolies and Mergers Commission. There is also scope for a more critical attitude towards the alleged benefits of mergers and dominant firms. Doubts arise about the capacity for investigation, the effectiveness and transactions costs of current UK regulatory policy. In the circumstances, serious consideration might be given to formulating a non-discretionary policy.[30] Also, following the changes in the 1973 Fair Trading Act there are substantial opportunities for inquiring into imperfections in the labour market and the activities of the nationalised industries. Within the labour market, it is an interesting exercise to apply to trade unions the current legislation on monopoly, mergers and restrictive practices. The market share and value of assets criteria could be used to identify monopoly unions and to assess proposed mergers. Presumably the public interest requires consideration of the effects of a union monopoly on entry conditions, factor substitution and any excessive rates of return on human capital (skills). In view of the recent history of industrial relations legislation, this is clearly a sensitive area for vote-conscious politicians. Further opportunities exist in the public sector.

Chapter 11

Monopoly, Bureaucracy and Competition in the Public Sector

INTRODUCTION: HOW DO BUREAUCRACIES BEHAVE?

Monopolies are not unique to private product markets. They also exist in the public sector. State agencies and Ministries are effectively single sellers of information and services to governments as buyers. For example, the Ministry of Defence is the sole supplier of information and defence services. A simple model of a monopoly Ministry is shown in Figure 11.1.[1]

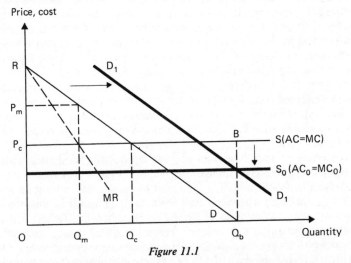

Figure 11.1

In Figure 11.1, demand and cost conditions are given by the D and S curves, respectively. A private competitive industry would produce the socially optimal output OQ_c at price P_c. A private monopolist would produce the smaller output OQ_m at the higher price P_m. A budget-maximising monopolistic bureaucrat would aim to offer an output of OQ_b, for which the government would be willing to pay a maximum sum shown by the entire area under the demand curve (ORQ_b). In this example, since Q_b is twice Q_c, the total budget would be equal to OP_cBQ_b and the output of the monopoly Ministry would be 'too large' in that it would exceed the social optimum. This result has implications for the behaviour of monopolistic bureaucrats. They have an incentive to confuse total with marginal costs and benefits. For example, at Q_c the bureaucrat can argue that total benefits exceed total costs and that a larger programme is justified. Such an argument is in serious error. The correct 'rule' for optimal size is to undertake an activity until, *at the margin*, the benefits which accrue to society are equal to the costs. However, the monopolistic bureau-crat can exceed the social optimum by persuading vote-conscious governments that only at Q_b are total benefits and costs finally equal: an outcome which will be further supported by the producer interest group favourably affected. On this basis, there is a presumption that industries and services which are directly supported by monopoly Ministries and state agencies will be 'too large'. Examples include the aircraft, car (Leyland and Chrysler), shipbuilding and weapons industries as well as transport, roads, education and local authority services. In addition, monopoly Ministries have no incentive to be technically efficient. In such cases as defence, hospitals, roads and schools, there are only single Ministries, so that there are no alter-native and independent checks on a bureaucrat's cost and demand estimates. For any chosen output, society could find itself paying more than the minimum level shown by the cost schedule (curve S) in Figure 11.1.[2] And yet, monopoly bureaucrats are likely to justify their preferred output of Q_b by creating an impression of allocative efficiency. This can be done by deliberately over-estimating demand or under-estimating costs, as shown by curves D_1 and S_0, respectively, in Figure 11.1.

External or social benefits provide monopoly Ministries with a basis for deliberately exaggerating demand in an effort to show that a project is worthwhile. The claims of technological fall-out or spin-off from aerospace projects and from basic research in universities are conspicuous examples of alleged external benefits. Others include domestic agriculture, health, education, regional policy, transport, local authority sports complexes and city centre re-development. One critic has suggested that, 'the force of these claims is perhaps exceeded only by the disclaimers that are often made that the benefits cannot be measured. Thus far there has been a limited attempt to pursue the hypothesis that the extreme difficulty of measurement may suggest that there is nothing to measure.'[3] Producer interest groups in the activity likely to benefit from a Ministry's increased spending will have every incentive to support the bureaucracy's (exaggerated) claims of substantial social benefits. If the potential beneficiaries are relatively scarce, specialised and articulate, as in the case of scientists, engineers and doctors, the increased demand will raise their relative earnings, hence their support for such spending programmes. At the same time, the vote-losses from any increased taxation and inflation required to finance greater state expenditures are likely to be relatively small, since their effects are widely diffused amongst the electorate. Whilst Ministries and interest groups are enthusiastic about external benefits, they are understandably silent on external costs. Recognition and accurate estimation of such costs will adversely affect the size of a Ministry's spending plans. The development of airports with their noise spillovers and the construction of motorways which increase traffic congestion in urban areas are obvious examples where it is in a Ministry's interest to ignore or underestimate social costs. Even in the absence of such externalities, a Ministry can deliberately under-estimate the costs of a project, ignore 'lifetime' costs and use an inappropriately low discount rate. Examples have occurred on advanced technology projects and on the construction of motorways, large bridges and nuclear power stations.

HOW CAN BUREAUCRACIES BE CONTROLLED?

Various proposals have been made to improve both the technical and allocative efficiency of monopoly Ministries. New management techniques such as cost-benefit analysis and programme budgeting have been introduced.[4] Inevitably, though, these have neglected the underlying budget-maximising behaviour of bureaucrats. People adjust to playing any games and bureaucrats are no exception. Whenever a planned spending programme appears politically attractive, a Ministry's staff is likely to find a cost-benefit ratio which exceeds unity. Indeed, there is a real danger that cost-benefit analysis and programme budgeting will be used to support, serve and reinforce the budget-maximising aims of monopoly Ministries. In the circumstances, alternative proposals have been made for creating and extending competition between government departments. Ministries might cease to have monopoly property rights in specific services. Thus, the Departments of Education, Employment and Industry together with the Manpower Services Commission and the Ministry of Defence might compete to supply the state's requirements for education and training services. Similarly, the Ministry of Defence might be split into separate Army, Navy and Air Force departments competing with each other, as well as with other Ministries, for the supply of defence services. Experiments might also be undertaken with the extended use of private markets and the private provision of services traditionally supplied by the state. In defence, greater use could be made of private markets in areas such as flying training, air and sea transport, and weapons maintenance. Elsewhere state finance could be retained but private provision could be extended in education, employment agencies, health and local authority services such as refuse collection and transport.[5] The aim would be to use competition to provide the Government as the buyer of services with comparative cost and demand information and to stimulate efficiency in the public sector.

TENDERING FOR GOVERNMENT CONTRACTS

Proposals to extend private provision would involve the increased allocation of government contracts to private firms. Already central and local governments make extended use of contracts for the building of bridges, hospitals, houses, power stations, roads, schools, telecommunications facilities and weapons. Choice problems arise in that the state as the buyer has to determine the product it requires, the stage in the product development at which competition should take place, the selection of a contractor and a contract. Consider a local authority requiring a new school. Should it invite competing firms to submit tenders for both design and construction? Or should it specify the design and time-scale, so restricting competition to the building stage and the price dimension? Should there be any limit on the number of firms invited to tender and what happens if there is only one supplier? Rules exist for competitive and non-competitive tendering for nationalised industry, central and local government contracts. The rules provide fascinating insights into policy-makers' interpretation of competition and the extent to which the state acts as a competitive buyer. A considerable stretching of the imagination is required to relate some of the tendering rules to the economic logic of the competitive model. And yet, such a dichotomy is not unexpected when it is remembered that the rules are inevitably the outcome of negotiations between the bureaucracy as the government's representative and producer interest groups. The pragmatism which characterises policy towards private monopolies occurs in the rules for tendering.

THE COMPETITIVE MODEL AND TENDERING RULES

If the state acted as a competitive buyer, it would create a set of tendering rules based on the economist's competitive model. These would provide for large numbers of firms, freedom of entry, so that all firms could submit a tender, with competition based on price criteria, using fixed price contracts. The general presumption is that competition will result in lower prices than monopoly. In the event, the central government's tendering rules frequently restrict competition to a limited number of firms from an approved list of contractors. This list consists of firms which the buyer's representatives have 'vetted' and deemed to be competent to undertake the work. Vetting involves an assessment of a firm's technical capacity, its financial position, quality control, past performance and reputation with the central or local government departments. State agencies are required to advertise the existence of an approved list with an invitation to new firms to apply for admission. The worry is that the selection process and the standard required for entry on to the list will reflect the *bureaucrat's* preference for avoiding and minimising risks. If so, the government as the buyer who has to choose and who might take a different view of risk, will not be presented with information on the price implications of alternative risks associated with different contractors.[6] Effectively, contractors who might offer lower prices but who are regarded as high risks are excluded from the approved list. Innovative and progressive firms are likely to be in this category, as too are consortia formed to bid for specific contracts. Moreover, not all firms on the approved list will be invited to tender for every contract of the appropriate size. Frequently, a short list of possible tenderers is compiled. For construction, defence, health and post office work, selective tendering can involve up to twenty firms, although the optimal number seems to be five to ten and frequently six. On building work, scales exist suggesting that the maximum number of tenderers should be five on contracts up to £10,000 (1972 prices); six for contracts of £10,000–£100,000; eight for work of £100,000–£1 million and six for projects of £1 + million.[7] Why reduce the maximum number of bidders from eight to six for the largest projects? In addition, whilst the competitive model does not provide a numerical definition of a large number of firms, it is difficult to accept five to eight as a large number. Oligopoly plus entry restrictions rather than competition with free entry appears to be the aim of selective tendering.

Since only a few firms will be invited to bid for any one contract, the buyer's representatives are required to compile a short list of approved bidders, and various criteria are used. Central and local government contracting departments consider a firm's past contractual performance including the quality of work, time slippages, cost escalation and its price tenders on recent contracts. Firms already operating at capacity are excluded, which raises the probability that the short list will include some marginal enterprises. When only a limited number of firms are invited to tender, at least one public corporation attempts to include a new entrant of its choice, to provide a competitive check on the established bidders. However, it has to be emphasised that, over the long term, the authorities aim to give all firms on the approved list the opportunity to tender. Such a rule is likely to conflict with technical efficiency and low price objectives, especially since it further reduces the already restricted opportunities for new entrants. More significantly, the general principle of selecting a short list of approved firms is incompatible with competitive buying behaviour. It means that without inviting all firms on the approved list to submit bids, the state buying agency restricts any price 'competition' to a small number of firms of its choice. In other words, the buyer selects firms for the short list using non-price criteria. The selected firms are then invited to submit tenders for a project and time period specified by the buyer. Competition is thus limited to price only. At this stage, the successful contractor will be the one offering the lowest tender.[8] As a description of the process, price competition subject to constraints is perhaps an under-statement. Nevertheless, the economic logic of the tendering rules is an issue which is the legitimate concern of economists.

WHAT IS THE UNDERLYING POLICY MODEL FOR SELECTIVE TENDERING?

From public pronouncements, interviews with civil servants and official reports, a model can be deduced and constructed showing that a selective tendering policy is based on propositions about transactions costs and the operation of markets. At the outset, it has to be recognised that requiring the state to act as a competitive buyer is not an unambiguous rule. The government might be aiming to maximise a social welfare function so that its tendering rules and choices will not be independent of its general policy objectives. A concern with obtaining 'the most suitable goods at the most satisfactory price'[9] provides opportunities for being subjective. 'Suitable goods' might be interpreted as British rather than foreign or supplied by 'lame ducks' located in Development Areas where regional employment is part of the 'product' being bought. Even if such conceptual difficulties are resolved, it is not costless for the state to organise a competition and to act as a competitive buyer.

Transactions costs arise in determining a product and subsequently printing and distributing details of the competition and later informing the unsuccessful bidders. Acting as a competitive buyer will require a search for the lowest price. Since search is a costly activity, there will be an optimal amount which is likely to be less than the extent of the market. If the buyer has to evaluate the reliability of each potential bidder, the costs of a complete search will be substantial. Lower prices might be obtained by approaching more firms, but searching will cease when its expected savings through lower prices equals the costs of obtaining the extra information. Selective tendering reduces some of the buyer's search costs since all firms on the approved list are of 'known reliability'. For example, in 1972 new quality requirements were introduced for defence contractors. The aim was to reduce search costs by ensuring that defence orders were only given to firms 'whose arrangements for quality and product reliability give the Department confidence to reduce its own direct inspection to a minimum level or even dispense with it entirely'.[10] Furthermore, it has been argued that selective tendering from an approved list has reduced bankruptcies. As a result, the buyer avoids all the bargaining costs involved when a contractor defaults and a replacement is required. One official report has asserted that '. . . experience shows that it is fallacious to suggest that the lowest tender obtained in open competition will necessarily result in the lowest final cost'.[11] Thus, part of the policy model for selective tendering is based on the transaction costs of organising and administering a competition and the costs of making choices. These costs mean that for a monopsonist such as the Government, there will be an optimal, but limited, amount of competition: hence selective tendering. The fact that this might mean inviting some six approved firms to tender can be further rationalised by reference to monopoly policy. Since the 1973 Fair Trading Act policy-makers have implicitly defined competition as occurring where there are five or more firms of similar size in the market. Using this criterion, six bidders represents competition!

A second element in the policy model for selective tendering concerns the operation of markets. A major argument seems to be that tendering can be a considerable element in a firm's costs. The larger the tender list becomes, the greater will be the costs of abortive tendering and, in the long run, it is believed that this will be reflected in higher prices to the government. Moreover, if too many firms are invited to tender, policy-makers feel that 'false expectations' will be raised and resources wasted as many firms spend time and effort on preparing tenders which have little prospect of winning. Finally, the policy model seems to assume that firms are profit-maximisers so that selective tendering will lead to prices based on cost-minimising operations. In total, none of the arguments for selective tendering are based on any obvious market failure. Instead, the policy is rationalised in terms of the 'excessive' costs of an open competition policy. Without selective tendering, the hypothesis seems to be that there would be much greater transactions costs for both buyer and sellers, some of the latter eventually being 'shifted' forward in higher prices. At this point, economists can contribute by critically evaluating the underlying policy model. Is it internally consistent? What are the implications of alternative behavioural assumptions? Are the empirical propositions consistent with the facts? What are the costs and benefits of alternative policies, ranging from open competition to negotiated solutions and public ownership? Although space does not permit a complete appraisal, some of the possibilities for critical assessment can be outlined. The exercise is intended to be illustrative rather than persuasive!

CONCLUSION: WHAT IS WRONG WITH
SELECTIVE TENDERING?

Theory shows that by not using an open competition policy, prices are likely to be higher. Also, the Paretian model immediately suggests that the state as a monopsonist, not acting as a competitive buyer, is a potential cause of resource misallocation. Second-best might be used to defend selective tendering, or any other policy. If so, it has to be recognised that since competition is a technical possibility, any second-best constraints are policy-created, raising questions as to whether the government is maximising community welfare or its own 'life'. Nor is the proposition about buyer search costs[12] conclusive since the model also predicts that the buyer will search more for lower prices when purchasing a high-priced item: a prediction which casts further doubts on a selective tendering policy which restricts the number of bidders regardless of the size of the contract.

The proposition about open competition increasing the risk that the successful bidder will go bankrupt raises both empirical and analytical issues. Evidence is required on the relationship between the number of bidders and the probability that a successful firm will default. Analysis points to a choice between alternative competitive and contractual arrangements to allow for uncertainty. There is no costless solution. Open competition is likely to achieve lower prices to be traded against a belief of a greater probability of bankruptcy. Selective tendering is believed to reduce, but not completely eliminate, the risks of default;[13] but this can only be achieved by paying a higher price to ensure that firms recover their expenditures. Moreover, in so far as selective tendering reduces competitive pressures, firms will tend to pursue objectives other than maximum profits. Any resulting X-inefficiency will lead to even higher prices! Similar worries apply to the proposition that the costs of abortive tendering will eventually lead to higher prices. The relevant point is that in the long run, competitive markets will promote technical efficiency and determine the optimal expenditure on tendering: if it does not have market value, it will not be supplied and the resources will be reallocated to more attractive alternative uses. Of course, in the final analysis, a selective tendering policy is attractive to vote-maximising governments and budget-maximising bureaucracies. Unlike open competition, it allows political decision-makers some discretion in the allocation of contracts and hence an ability to pursue their own objectives.

Chapter 12

Subsidy Policy and the Regions

Subsidies enable governments to achieve specific objectives such as higher employment, lower prices, import savings and income re-distribution. British governments have used a variety of subsidies, with regional policy as one element in the total. Subsidies can be classified in various ways. For example, a distinction can be made between general and specific types.[1] General schemes have been the traditional method of subsidising British industry. They are blanket subsidies available to all firms which satisfy certain conditions, for example, relating to investment, employment, training or location. General schemes aim to influence the operation of markets without detailed and costly involvement in the affairs of individual firms. In contrast, specific subsidy schemes provide a 'tailor-made' subsidy to an individual firm or person for a particular purpose, such as the survival of a unit, the re-structuring or re-equipment of an enterprise or the development of a new airliner. Specific subsidies have increased in importance with the Industry Acts of 1968, 1972 and 1975. In contrast to macro-economic policy, they represent an attempt at 'fine tuning' through state intervention at the extreme micro-level, namely, the firm. A selective, discriminating approach is used in which the amount of subsidy is negotiated for each case and, ideally, set at the minimum level required to influence decisions. However, attempts to negotiate specific subsidies with individual firms will usually take place in a non-competitive situation, where the firm's cost levels are likely to be X-inefficient (see Chapter 10).[2] The Government and the enterprise will be in a bilateral monopoly bargaining situation, the outcome of which is indeterminate! Without alternative cost yardsticks, the resulting state subsidy is likely to be based on inefficient cost levels. Moreover, if the state imposes profit controls on subsidised firms, the enterprise will have a further incentive to pursue objectives other than maximum profits.[3] For present purposes, it is sufficient to note that subsidies to an individual firm will have a locational dimension.

An alternative classification scheme distinguishes between subsidies for outputs and inputs. British examples of the former include agriculture and subsidies to the nationalised airline for the higher costs of operating domestic aircraft. Input subsidies embrace R&D (see Chapters 7 and 13), investment, labour and the location of factors. Once again, regional policy forms one aspect of overall subsidy policy. Investment incentives are available throughout Britain, with higher rates in the Development Areas.[4] Labour subsidies have distinguished between the employed and unemployed, school-leavers and adults, training and the unskilled, manufacturing and other sectors and the Development Areas compared with the rest of the UK. In the mid-1970s, a Temporary Employment Subsidy was introduced whereby firms throughout Britain obtained a temporary lump sum subsidy for each job they maintained. A recruitment subsidy for school-leavers was also introduced under which firms received a lump sum subsidy for each school-leaver taken on.[5] In some cases, labour subsidies are 'tied' to the Development Areas. Cash to help a jobless worker move to another area and the Regional Employment Premium (REP) are examples.

In view of the extensive and inter-related nature of subsidy policy, attention will be focused on two related aspects, namely subsidies to 'lame duck' regions and private firms. Each provides examples of the general issues raised by subsidies. Does analysis suggest any 'guidelines' for subsidy policy? Why subsidise certain regions and firms? Since state support for private firms is often justified on local employment grounds, we begin with regional issues. Why do governments require a policy towards the regions? Should policy aim to take work to workers or vice versa? And has regional policy been successful?

WHAT IS THE REGIONAL PROBLEM?

British governments have regarded the regional problem as one of a permanent 'imbalance' in economic activity in the economy. There have been regional differences in unemployment rates, activity rates, net outward migration, average incomes per head and growth rates. The problem is not new and has existed since the 1930s. Usually, it is reflected in unemployment rates varying between different regions in the UK. In mid-1976, when the UK unemployment rate was 5·4 per cent, the Northern rate was 7 per cent and that for the South-East was 3·9 per cent. Traditionally, excess labour supply has dominated the Development Areas of the North, North-West, Scotland, Wales and Northern Ireland, whilst the Midlands and South-East have been characterised by excess demand. Because of differential regional unemployment rates, congestion and dis-economies of concentration are reputed to exist in the South and the under-use of resources, especially labour, in the declining or Development Areas.

WHY IS THERE A REGIONAL PROBLEM?

For simplicity, it will be assumed that the policy objective is to reduce the differentials in regional unemployment rates. This is a useful proxy for such other regional characteristics as activity rates, migration and income levels. Differences in regional unemployment rates are most likely to be explained by the operation of local labour markets. In a competitive system, relative wage rates will reflect scarcities in each regional labour market, with prices adjusting to clear markets. On this view, regional differences in unemployment rates are due to imperfections in the labour market. For example, markets might be failing to provide information on job opportunities and labour supplies in different regions. Alternatively, labour might be immobile or collective bargaining might impose constraints on the extent to which regional wage differentials can reflect relative scarcities.

Another explanation has concentrated on the demand side of the labour market and has attempted to explain regional unemployment rates in terms of employment opportunities in a region. Two related hypotheses have been formulated, based on structure and comparative costs.[6] The former asserts that the relatively high unemployment regions tend to have an unfavourable industrial structure containing a high proportion of declining industries. Examples include coal, shipbuilding and textiles. Consequently, the regional problem is one of structural unemployment which is concentrated in certain geographical areas (see Chapter 4). If this is the case, policy could aim to change the industrial structure of the less prosperous regions. But which industries should policy-makers choose? How do they select between activities with different ratios of capital to labour, males to females and skilled to unskilled? Should they prefer manufacturing to services and activities which use local factor inputs and 'export' their output to other regions in the UK?[7] Costs will not be irrelevant in such an exercise. This brings us to the second hypothesis which maintains that the less prosperous regions are at a comparative disadvantage or are higher-cost locations. They might, for example, be remote from the major consumer markets in the London area and in the EEC. As a result, the modern, expanding growth industries, such as cars and electronics, have not been attracted to the Development Areas. Policy might reduce some of the cost disadvantages of the Development Areas by improving their 'infrastructure' through increased investment in, say, road and rail communications with the major markets. For policy-makers, however, problems arise because markets are not static. Consumer demands and technology are continually changing, both in the UK and abroad, so that the comparative advantages and disadvantages of regions is not fixed in perpetuity. For example, in the 1970s, the development of North Sea oil has favourably affected the growth and employment prospects of Scotland, whilst the lack of competitiveness of British Leyland and Chrysler has adversely affected the Midlands.[8] Thus, the regional problem is part of the general problem of resource re-allocation required in any changing economy. Some of the changes, and hence regional 'imbalances', will reflect search behaviour and market adjustments which might be too costly to eliminate completely. Elsewhere, the imbalances might reflect market failure, requiring state intervention to improve the operation of markets.

WHAT ARE THE REGIONAL POLICY INSTRUMENTS?

Since the Development Areas are characterised by an excess supply of labour at the ruling wage rate, the standard demand and supply framework shows three general possibilities for policy.[9] First, flexible wage rates might be introduced, so allowing local labour markets to be cleared. Local wage bargains could, for example, replace national bargains. However, owing to possible opposition from trade union interest groups, governments might wish to accept the existing system of collective bargaining as a constraint. In which case, the second possibility would require policy to increase the demand for labour at the ruling wage rates in Development Areas. Public expenditure could be increased in the form of consumption purchases, investment or subsidies to firms, industries and employment. Also, the state can 'encourage' firms to move to the high unemployment regions: measures to promote the mobility of firms have been the basis of successive government's location of industry policies. Thirdly, policy might aim at decreasing the supply of labour in Development Areas through promoting greater labour mobility. What criteria might be used to choose between these alternatives?

IS LABOUR MOBILITY THE SOLUTION?

If there are rigidities in the structure of relative wages and if the government wishes to allow market forces to determine the location of firms, it would seem that labour mobility is the appropriate solution to the regional problem. Labour mobility involves a geographical adjustment of labour supply to changes in demand. Using a worker's available skills, it embraces movements both within and between regions, between rural and urban areas and between industries within an economy, as well as between economies. In Britain, the costs of much mobility are borne by individuals and/or firms. Some financial incentives are offered by the state to assist unemployed workers to move to other areas. The unemployed can obtain state assistance for job search, housing expenses, removal and re-housing costs. State involvement in financing labour mobility can be explained in terms either of market deficiencies or a general reluctance to allow individuals to express their preferences. The latter explanation is easily dealt with. The existence of a large amount of unaided mobility in the UK suggests that policy-makers accept the desirability of individual choice in this sphere. As for the market deficiency explanation, the major issue is whether both the employed and the unemployed can obtain sufficient funds to finance worthwhile moves. Will private markets provide funds for mobility? Training and re-training raise similar issues.[10]

MARKETS AND MOBILITY: WILL THE CAPITAL MARKET FINANCE HUMAN INVESTMENTS?

Labour mobility, like training, involves present costs being incurred in return for expectations of a higher future income. It is an investment in human beings and will be undertaken as long as it is expected to be worthwhile. Policy problems arise because human investments differ from physical capital in that the ownership of the investment remains with the individual, regardless of who bears the costs of mobility. Even so, firms will be willing to bear the costs of labour mobility so long as they expect to obtain a return on their investment. Examples might include the case of movement where a firm requires specific skills which only have value to one employer. A firm might also finance labour mobility where it is the sole employer in a locality or where it can arrange a voluntary contract in which the employee would agree to remain with the firm for a specified time, with compensation being required for breach of contract. In contrast, firms will usually be reluctant to finance mobility where the local labour market contains a relatively large number of alternative employers for migrant labour. In this situation, mobility is of a general character and has value to more than one firm. Without a low-cost contracts, system, an individual firm's prospects of obtaining a return on its general mobility investments are correspondingly reduced. There remains the possibility that individuals will finance mobility.

Individuals will bear the costs of mobility if they expect it to be worthwhile. Difficulties arise because of a difference in the time stream of mobility costs and rewards. Take the case of employed shipyard workers, miners and aero-engine workers living in, say, Scotland or the North-East and who believe that a move to the South-East would be worthwhile. For these workers, mobility costs will take the form of any forgone earnings, direct outlays on movement and adjustment costs. In the circumstances, mobility which requires a substantial investment may not be undertaken simply because individuals may not be able to finance (afford) the present costs, even though the investment is expected to be worthwhile. If individuals have insufficient income and savings to finance mobility, it might be expected that the private capital market would provide funds for profitable mobility investments. For reasons to be outlined below, private capital markets will tend to under-invest in mobility.

The nature of the property rights in human capital provides the basic explanation for the general absence of private funds for mobility. Without acceptable collateral, a worker's future earnings are a relatively unattractive prospect for inducing investors to provide finance for mobility. Unlike the investor in physical capital who pledges the equipment, potentially mobile labour cannot offer itself as collateral. Private capital markets might attempt to solve this problem through the use of *voluntary* contracts in which individuals would obtain funds for mobility and in return agree to repay the lender from future earnings.[11] Whether finance for mobility should be provided to the individual in the form of a loan or equity-type investment is something which might be settled – as with physical investment – by private contracts on the capital market. A possible factor inhibiting the development of such contracts might be their relatively high administration and enforcement costs resulting from the freedom of labour to move between areas. Thus, private capital markets are likely to under-invest in mobility, such deficiencies constituting a case for state intervention. One possibility would be to create a state manpower bank to provide loan and equity finance for mobility. State involvement in this area can be rationalised on technical monopoly grounds. The state has extensive property rights which would enable it to reduce the administration, collection and enforcement costs of a loans scheme, especially if repayments were combined with the existing income tax system. How might such a scheme operate?

A STATE MANPOWER BANK

Is there 'too much' or 'too little' mobility? The question is more appropriately answered in terms of the amount of investment in human beings rather than in terms of the numbers who move. We have established a general presumption of under-investment in labour mobility. It does not follow, however, that mobility must be provided free. The real difficulties arise because borrowers who would be capable of satisfying lenders of their ability to repay are unable to pledge themselves or their future earnings as security for a loan. In other words, deficiencies in the human capital market lead to an inability to raise cash for mobility which individuals believe to be worthwhile. The case for some form of loans system as a solution to this problem is based on a series of related propositions.

Mobility gives returns to individuals but requires scarce resources and hence is not a costless process (no free lunches). A loans system administered by a state manpower bank would ensure that the beneficiaries of mobility would bear the costs and that existing deficiencies in the human capital market would not prevent mobility investments where individuals are willing to pay. Also, by providing finance at market rates, a loans system would tend to reduce the possibility of over-investment in mobility. Policy would aim to supply funds on similar terms between mobility and physical capital investments. But clearly, the proposition about under-investment in mobility applies to other aspects of labour market investments in human beings. Thus, the state manpower bank would provide loans not only for mobility but also for training, re-training, job search, vocational guidance and labour market information: the aim should be to induce investment in these activities until the additional costs are justified by the extra returns.

THE OBJECTIONS TO A LABOUR MOBILITY POLICY

A labour mobility policy would encourage workers to move between different jobs and different areas and from the declining to the expanding sectors of the economy. Areas of relatively high unemployment would be encouraged to 'export' their unemployed. Why have post-war governments failed to adopt a labour mobility solution to the regional problem?

The Downs model would explain current UK regional policy in terms of its vote-winning attributes. Where policies are presented as costless, voters are likely to prefer current locations and immobility. At the same time, policy has been influenced by the desire to achieve something called 'balanced' regional development. This rather vague concept has involved more than a reduction in regional unemployment rates. It has also aimed to prevent the drift of population from North to South, such moves being opposed because of their alleged damage to community life in the declining areas. Furthermore, policy has tried to prevent congestion, housing shortages and over-crowding in the more prosperous regions of the South. Doubts might be raised about the meaning, empirical validity and the associated costs and benefits of these preferred 'commodities'. What, for example, is the exact nature of the alleged harm to community life as the size and composition of a local community undergoes change? What are the costs of different rates of migration? And until congestion, housing shortages and over-crowding are given empirical content, it is by no means obvious that the problems are confined to the South-East: what about Glasgow, Liverpool, Newcastle and Lancashire? For those who argue that current regional policy reflects the existence of obstacles to labour mobility, such as rent control, an alternative approach might propose the removal of policy-created constraints. Such examples show the opportunities for a critical appraisal of existing policy and its objectives.[12]

The concern of policy-makers with population movement and congestion has led to the rejection of labour mobility as the only solution to the regional problem. Instead, governments have been committed to a regional policy which includes the location of industry as one of its major components. Location policy aims to persuade and stimulate firms to establish new plants in areas of high unemployment. It is a policy of taking work to workers and has been supported by financial incentives, and Industrial Development Certificates (IDCs) which are required for factory building and extensions.

LOCATION OF INDUSTRY POLICY: WHY STATE INTERVENTION?

Theory predicts that a profit-maximising firm will locate a new plant in the area where its total costs are at a minimum. Two categories of private costs can be distinguished, namely, transport and production costs. Cost-minimisation means that plant location will be influenced by the sources of material inputs, by consumer markets and by the relative prices and local supplies of factors of production. Using this model, the critics of location policy argue that without state intervention, firms will locate plants in areas where their costs are lowest. If state location policy involves the development of industry in areas other than the least-cost locations, there will be an adverse effect on the economy's real income.[13] To assess this criticism, three questions have to be answered. First, can state location policy be assessed on criteria other than the minimisation of private costs? Secondly, what is the evidence on the efficiency of plant location in different areas? Thirdly, is the theory consistent with the facts, at least to the extent that firms build plants in the least-cost locations?

The Location of Industry and Social Costs and Benefits

Theory explains location decisions in terms of the minimisation of private costs or those borne by the firm. Supporters of a state location policy argue that a location decision involves some costs which are not borne by individual firms but are thrown on to other people in the community. Congestion costs are an example, resulting in a divergence between private and social costs. On this basis, state intervention might be justified on grounds of market failure due to externalities. A state location policy is required because when social costs are considered, the most preferred private location might not necessarily be the most advantageous from the community's viewpoint. Whether IDCs or general tax-subsidy measures are the most 'appropriate' form of state intervention is a policy issue separate from the technical question of the causes of market failure.

Evidence on Industrial Location in Different Areas

In addition to the social cost argument, a state location policy is often justified on the basis of the 'footloose' nature of a large part of manufacturing industry. Footloose means that a firm can function economically in a variety of locations. If it can be shown that a large part of manufacturing industry, especially the new plants located in Development Areas, is of the footloose type, then the criticism that state intervention adversely affects efficiency is invalid.

An early study found that 70 per cent of employment and net output in manufacturing industry was by trades which were fairly well-dispersed over the UK.[14] Footloose trades included food, chemicals, engineering and plastics. The study also found that the footloose activities had been the subject of the state's location policy. It was concluded that since location policy involved 'footloose' firms, it was unlikely to have adversely affected the economy's real income levels.

A further study estimated that about two-thirds of manufacturing industry (by employment) was footloose.[15] It was also found that plants established in Development Areas as a result of government policy experienced some *initial* cost disadvantage although in the long run, say five years, this was neither serious nor continuing. Nevertheless, evidence of a short-run cost disadvantage confirms continued reservations about the efficiency implications of existing location policy. Presumably, policy-makers can rationalise the situation by claiming that the resulting social benefits make the policy worthwhile. Critical assessment of such a claim is difficult in the absence of any quantification of the relevant, *ex ante*, costs and benefits. The situation is further complicated by the existence of budget-maximising state agencies responsible for regional policy. They have an incentive to deliberately exaggerate the alleged social benefits, and to underestimate the costs, of regional policy (see Chapters 3 and 11).

Are Firms Cost-Minimisers Selecting the Least-Cost Location?

Some economists have suggested that within British industry, location decisions often appear to be unsystematic and sometimes casual. Firms seem to be concerned with selecting a site that is satisfactory or adequate rather than searching for the best or optimum location. If location decisions rarely appear to be based on detailed calculations of the relative transport and production costs at alternative sites, it *might* be concluded that firms are not cost-minimisers and that they are pursuing objectives other than maximum profits. Such a conclusion would provide further support for location policy. There are, though, reservations about the methodology of some of the research into the location behaviour of firms. Even if a firm's decision-maker can be identified, difficulties arise in obtaining *ex ante* information rather than *ex post* rationalisations of location decisions. There are doubts about the appropriateness of tests of profit-maximising behaviour which ask people what they believe they do, as distinct from observing their response to changes in demand and costs.[16] Finally, evidence of 'incomplete' search does not constitute a refutation of profit-maximisation. To obtain information involves search costs, so that there will be an optimal amount of ignorance![17]

To summarise, state intervention in location decisions can be explained in terms of market failure due to externalities. Where firms are footloose, location policy might not adversely affect efficiency. Finally, if firms pursue objectives other than maximum profits, the efficiency objections to state intervention might not be valid. In this case, state intervention might be further justified on grounds of market failure due to imperfections: only in imperfect markets can firms pursue objectives other than maximum profits. Once the causes of market failure have been identified, questions arise about the appropriate policy solutions, their costs and likely benefits. Location policy is one possibility. Others include tax-subsidy policy or state ownership to 'correct' externalities and competition policy to remove imperfections. In view of the popularity of labour subsidies, the REP has to be considered as an alternative policy solution.

THE ECONOMICS OF THE REGIONAL EMPLOYMENT PREMIUM

The REP is a labour subsidy offered to manufacturing firms located in Development Areas. Introduced in 1967, it was designed to raise employment in two ways. First, for manufacturing as a whole, it lowered labour costs in Development Areas. By doing so, it aimed to attract more new plants to the high unemployment regions. Secondly, within the Development Areas, it reduced the costs of labour relative to capital, so encouraging the substitution of labour for capital. Effectively, the REP might be explained by visualising the UK economy confronted with external and internal balance of payments problems. The external problem is reflected in the exchange rate. The internal payments or regional problem results from the pattern of trade flows and the level of activity associated with different regions in Britain. REP aimed to reduce the internal payments problem by changing relative manufacturing costs and prices within the economy in favour of the Development Areas. Micro-economics can be used to predict the effects of such a labour-subsidy.

Assume that the REP reduces costs and product prices and is not absorbed in wage increases. For simplicity, assume that there are two manufacturing firms in the economy, firm S located in the South and firm N in the North, as shown in Figure 12.1.[18] If the REP is introduced for firm N, its MC curve will shift downwards, whilst firm S will be unchanged. For N, price falls and output rises following the introduction of REP, with N now producing a larger proportion of the economy's output. Also, the increased profits for N will attract new firms to locate in the Development Areas.

The employment effects of REP are shown in Figure 12.2.[19] Firm N is initially in equilibrium at point A, where iso-cost line C_1 is tangential to iso-quant Q_1. For N, the REP results in both substitution

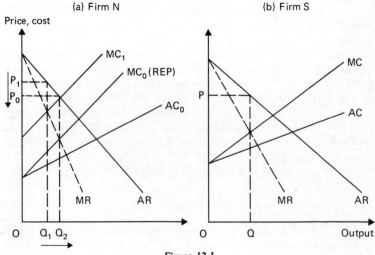

(a) Firm N   (b) Firm S

Figure 12.1

and scale effects. The substitution effect leads to the substitution of labour for capital and increases employment from L_1 to L_2. The scale effect results from the lower price for N's output. If both labour and capital are normal factors, the scale effect will reinforce the substitution effect and further increase employment from L_2 to L_3. A new equilibrium is achieved at point B and the predicted outcome is higher employment in the Development Areas. Does the evidence support this prediction?

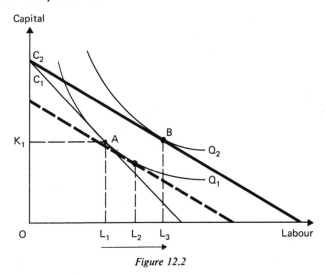

Figure 12.2

CONCLUSION: THE RESULTS OF REGIONAL POLICY

Ultimately, the choice between alternative policy instruments and the assessment of UK regional policy as a whole depends on the evidence. What has policy achieved? Differential regional unemployment rates still exist, as can be seen in Table 12.1. Indeed, compared with the national average, the unemployment differentials for the North, North-West and Wales actually increased between 1965 and 1975. Moreover, when the REP was introduced, it was expected to halve the disparity in unemployment between the Development Areas and the rest of the country. Instead, by 1973, the unemployment differential had doubled![20]

Although regional imbalances persist, it is possible that the situation would be much worse in the absence of policy. There is support for this view. It has been estimated that the UK regional policies of the 1960s created about 300,000 jobs in the Development Areas by 1971.[21] Investment incentives, building grants and selective assistance made

Table 1.21

| Region | Regional unemployment rates (%) | |
	1965	1975
North	2·5	6·0
North-West	1·6	5·4
Yorkshire	1·1	4·1
East Midlands	0·9	3·8
West Midlands	0·7	4·4
East Anglia	1·3	3·7
South-East	0·9	3·0
South-West	1·6	4·9
Wales	2·6	5·8
Scotland	2·8	5·3
N. Ireland	6·0	7·9
UK	1·5	4·3

Source: Central Statistical Office, *Economic Trends, Annual Supplement, 1975* (London, HMSO, 1975).
Note: Unemployment rates are third quarter averages, seasonally adjusted.

a major contribution, creating over 50 per cent of the new jobs. Government factory building and IDC policy contributed about 90,000 jobs, with REP accounting for only 10–15 per cent of the total impact of regional policy on employment in Development Areas. However, the evidence on job creation does not provide a verdict on the cost-effectiveness of alternative policy instruments. Even if it is accepted that, owing to unemployment, the alternative-use value of labour in Development Areas is zero, there remains a lack of evidence on the job-creating effects per unit of state expenditure allocated to different policies. Nor do we have any evidence on whether alternative policies would have been more successful. For example, some economists argue for more selective policy measures offering subsidies for *extra* employment created in Development Areas rather than for *existing* jobs. Others have suggested a more dis-aggregated policy, perhaps operating at the level of the town. One estimate has shown that a 1 per cent reduction in unemployment in the average town could be achieved by spending £4 million on training 4,000 unskilled men.[22] To some, however, the most satisfactory solution to the regional problem is a lower level of national unemployment.

No wonder an official report commenting on regional policy, declared that 'There must be few areas of government expenditure in which so much is spent but so little known about the success of the policy'.[23] Similar worries apply to state support for lame ducks.

Chapter 13

Subsidy Policy and Lame Ducks

INTRODUCTION

British governments have subsidised private firms and industries. Examples have included British Leyland, Chrysler, Upper Clyde Shipbuilders and Rolls Royce together with the aircraft, agricultural, computer, cotton, machine tool and shipbuilding industries.[1] Support for individual firms has increased since the early 1970s and the debate about 'lame ducks'. These were private firms which were unable to remain in business as commercially-viable enterprises without state financial assistance. The Industry Acts of 1972 and 1975 provided a general policy framework enabling governments to support the private sector. In the public sector, nationalised industries, such as coal and rail, have also been subsidised. Subsidisation means that enterprises remain in business and whole industries can avoid or postpone contraction. In other words, subsidies to firms interfere with the operation of markets and the allocation of resources in the economy. Nor are subsidies the only form of state support for private firms and industries. Others include tariff protection, quotas on imports and non-competitive, preferential purchasing by central and local governments (see Chapters 6 and 11).

SHOULD PRIVATE FIRMS RECEIVE STATE FINANCIAL AID?

Theory suggests two general arguments for state subsidies to private firms. Both are based on propositions about market failure. First, if society wishes to achieve an optimum allocation of resources, private firms will be required to charge prices equal to marginal costs (see Chapter 2).[2] For technical monopolies in decreasing cost activities, such a pricing policy requires subsidies. Needless to say, the marginal cost pricing argument was *not* used in the classic examples of state support in the 1970s, namely, Upper Clyde, *Concorde*, British Leyland and Chrysler. Secondly, externalities can cause market failure and subsidies enable the expansion of socially desirable activities. Indeed, the social benefits argument is most frequently used. It provides a general rationalisation for many activities which governments claim to undertake in the 'national interest'. Subsidies to firms and industries are often justified on grounds of advanced technology, defence, balance of payments, regional employment and the short-comings of the capital markets.[3] Such arguments have to be critically assessed.

   The alleged social benefits have to be identified and measured and the resource costs have to be estimated. Consideration has also to be given to the possibilities of alternative and lower-cost methods of achieving the same ends. For example, subsidies to the British air-craft industry are partly justified because they provide external economies in the form of technological fall-out. Certainly, analysis shows that competitive markets will under-invest in invention and research because of the difficulty of establishing property rights in marketable information. Whilst such market failure provides a general case for state intervention, it does not follow that the British aircraft industry should be subsidised. Much depends on which sectors of the economy are expected to make the best use of scarce technical resources. Would some of the technical resources employed in aircraft yield larger technological benefits if they were employed elsewhere in the economy? A similar question can be asked about the balance of payments contribution of a subsidised British aircraft industry. In fact, UK evidence shows that there are sectors other than aircraft which make greater contributions to technology and the balance of payments.[4]

   Governments frequently support firms located in high unemploy-ment regions, the aim being to maintain local employment. This intervention forms part of regional policy. In some instances, policy might be concerned not so much with preventing any re-allocation of resources but more with the time period required for resource re-adjustments. In other words, policy might aim to re-allocate resources in the long run rather than in the short run. Attractive though this might seem, it cannot avoid the conflict between job preservation and resource re-allocation. Like the infant industry argument, the worry is that we shall always be in the short run, with the long run perma-nently postponed on the principle of 'unripe time'. In this context, mention must be made of the shadow pricing argument for subsidies. This is based on market failure in the form of imperfections which prevent wage rates adjusting to clear local labour markets. As an example, take the case of state aid to Chrysler and its car factories located in Scotland. These factories employ labour which in the short run would be otherwise unemployed. Consequently, wage payments to Scottish car workers do not reflect the fact that the alternative-use value of labour in the region is zero: no real sacrifices are incurred in using this labour because it would be otherwise unemployed. Society does not forego any goods and services by using the labour for producing cars. Shadow prices allow policy-makers to consider the real resource costs of an activity which, in Development Areas, will differ from the ruling transactions prices. Thus, when governments are assessing projects in such Areas, the relevant shadow price of labour might be regarded as zero, rather than the wage bill. However, the concept has its limitations as a guideline for subsidy policy. Whilst the resource costs of Chrysler's Scottish workers may be zero, this is equally true for other policies which provide jobs for them in Scotland. Thus, some criterion other than shadow pricing is require to justify state subsidisation of Chrysler's Scottish plants. Moreover, shadow pricing is only relevant to labour which would be otherwise unemployed. This does not apply to all Chrysler workers. Some, such as the skilled and the young, would obtain alternative jobs quite quickly, so that their alternative-use value ceases to be zero. Others, such as the elderly and unskilled would be unemployed for longer periods, depending on their willingness to revise downwards their supply prices and search for jobs elsewhere (see Chapter 4). In the limit, shadow pricing is only applicable for the *expected* duration of unemployment. In forming such expectations, policy-makers cannot avoid judgements about wage rates and the mobility of labour, both of which will affect the extent of market clearing. Nor can the shadow pricing and social benefits arguments for subsidies be divorced from the economics of politics. It is possible that budget-maximising agencies and producer interest groups might combine to over-estimate the demand for an activity and persuade vote-conscious governments that the alleged (over-estimated) social benefits of a project are sufficient to make it worthwhile. State agencies might also aim to maximise their budgets by under-estimating the costs of a project, with shadow pricing offering some attractive possibilities! In the circumstances, it seems that 'unless objectives can be reasonably clearly set out and policies monitored so that their effectiveness is known, policy is at the mercy of whatever plausible arguments hold the scene'.[5] Indeed, the policy guidelines of economic theory are so general and have to be operated within the political market, that it might reasonably be asked whether there are any firms in the UK which would *not* qualify for a subsidy?

THE POLICY OPTIONS

Where market failure analysis justifies state subsidies, there are a variety of alternative policy options. These include adjustment policies, nationalisation and worker's co-operatives or labour-managed firms. Adjustment policies would *not* subsidise lame ducks.

Instead, the state would offer financial assistance for labour mobility, training and job search to assist the re-allocation of resources from lame ducks to other activities in the economy. Such financial assistance would be rationalised on grounds of deficiencies in the human capital market (see Chapter 12). If, however, governments do not believe individuals are the best judges of their welfare and wish to prevent market re-allocation, they might prefer the alternative policy of subsidising lame ducks. Either way, governments cannot avoid a decision on society's attitude to change. They have to choose between preventing change or accepting it and being more concerned with the adjustment period and the adequacy of arrangements for re-allocating resources.

Where the state decides to subsidise private firms, it still has to resolve a number of difficulties. Are the subsidies to be of the fixed-sum or open-ended (cost-plus) type, as used on *Concorde*? Will they be given to a firm or earmarked for a specific activity or factor of production? Are they to be temporary or permanent? If the former, and subsidies are supposed to restore lame ducks to health, so that they can survive without further aid, why are subsidies required: why not loans? On this point, it is usually argued that the capital market is dominated by private commercial criteria: the possibility of capital market failure has been analysed elsewhere (see Chapters 7 and 9). Governments will also have to decide whether to be concerned with the internal efficiency of private firms or to accept as constraints the existing employment level and skill composition of a unit's labour force. For subsidised firms the state might wish to impose price or profit controls and require an equity stake. A choice will also be required between subsidising private firms, nationalisation and creating a labour-managed firm, each being alternative forms of ownership for lame ducks. Perhaps those 'terrible' markets are not too bad after all. It is amazing the number of problems we create for ourselves when we try to replace them.[6]

NATIONALISATION

Nationalisation of lame ducks creates many of the problems raised by subsidies to private firms, as well as some new ones. Objectives have to be specified and associated pricing and investment rules are required. The efficiency and performance of state enterprises has to be monitored and their decisions can be modified by governments wishing to manage the economy.[7] Does theory offer any 'guidelines' on decision-making by state enterprises?

Pricing and investment policies are related and cannot be separated from the objectives of state enterprises. A range of alternative pricing solutions exist. A state enterprise could be required to act commercially and charge a profit-maximising price. Or, it could be required to 'break even', using average cost pricing. Alternatively, prices could equal marginal costs or could be set so as to maximise sales revenue. Finally, zero pricing is a possibility, as with bridges, museums, parks and the health service. Theory shows that each alternative has different price, output, employment, investment and financial implications. Presented with a set of predictions, governments can choose the pricing solution which makes the greatest contribution to their policy objectives. Economists frequently advocate marginal cost pricing.

If society wishes to achieve an optimum allocation of resources, welfare economics suggests that marginal cost pricing is desirable.[8] Such a pricing 'rule' maximises welfare. However, it is not without ambiguities and difficulties.[9] Marginal cost has to be defined and measured and will differ according to the time horizon. Lumpiness could mean that the marginal cost of an extra passenger on an empty train is almost zero whilst, for a full train, the marginal cost is the price of another train! Short- and long-run costs exist and the appropriate rule is to make price equal to long-run marginal cost, which will also be a point on a short-run marginal cost curve. But state enterprises, especially recently acquired lame ducks, are unlikely to be in long-run equilibrium. Accordingly, it is frequently argued that prices should equal short-run marginal cost to ensure optimal use of *existing* assets, with price equal to long-run marginal cost for determining the optimum size of an activity and the associated investment decisions. But what is the short- and long-run as an operational concept?[10] Moreover, for optimum resource allocation, the relevant costs are marginal social costs rather than the enterprise's private costs.

Marginal cost pricing has financial and income distribution implications. With decreasing or increasing costs, it leads to losses or surpluses, respectively. Losses financed out of general taxation are likely to interfere with optimum allocation, as well as involving a redistribution of income from society in favour of the consumers of the state-owned activity.[11] Surpluses also have distributional implications. Worries about the distributional effects of marginal cost pricing has led some economists to argue that those consumers who benefit from a service should pay for it, hence the attractiveness of pricing to cover total outlays. Second-best provides further objections to marginal cost pricing. Since the conditions for optimum resource allocation are unlikely to be satisfied throughout the economy, the second-best pricing rule for state enterprises is likely to involve a departure from strict marginal cost pricing (see Chapters 2 and 10). Finally, the economics of bureaucracies casts further doubts on the relevance of marginal cost pricing, or any other solution. A state enterprise aiming to maximise its budget has every incentive to set prices where demand elasticity is unity. It could rationalise such a price by claiming that it reflected 'true' marginal costs. And since state enterprises are usually monopolies, there would be no alternative cost yardsticks against which such a claim could be assessed and monitored. Effectively, marginal cost is whatever the chairman of a nationalised industry asserts it to be![12] Clearly, the opportunities for technical inefficiency are substantial.

Some of the principles of marginal cost pricing as well as its difficulties have been reflected in policy towards the British nationalised industries.[13] In 1967, policy adopted marginal cost pricing but, in addition, revenue had to cover accounting costs. Two-part tariffs have been used as one method of breaking even, with a fixed charge to recover overheads and a further tariff based on variable costs. Such tariffs are unlikely to result in optimum allocation. This is because the fixed charge for overheads might prevent some people from consuming the service who would otherwise be willing to pay its marginal cost. In the 1970s, however, the pricing and investment policies of the nationalised industries were modified as governments became increasingly concerned with inflation and unemployment. Thus, one official report concluded that between 1969 and 1974 '. . . the impetus towards a more rational control of the nationalised industries has tended to decrease. Departments, including the Treasury, have paid insufficient attention to the more general problems of the industries.'[14] Nationalisation of lame ducks would not be without its difficulties.

ARE LABOUR-MANAGED FIRMS PREFERABLE?

An alternative policy for lame ducks might involve subsidies being conditional on the formation of a workers' co-operative or labour-managed firm. Examples of workers' co-operatives have included the Meriden motor cycle plant and the ill-fated *Scottish Daily News*. What is likely to happen if workers hired capital instead of capitalists hiring workers? Theory has recently developed models of labour-managed firms which predict possible outcomes and which also provide insights into the likely results of Planning Agreements and industrial democracy (see Chapter 7).[15]

For simplicity, it is assumed that labour-managed firms (LMFS) maximise the net earnings or return per worker after meeting non-labour costs. Capital would be hired and the co-operative's products would be sold at market prices. Labour would bear the risks, with any surpluses or losses being distributed between workers, each individual of a given skill receiving an equal share. Consequently, incentives are likely to differ between LMFs and profit-maximisers in capitalist economies (PMFs). The argument is that in a large capitalist enterprise, a worker '. . . may well have little or no social partici-patory motivation to behave in a way which will promote the profit-ability of the enterprise . . . since any extra profit due to his extra effort will in the first place accrue to the entrepreneur'.[16] It is believed that with a workers' co-operative, the sense of participation may be greater, so providing a stronger social motivation to do the best for the firm in the form of the 'whole partnership of fellow workers'.

Using this model, it has been shown that in the long run, both LMFs and PMFs will result in an efficient, Pareto-optimal, allocation of resources, so long as markets are competitive in the sense of free entry and price-taking behaviour. Although the final outcome is identical, the adjustment process differs. With PMFs, labour will be attracted to the sectors where its marginal value product is highest. For LMFs, if the average earnings are higher in one industry than in another, workers will be attracted from low-earnings co-operatives to establish new co-operatives in the higher-earnings sector. Interest-ingly, even with LMFs, resource re-allocation and adjustment cannot be ignored.

The short-run adjustment process under competition is different. Consider the response of firms to a rise in the demand price offered for their product. PMFs will respond by increasing employment and output. But in the short run, a LMF will respond by *reducing* employ-ment and output in order to continue maximising average income per worker. Assuming that the rules of the co-operative allow it to dis-miss workers, such a short-run response would be highly inefficient. Optimal resource allocation requires that in the short run, labour as the variable factor should be attracted *towards*, not rejected from, its most highly valued employment: an example of the possible costs of co-operatives. The implications of LMFs for macro-economic employment policy are certainly non-trivial. In an economy of LMFs, to rely on Keynesian aggregate demand policies to reduce un-employment 'would be at best ineffective, and at worst might lead to a reduction in output and employment. Indeed, as a short-run policy to induce existing firms to give more employment it would be necessary to *decrease* total demand . . .'[17] In the circumstances of LMFs there are reservations about the employment effects of monetary and fiscal policies which operate through general changes in aggregate demand.

Further reservations apply to the basic model of LMFs. For example, some criteria are required to determine whether there will be any skill differentials for sharing in surpluses and losses. The criteria are likely to be the result of negotiations and bargains with the possibilities of conflict between labour groups replacing the traditional capital-labour struggle. Even if LMFs improve incentives, there might be difficulties of disciplined administration and internal 'policing' in a self-governing co-operative. Such difficulties are likely to be re-inforced if the members have different preferences for income and leisure. In some cases, co-operatives might be utility-maximising agencies, satisfying their preferences for income, staff, employment and leisure. Ultimately, of course, the acceptance or rejection of these hypotheses will depend on their empirical validity. Unfortunately, this is an area where we have very little empirical evidence, some of it being of an indirect kind. For example, evidence on the effects of worker participation on efficiency indicates that 'many of the fears of management that participation would greatly reduce efficiency are not founded in fact'.[18] Both analytical and empirical work on workers' co-operatives is in its infancy. Analysis does, however, suggest that the principle of LMFs in itself cannot provide all the answers.

CONCLUSION: A RULE FOR SUBSIDY POLICY?

Industrial subsidy policy is a classic example of the problems of economic policy and forms an appropriate conclusion for the whole book. There are disputes about the objectives of subsidy policy and society's attitude to change. Some economists and politicians prefer job preservation, others are more concerned with resource re-alloca-tion. Controversy exists over the causes of the policy problem. Some use market failure explanations, but disagree about whether the sources of failure are in externalities, the labour market or the capital market. Others use an alternative explanation which recognises the 'problems of firms trapped in a cumulative spiral of decline' and the influence of organised labour on managerial decisions.[19] Inevitably, the perceived causes of the policy problem results in alternative policy solutions. For lame ducks, these include adjustment policies, subsidies to private firms, nationalisation and workers' co-operatives, much depending on a government's preference for market-improving or market-displacing policies. Throughout the debate, there are numerous examples of economic principles versus pragmatism, and *ad hoc*ery; of uncertainty about the aims of subsidy policy and of the *ex post* economic rationalisation of government subsidy decisions made perhaps on electoral grounds. Elsewhere, theory is seen to have its limitations as a guide for subsidy policy; this is especially so in the case of recent developments, such as our understanding of workers' co-operatives.

A quotation from J. S. Mill summarises the debate not only about subsidies, but also about the whole of economic policy.

'There are some things with which governments ought not to meddle and other things with which they ought; but whether right or wrong in itself, the interference must work for ill, if government, not understanding the subject which it meddles with, meddles to bring about a result which would be mischievous.'[20]

Economic policy abounds with mischief.

Notes

Chapter 1   The Economists' Approach to Policy Problems

1   See, for example, T. W. Hutchison, *Economics and Economic Policy in Britain, 1946–1966* (London, Allen & Unwin, 1968); see also Sir J. Hicks, 'What is Wrong with Monetarism?', in *Lloyds Bank Review* (October 1975), and H. G. Johnson, 'What is Right with Monetarism?', in *Lloyds Bank Review* (April 1976).

2   Figure 1.1 could have shown future consumption instead of investment so that the frontier would then show various combinations of present and future consumption. R. G. Lipsey, *An Introduction to Positive Economics* (London, Weidenfeld & Nicolson, 1975), ch. 4.

3   Reference to policy objectives can be found in *Hansard* and in various White Papers, for example, *Report of the Committee on the Working of the Monetary System*, Cmnd 827 (London, HMSO, 1959), ch. 2. By 1976, the full employment target was being defined as 700,000 unemployed. See also Chapters 4–7.

4   Op. cit., ibid.

5   The starting date of 1964 was chosen because it coincided with a new government and the National Plan.

6   See, for example, M. Friedman, 'The Methodology of Positive Economics', in *Essays in Positive Economics* (Chicago, University of Chicago Press, 1953).

7   *The Regeneration of British Industry*, Cmnd 5710 (London, HMSO, 1974), p. 2.

8   Government indecision, or no action (a choice), will cause some automatic mechanism to operate.

9   J. Tinbergen, *On the Theory of Economic Policy* (Amsterdam, North-Holland, 1952). Also, N. Kaldor, 'Conflicts in National Economic Objectives', in *Economic Journal* (March 1971). This principle does not mean that conflicts can be removed completely: at best, the trade offs might be reduced.

10   The reader might be genuinely worried about the use of the subjective concept of a 'satisfactory' test of a hypothesis.

Chapter 2   Why Do Governments Intervene in the Economy?

1   The principles have general applicability – for example, for cars and TVs substitute North Sea oil and coal, or the Midlands–South East and the Development Areas.

2   Perfect competition is a sufficient but not a necessary condition for reaching a Pareto optimum: a socialist state is also capable of achieving such an optimum. See D. M. Winch, *Analytical Welfare Economics* (Harmondsworth, Penguin, 1971), pt 1.

3   Public goods are those for which one person's consumption does not reduce anyone else's consumption – for example, defence, music, ideas, theories and information. A. Alchian and W. Allen, *University Economics* (London, Prentice-Hall, 1974).

4   Unemployment might also reflect the failure of markets to transmit to producers the correct market clearing signals about present and future consumer demands. Markets might fail to correctly inform producers that the offer of labour services by the unemployed constitutes a demand for additional output. Similarly, markets might not exist which enable firms to correctly identify the specific future product demands of current savers. See, for

example, A Leijonhufvud, *Keynes and the Classics*, IEA, Occasional Paper 30 (London, 1969), pp. 35–7; also Chapter 4.

5   This general form of the welfare function can be expressed more specifically – for example, it might be linear

$$W = a_0 + a_1E + a_2P + a_3B + a_4G + a_5Y$$

or multiplicative

$$W = a_0E^{a_1}P^{a_2}B^{a_3}G^{a_4}Y^{a_5}$$

where $a_0 \ldots a_5$ are the 'weights' (importance) attached to each target. Each variable and its influence on W has to be specified. See Winch, op. cit.

6   The principle was formulated by Kaldor–Hicks–Scitovsky. More specifically, it is usual to include two additional conditions:
    (1) that a reversal of the change does *not* result in an improvement;
    (2) that the resulting income distribution is 'desirable'.
    See, for example, I. Little, *A Critique of Welfare Economics* (Oxford, Oxford University Press, 1960), p. 123.

7   See, for example, D. W. Pearce, *Cost-Benefit Analysis* (London, Macmillan Studies in Economics, 1971).

8   R. G. Lipsey and K. Lancaster, 'The General Theory of Second-Best', in *Review of Economic Studies*, vol. 24, pp. 11–32. Also Winch, op. cit.

9   C. K. Rowley, *Anti-Trust and Economic Efficiency* (London, Macmillan, 1973), p. 17.

Chapter 3   An Alternative Explanation of Public Policies: An Economic Theory of Politics

1   Arrow's General Possibility Theorem has shown that it is impossible to devise a constitution which has certain apparently desirable attributes. See, for example, D. M. Winch, *Analytical Welfare Economics* (Harmondsworth, Penguin, 1971), ch. 10.

2   Anthony Downs, *An Economic Theory of Democracy* (New York, Harper, 1957), chs 15–16.

3   Compare the similarity of products which emerge under duopoly – for example, in the car market.

4   Downs, op. cit., p. 198.

5   Some exist, such as Ralph Nader's organisation in the USA, and the Consumers Association, publishers of *Which* in the UK.

6   Downs, op. cit., p. 203.

7   Also W. A. Niskanen, *Bureaucracy and Representative Government* (Chicago, Aldine-Atherton, 1971).

8   Downs, op. cit., p. 299.

9   See, for example, A. Wildavsky, 'Budgeting as a Political Process', in *International Encyclopaedia of the Social Sciences* (London, Macmillan, 1968), vol. 2; also D. McFadden, 'The Revealed Preferences of a Government Bureaucracy', in *The Bell Journal of Economics* (Autumn 1975 and Spring 1976).

Chapter 4   Unemployment

1   The demand curve (D) reflects labour's marginal physical product; the supply curve (S) is based on a worker's exchange between income and leisure (see Chapter 8 and Figure 8.5). The price is the real wage rate (W/P), namely, the money wage rate divided by the price level. The analysis will be used to explain the natural unemployment rate in Chapter 5. See, for example,

E. Shapiro, *Macro-Economic Analysis* (New York, Harcourt, Brace, 1966), pp. 339f.

2 It is assumed that workers are *not* prevented by unions nor custom from reducing their offer price to as low as they wish. Adjustment takes time because workers have to learn from experience. See Chapters 5 and 12; also A. Alchian and A. W. Allen, *University Economics* (London, Prentice Hall, 1972), ch. 25.

3 Until late 1972, the temporarily unemployed were included in the total register of unemployed; they are no longer included in the count. See J. Hughes, 'How Should We Measure Unemployment?', in *British Journal of Industrial Relations*, vol. 13, no. 3.

4 The incentive to register as unemployed is much weaker for those ineligible to claim benefit.

5 J. Bowers, *The Anatomy of Regional Activity Rates* (London, NIESR, 1970). Variations in activity rates could be positively related to employment opportunities in the economy.

6 Institute of Manpower Studies, *Monitor* (Autumn 1972).

7 D. Healey, Chancellor of the Exchequer, Debate on the Address, *Hansard* (26 November 1975).

8 It has been suggested that unemployment of up to eight weeks duration should be classed as frictional; those who have been unemployed for between eight and twenty-six weeks should be regarded as voluntarily un-employed: twenty-six weeks is the period during which earnings-related unemployment benefit can be drawn. J. B. Wood, *How Much Unemployment?*, IEA, Research Monograph, no. 28 (London, 1972).

9 D. Gujarati, 'The Behaviour of Unemployment and Unfilled Vacancies', in *Economic Journal* (March 1972). Alternative hypotheses have been formulated including 'shake-outs' and the effects of the Industrial Training Act, 1964 (see Chapter 5).

10 D. MacKay and G. Reid, 'Redundancy, Unemployment and Manpower Policies', in *Economic Journal* (December 1972).

11 See also K. Hartley, 'Industry, Labour and Public Policy', in R. Grant and G. K. Shaw (eds), *Current Issues in Economic Policy* (London, Philip Allan, 1975).

12 ibid.

13 See Chapter 6 on import controls; Chapter 7 on growth; Chapter 12 on regional policy and Chapter 13 on lame ducks.

14 See any basic economics text: for example, R. Lipsey, *Positive Economics* (London, Weidenfeld & Nicolson, 1975).

15 The model is:
$$N = f(Q)$$
where N is employment, Q is output and $f > 0$;
$$Q = f(AD)$$
where AD is aggregate demand and $f > 0$;
$$AD = Y = C + I + G + X - M$$
with G and $X - M$ assumed given or autonomous (see Chapter 6 on balance of payments);
$$C = a + bY$$
with a and $b > 0$;
$$I = f(mec, r)$$
where mec is marginal efficiency of capital and r is rate of interest, negatively

related to I (a distinction has to be made between the mec, which relates to a *stock* of capital, and the marginal efficiency of investment, which relates to a *flow* of I);

$$r = f(L, M)$$

where L is the demand for money or liquidity preference and M is the supply of money (see Chapter 5 for alternative definitions of M).

16   The model can be summarised as

$$M \rightarrow r \rightarrow I \rightarrow Y$$

For the UK, the multiplier has been estimated to be under 1·5.

17   The model of the banking system can be generalised to incorporate some of the changes since 1945. For example, in the late 1950s, concern was expressed about the wider structure of liquidity. The definition of the money supply was expanded to include other liquid assets such as Treasury and commercial bills and short-term government securities, as well as financial institutions like building societies, hire purchase and insurance companies together with trade credit (*Radcliffe Report*, 1959). In 1971, a new Competition and Credit Control Policy was introduced. A 12½ per cent reserve assets ratio was applied to *all* UK banks and not solely to the clearing banks. More reliance has also been placed on special deposits which are effectively a method of varying the banking system's reserve assets requirements. M. Artis and M. Parkin, 'Competition and Credit Control', in *The Bankers' Magazine* (September 1971).

18   Curve L is the demand or liquidity preference schedule, corresponding to a given level of real income.

19   R. Levacic, *Macro-Economics* (London, Macmillan, 1976), p. 172.

20   ibid., p. 105. See also Chapter 7 which introduces the accelerator.

21   The modern Quantity Theory can be summarised $M \rightarrow Y$ compared with the indirect relationships of the Keynesian model (see Chapter 5).

22   There were loops in the Phillips curve: anti-clockwise for the nineteenth century and clockwise since 1945 – that is, for any given level of unemployment, the rate of wage change was higher if unemployment was rising and lower if unemployment was falling. D. Laidler and M. Parkin, 'Inflation – A Survey', in *Economic Journal* (December 1975), p. 754.

23   Both inflation and unemployment can be viewed as 'bads' (undesirable). Each indifference curve (I) shows that inflation and unemployment are substitutes, with an increasingly large reduction in U needed to justify each successive percentage point increase in $\dot{p}$. Higher levels of utility arise in moving from I_1 to I_2 to I_3 – that is, towards the origin in Figure 4.6. See R. Lipsey, 'Structural and Deficient-Demand Unemployment Reconsidered', in B. McCormick and E. Smith (eds), *The Labour Market* (Harmondsworth, Penguin, 1968), p. 246.

Chapter 5   Inflation

1   Labour Government, *Attack on Inflation, A Policy for Survival*. A guide to the Government's Programme (London, HMSO, 1975).

2   ibid.

3   ibid.

4   ibid.

5   For a change the Government specified some price stability targets for its policy. Price rises to be reduced from 26 per cent per annum in 1974–75 to 10 per cent by the end of summer 1976 and to single figures by the end of 1976; ibid., p. 6.

6 A. Marshall, *Principles of Economics*, 8th edn (London, 1920), p. 348.

7 (a) The demand-pull sequence is $+P_t \rightarrow +W_{t+1}$.
   (b) The cost-push sequence is $+W_t \rightarrow +P_{t+1}$.

8 The modern version has two characteristics: it is concerned with nominal income (Y) and is a theory of the demand for money (reflected in V) as a specific application of the standard theory of consumer choice. It can be represented thus:

$$Y = MV$$

where Y = nominal income ($=PQ$ where P is price level and Q is real output);
   M = quantity of money defined as coins, notes and bank deposits;
   V = income velocity of circulation of money – that is, the number of times money changes hands in payment for final goods and services. Changes in the quantity of money demanded will be reflected in V.

9 Whilst interdependence between demand and supply curves undermines partial equilibrium analysis, it does not affect the Quantity Theory as a theory of the demand for money. Such a demand function 'fits the facts' with a low substitutability between money and financial assets. Thus: '... although the price level cannot be determined simply by analysing the supply of and demand for money, the money market will, nevertheless, play a crucial part in a more complete and general analysis'. D. Laidler and M. Parkin, 'Inflation – A Survey', in *Economic Journal* (December 1975), p. 751.

10 Such short-run problems have been analysed with the Phillips curve.

11 M. Friedman, 'Statement on Monetary Theory and Policy', in *Employment Growth and Price Levels*, Joint Economic Committee, us Government (May 1959); reprinted in R. Ball and P. Doyle (eds), *Inflation* (Harmondsworth, Penguin, 1969) (author's italics).

12 S. Weintraub, *Keynes and the Monetarists* (usa, Rutgers University Press, 1973).

13 A. A. Walters, *Money in Boom and Slump*, iea, Hobart Paper 44 (London, 1970), p. 50.

14 M. Friedman, *The Counter-Revolution in Monetary Theory*, iea, Occasional Paper 33 (London, 1970), p. 24.

15 J. Hicks, 'The Permissive Economy', in *Crisis 75 . . . ?*, iea, Occasional Paper Special 43 (London, 1975). Interestingly, if sociological explanations are reflected in changing inflationary expectations (caused by ? Why the explosion in the late 1960s and not earlier ?) it is relevant that expectations are also central to the Monetarist explanation of the Phillips curve (see below). How do we distinguish between the alternative models ?

16 N. Kaldor, 'The New Monetarism', in *Lloyds Bank Review* (July 1970).

17 Walters, op. cit.

18 Autonomous of Y – that is, $A = I + G + X - M$.
   (a) Keynesian hypothesis: $\Delta A \rightarrow \Delta Y \rightarrow \Delta C$:

$$\Delta C = a + b\Delta A$$

   (b) Quantity Theory hypothesis: $\Delta M \rightarrow \Delta C$:

$$\Delta C = a_1 + b_1 \Delta M$$

19 C. Barrett and A. Walters, 'The Stability of Keynesian and Monetary Multipliers in the uk', in *Review of Economics and Statistics* (November 1966).

20 C. Goodhart and A. Crockett, 'The Importance of Money', in Bank of England *Quarterly Bulletin* (June 1970), p. 77.

21 For a review of evidence, see D. Pierce and D. Shaw, *Monetary Economics* (London, Butterworths, 1974), ch. 8; also, A. A. Walters (ed.), *Money and Banking* (Harmondsworth, Penguin, 1973). UK evidence indicating the direction of causality between money, income and prices is less clear cut than that for the USA. UK evidence shows *both* unidirectional causality from nominal incomes to money and also unidirectional causality from money to prices: see D. Williams *et al.*, 'Money, Income and Causality: The UK Experience', in *American Economic Review* (June 1976).

22 HM Treasury, *Economic Progress Report* (London, HMSO, April 1975).

23 No one would criticise demand theory if it was found that the price and income elasticities for, say, cars varied over time: the theory does not predict constant unchanging empirical magnitudes. See also, H. G. Johnson, 'What is Right with Monetarism', *Lloyds Bank Review* (April 1976).

24 M. Artis, 'Monetary Policy in the 1970s', in H. Johnson and A. Nobay (eds), *Issues in Monetary Economics* (Oxford University Press, 1974).

25 Laidler and Parkin, op. cit.

26 Artis, op. cit., p. 535.

27 IS–LM analysis is useful for this section of the argument: see R. N. Waud, 'Proximate Targets and Monetary Policy', in *Economic Journal* (March 1973).

28 G. Mrydal, *Against the Stream* (London, Macmillan, 1974), p. 315.

29 In fact, demand models postulate that $W = f(P)$, so that W is not ignored.

30 $$\dot{W} = f(\Delta T, T)$$

where ΔT is rate of change of unionisation and T is level of unionisation (proportion of labour force in unions). A. Hines, 'Trade Unions and Wage Inflation in the UK, 1893–1961', in *Review of Economic Studies* (October 1964); also D. Digas and A. Hines, 'Trade Unions and Wage Inflation in the UK: A Critique of Purdy and Zis', in *Applied Economics* (September 1975).

31 *Applied Economics* (September 1975), p. 210.

32 L. Godfrey and J. Taylor, 'Earnings Changes in the UK, 1954–1970', in *Oxford Bulletin of Economics and Statistics*, Vol. 35, No. 3 (1973).

33 For an explanation of these exceptions, see Chapters 8 and 10 on minimum wage legislation and monopoly.

34 Hines, op. cit.

35 British unions might have raised their members relative hourly earnings by 0–10 per cent in the early 1960s with the union differential probably increasing to some 25 per cent in the 1968–73 period of greater union militancy. C. Mulvey, 'Collective Agreements and Relative Earnings in UK Manufacturing in 1973', in *Economica* (November 1976). A prices or profits push variant of cost models explains inflation in terms of the exercise of market power in highly concentrated industries. US evidence provides no support for any relationship between price changes and concentration. Also, it has to be remembered that the UK and US economies do not consist entirely of manufacturing firms: a point frequently ignored by advocates of the administered pricing hypothesis. See Chapters 9 and 10.

36 To resolve the controversy between cost and demand explanations of inflation, a test of causality has been developed (C. Sims, *American Economic Review*, September 1972). This asserts that if causality runs from X to Y *only*, then future values of X in a regression equation should not have significant coefficients. When applied to US data for 1949–70, it was found

that *future* values of the money supply were not significant in explaining prices so that the tests were consistent with a undirectional causality from money to prices. Similarly, future values of prices did not explain wages (cost-push) and the causal chain was from prices to wages and not vice versa. Thus, these findings support the Monetarist view. J. Barth and J. Bennett, 'Cost-Push versus Demand-Pull Inflation', in *Journal of Money, Credit and Banking* (August 1975).

37 Phillips curves have been estimated for Australia, Canada, Germany, Italy, Japan and South Africa.

38 In Figure 5.2 D_L and S_L are the demand for, and supply of, labour, respectively. Excess demand is shown by $(D_L - S_L)/S_L$. The annual rate of change of money wage rates is w and U is the unemployment rate.

39 For the UK, a positive relationship has been found between increases in rates of tax on wages and subsequent rates of wage increase: J. Johnston and M. Timbrell, 'Empirical Tests of a Bargaining Theory of Wage Rate Determination', in *Manchester School* (June 1973).

40 R. Thomas and P. Storey, 'Unemployment Dispersion as a Determinant of Wage Inflation in the UK, 1945–1966', in *Manchester School* (June 1971).

41 D. Gujarati, 'The Behaviour of Unemployment and Unfilled Vacancies', in *Economic Journal* (March 1972); also, G. Evans, 'A Note on the Trends in the Relationship between Unemployment and Unfilled Vacancies', in *Economic Journal* (March 1975).

42 J. Taylor, *Unemployment and Wage Inflation* (Harlow, Longman, 1974).

43 E. S. Phelps *et al.*, *The Micro-economic Foundations of Employment and Inflation Theory* (New York, Norton, 1970); also, M. Friedman, 'The Role of Monetary Policy', in *American Economic Review* (March 1968).

44 A similar result is obtained using a Keynesian model and distinguishing between the nominal and the real interest rates. If the nominal r only partly adjusts to a rise in expected inflation the real r will fall, causing investment to rise and, via the Keynesian multiplier, output and employment.

45 A similar distinction applies to average cost curves: the long-run cost curve maps out single points on different short-run curves but any point on a short-run curve is not necessarily a long-run equilibrium. Figure 5.3 can be redrawn using a single Phillips curve relationship between unemployment and *deviations in the rate of inflation from the expected rate*: see P. Wannocott, '*Macro-Economics* (Illinois, Irwin, 1974), p. 287. Alternatively, a long-run trade off can be obtained between not the level of, but the rate of change of, the rate of inflation and the level of unemployment.

46 Keith Hartley, 'Industry, Labour and Public Policy', in G. K. Shaw and R. Grant (eds), *Current Issues in Economic Policy* (London, Phillip Allan, 1975), see Chapters 4 and 12.

47 M. Friedman, *Unemployment versus Inflation*, IEA, Occasional Paper No. 44 (London, 1975).

48 The timing of the change in the 1960s is explained in terms of exchange rate policy. Fixed rates ensured that to the mid-1960s, relatively low unemployment created a balance of payments deficit rather than accelerating inflation. The inflation explosion of the 1960s was world-wide, a common factor being the expansion of world demand from US reflationary fiscal policy after the mid-1960s. The creation of excess international money (mainly dollars) in a system of fixed exchanges led to the over-expansion of national money supplies in almost every major industrial country (a world Quantity Theory). The sterling devaluation of 1967 further contributed to inflationary pressure in the UK; see Chapter 6.

49 This can be represented by

$$\dot{w} = f(u) + b\Pi$$

where Π is the anticipated inflation rate and b is the extent to which inflationary expectations are reflected in current wage changes. In this model, if $f(u) = 0$, then $\dot{w}$ depends on $b\Pi$. Phillips assumed $b = 0$, whilst the vertical Phillips curve requires $b = 1$. All the evidence suggests $b < 1$, typically in the range 0·3–0·8. S. J. Turnovsky, 'On the Role of Inflationary Expectations in a Short-Run Macro-Economic Model', in *Economic Journal* (June 1974).

50 A fixed exponential weighting system is used and this means that the anticipated rate of inflation will *always* be lagging behind current inflation! Also, it has been shown that even if inflation is completely anticipated, the influence of other variables (for example, demand and supply of money) means that an empirically-estimated $b < 1$ could, in fact, be consistent with the absence of money illusion; see Turnovsky, op. cit.

51 Similar estimation problems occur with empirical work on long-run cost-curves. However, some recent studies have found no long-run trade off, so supporting the natural rate hypothesis and a vertical curve. Laidler and Parkin, op. cit.

52 E. S. Phelps, 'Inflation, Expectations and Economic Theory', in N. Swan and D. Wilton (eds), *Inflation and the Canadian Experience* (Toronto, Queen's University, 1971). For the UK, U_n was estimated to be slightly less than 2 per cent in the mid-1960s and almost 4 per cent since 1967; see D. Laidler, in M. Friedman, *Unemployment vs. Inflation*, IEA, Occasional Paper 44 (1975).

53 By maintaining real incomes, the economy would tend to operate around U_n.

54 Using the models,

$$\dot{w} = f(\dot{p}, \ e, \ S, \ Y)$$
$$\dot{p} = g(\dot{w}, \ e, \ \dot{y}, \ Z)$$

where e is inflationary expectations, S is union militancy, $\dot{y}$ is productivity, and Y and Z are any other relevant variables. Incomes policies can
   (a) act on either the wage or price equations or both – that is, act on the independent variables $\dot{p}, \dot{w} \ldots Y, Z$ – and/or
   (b) change the functional relationships shown by f and g.

55 M. Parkin and M. Sumner, *Incomes Policy and Inflation* (Manchester University Press, 1972), pp. 13, 25.

56 J. Carlson and M. Parkin, 'Inflationary Expectations', in *Economica* (May 1975).

57 A. B. Askin and J. Kraft, *Econometric Wage and Price Models* (London, Lexington, 1974).

58 M. Parkin, 'Incomes Policy: Some Further Results on the Rate of Change of Money Wages', in *Economica* (November 1970).

59 F. Blackaby (ed.), *An Incomes Policy for Britain* NIESR (London, Heinemann, 1972), p. 221.

60 First National City Bank, 'Price Controls Flunk the Inflation Test', in *Monthly Economic Letter* (July 1973).

61 K. Hartley, 'Industrial Training and Public Policy', in A. Culyer (ed.), *Economic Policies and Social Goals* (London, Martin Robertson, 1974).

62 National Board for Prices and Incomes, *Standing Reference on the Pay of the Armed Forces*, Third Report, Cmnd. 4291 (London, HMSO, 1970).

63 *Report* of a Court of Inquiry into a dispute between NCB and NUM (Wilberforce), Cmnd. 4903 (London, HMSO, 1972).

64 ibid., p. 8.
65 ibid., p. 10.
66 O. E. Williamson, *Economics of Discretionary Behavior* (Chicago, Markham, 1964). A profit maximiser will have a horizontal utility function and will locate at the maximum profit position.
67 J. Burton, *Wage Inflation* (London, Macmillan Studies in Economics, 1972), p. 86.
68 D. Laidler, 'Inflation and its Control', in Grant and Shaw (eds), op. cit.

Chapter 6   The Balance of Payments

1   Compared with W. Germany and France, Britain's average propensity to import and its income elasticity of demand for imports (1·82) have been higher and its price elasticity of demand for imports lower ($-0·86$). Difficulties emerge because the UK's income elasticity of demand for imports exceeds the world income elasticity of demand for Britain's exports (0·9). Thus, if exchange rates remain unchanged, Britain can only grow half as fast as the rest of the world in the long run. See H. Houthaker and S. Magee, 'Income and Price Elasticities in World Trade', in *Review of Economics and Statistics* (May 1969); also M. Panic, 'Why the UK's Propensity to Import is High', in *Lloyds Bank Review* (January 1975).

2   In Figure 6.1 aggregate demand is AD, resulting in full employment Y_f, as in quadrant I. Investment is I_0 and is determined by the rate of interest r_0, as shown in quadrant II. Capital inflows (K) are shown in quadrant III and are K_0 at interest rate r_0. At Y_f, there is a trade deficit of B_0, shown in quadrant IV.

3   See Figure 6.1, where any improvement in the trade deficit requires a reduction in aggregate demand and hence lower employment.

4   F. Hirsch, *The Pound Sterling: A Polemic* (London, Gollancz, 1965). P. Oppenheimer, 'Employment, Balance of Payments and Oil in the UK', in *Three Banks Review* (March 1976).

5   H. Junz and R. Rhomberg, 'Prices and Export Performance', in *Staff Papers*, (IMF, July 1965).

6   L. Krause, 'British Trade Performance', R. Caves (ed.), *Britain's Economic Prospects* (London, Allen & Unwin, 1968).

7   G. M. McGeehan, 'Competitiveness: A Survey', in *Economic Journal* (June 1968).

8   M. Panic, 'Why the UK's Propensity to Import is High', in *Lloyds Bank Review* (January 1975).

9   *The Regeneration of British Industry*, Cmnd. 5710 (London, HMSO, 1974).

10 The mirror image of this situation will be an excess demand for dollars at the ruling sterling price of dollars. The demand for pounds reflects a supply of dollars and the supply of pounds represents a demand for dollars. The excess demand will be associated with black market pressures.

11 A similar difficulty arises when governments introduce minimum price controls for agricultural products (for example, USA and EEC Common Agricultural Policy) and are then required to purchase surplus crops and in some cases pay farmers to leave their fields unplanted.

12 The analysis of discriminating monopoly is presented in the section on deflation. The discriminating monopoly model provides a framework for analysing claims by foreigners (for example, USA) that British firms are involved in 'dumping' (for example, cars).

210 *Problems of Economic Policy*

13 This can be seen with the aid of the following diagrams:

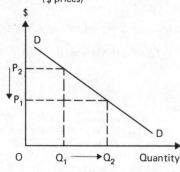

(a) Demand for British exports ($ prices)

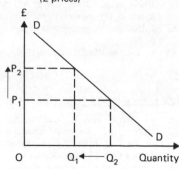

(b) British demand for imports (£ prices)

14 NIESR, 'The Effects of the Devaluation of 1967 on the Current Balance of Payments', in *Economic Journal* (Supplement) (March 1972).

15 For an outline of the Marshall-Lerner conditions see, for example, W. Scammell, *International Trade and Payments* (London, Macmillan, 1974), p. 307.

16 The foreign trade multiplier is:

$$\Delta Y = \Delta X/(s + m)$$

where X is exports, s is marginal propensity to save and m is marginal propensity to import.

17 D. C. Hague *et al.*, *Devaluation and Pricing Decisions* (London, George Allen & Unwin, 1974).

18 A. P. Thirlwall, 'The Panacea of the Floating Pound', in *National Westminster Bank, Quarterly Review* (August 1974); also M. Friedman, *Capitalism and Freedom* (Chicago, Chicago University Press, 1962), ch. 4; S. Brittan, *The Price of Economic Freedom* (London, Macmillan, 1970).

19 G. E. J. Llewellyn, 'The Determinants of UK Import Prices', in *Economic Journal* (March 1974).

20 A. Thirlwall, op. cit., p. 21; also F. Hirsch and D. Higham, 'Floating Rates – Expectations and Experience', in *Three Banks Review* (June 1974).

21 Even with fixed parities it is possible for one country's inflation rate to persistently differ from the world inflation rate. For example, if there are two sectors, a foreign trade and a closed or domestic sector, inflation rates can differ between the two. Since a country's overall inflation rate is an average of the two sectors, there is scope for its inflation to persistently differ from the world rate. D. Laidler and M. Parkin, 'Inflation – A Survey', in *Economic Journal* (December 1975), p. 784.

22 M. Fg. Scott, *A Study of UK Imports* (London, NIESR, 1963), p. 70. The import function is

$$M = a + mY$$

where m is marginal propensity to import.

23 R. Cooper and K. Hartley, *Export Performance and the Pressure of Demand* (London, George Allen & Unwin, 1970), ch. 4.

24 This suggests a model in which UK exports depend upon relative prices (P_r) and domestic and overseas demand (D_d and D_w, respectively):

$$X_{\text{UK}} = f(P_{\text{r}}, D_{\text{d}}, D_{\text{w}})$$

25 R. Ball *et al.*, 'The Relationship between UK Export and Performance in Manufactures and the Internal Pressure of Demand', in *Economic Journal* (September 1966).

26 Cooper and Hartley, op. cit.

27 A. Prest and D. Coppock, *The UK Economy: A Manual of Applied Economics*, 5th ed., (London, Weidenfeld & Nicolson, 1974) p. 137.

28 K. Hartley, *A Market for Aircraft*, IEA Hobart Paper 57 (London, 1974), p. 66.

29 The emphasis on current relative costs allows the infant industry (externalities) argument to remain.

30 R. G. Lipsey, *Positive Economics* (London, Weidenfeld & Nicolson, 1975), p. 675.

31 R. N. Cooper, 'The Balance of Payments', in Caves (ed.), op. cit., p. 196.

32 M. Goldstein, 'The Effects of Exchange Rate Changes on Wages and Prices in the UK: An Empirical Study', in *IMF Staff Papers* (November 1974), p. 736. The 1·2 per cent decrease in real wages reflects the 2·7 per cent price rise and a 1·5 per cent rise in money wages.

33 G. Bispham, 'New Cambridge and Monetarist Criticisms of Conventional Economic Policy-Making', in *NIESR Review* (November 1975); also D. Kerns, 'Public Sector Deficits', in *National Westminster Bank Quarterly Review* (May 1974).

Chapter 7 Economic Growth

1 I. Kravis, 'A Survey of International Comparisons of Productivity', in *Economic Journal* (March 1976).

2 J. Jewkes, *The New Ordeal by Planning* (London, Macmillan, 1968), p. 16.

3 M. Kennedy, 'The Economy as a Whole', in A. Prest (ed.), *The UK Economy* (London, Weidenfeld & Nicolson, 1972), p. 48. By 1976, the Labour Government announced that 'to reduce unemployment to 700,000 in 1979 . . . the GDP must grow at an average rate of 5½ per cent' (Chancellor of Exchequer, *Hansard*, 9 March 1976). This is an ambitious target, especially in relation to Britain's past performance.

4 R. Bacon and W. Eltis, 'Stop-Go and De-Industrialisation', in *National Westminster Bank, Quarterly Review* (November 1975).

5 D. Smith, 'Public Consumption and Economic Performance', in *National Westminster Bank, Quarterly Review* (November 1975). A. Whiting, 'Is Britain's Poor Growth Performance due to Government Stop-Go Induced Fluctuations?', in *Three Banks Review* (March 1976).

6 Bacon and Eltis, op. cit.

7 The production function approach has been chosen because of its simplicity. Alternative growth models exist. Harrod-Domar models stress the importance of capital-output and savings-output ratios, as well as increases in the labour force and technical progress; neo-classical growth models stress the role of variations in the capital-output ratio and flexibility of relative factor prices; Cambridge models emphasise that the savings of capitalists and workers depends on income distribution; Arrow introduced technical progress through learning-by-doing. See A. Peaker, *Economic Growth in Modern Britain* (London, Macmillan, 1974).

8 *Budget Statement* (1972); also *Regeneration of British Industry* Cmnd. 5710 (London, HMSO, 1974), p. 1.

9 *Budget Statement* (1972).

10   The accelerator is

$$I = v(\Delta Y)$$

where v is the capital output ratio, and ΔY is the change in output or the current output in relation to previous period's output.

11   P. Junankar, *Investment: Theories and Evidence* (London, Macmillan, 1972), p. 69.

12   D. Smith, 'Public Consumption and Economic Performance', in *National Westminster Bank, Quarterly Review* (November 1975).

13   The residual is shown by the 'A' term in the Cobb-Douglas production function: see, for example, M. Blaug, *An Introduction to the Economics of Education* (London, Allen Lane, 1970), p. 92.

14   K. Hartley, 'The Learning Curve and its Application to the UK Aircraft Industry', in *Journal of Industrial Economics* (March 1965).

15   G. Becker, *Human Capital*, NBER (Columbia UP, 1964); also K. Hartley, 'Industrial Training and Public Policy', in A. Culyer (ed.), *Economic Policies and Social Goals* (London, Martin Robertson, 1975); see Chapter 12.

16   M. Blaug, *An Introduction to the Economics of Education*, op. cit., chs 6 and 7.

17   P. Layard *et al.*, *Qualified Manpower and Economic Performance* (London, Allen Lane, 1971).

18   Computers might lead to twenty-seven man years of labour *saved* per year of operation over a seven year life, whilst the construction of a computer might require fifty man years over two years. See P. Stoneman, 'The Effects of Computers on the UK Demand for Labour', in *Economic Journal* (September 1975).

19   Do new factories embody best practice technology? See 'An Interchange', B. Haigh, R. Gregory and D. James, *Economic Journal* (June 1975).

20   A. Whiting (ed.), *The Economics of Industrial Subsidies* (London, HMSO, 1976), p. 56.

21   ibid., p. 149.

22   C. Kennedy and A. Thirlwall, 'Technical Progress: A Survey', in *Economic Journal* (March 1972), p. 47. For an analysis of the micro-economics of R&D, see Chapter 9.

23   E. Denison, 'Economic Growth', in R. Caves (ed.), *Britain's Economic Prospects* (London, Allen & Unwin, 1968).

24   N. Kaldor, *Causes of the Slow Rate of Growth of the UK* (Cambridge University Press, 1966). The basic equation relating to the growth of GDP and the growth of manufacturing output (MF) was

$$q_{GDP} = 1 \cdot 15 + 0 \cdot 16 q_{MF} \qquad R^2 = 0 \cdot 96$$
$$(0 \cdot 08)$$

25   See Chapter 12 for an analysis of the related Regional Employment Premium; economies of scale are analysed in Chapter 9.

26   R. Rowthorn, 'What Remains of Kaldor's Law', in *Economic Journal* (March 1975).

27   N. Kaldor, 'Economic Growth and the Verdoorn Law', in *Economic Journal* (December 1975), p. 895.

28   ibid., pp. 895f.

29   This is a proposal for extending the supply of alternative information, rather than relying on a single source which is more likely to be wrong! Nor is it a proposal for perfect information since, in uncertainty, no economic agent has perfect foresight.

30   *The Regeneration of British Industry*, Cmnd 5710 (London, HMSO, 1974).

31 ibid., p. 1.
32 ibid., p. 1; also Chapters 9, 10, 12 and 13.
33 ibid., p. 6; also Tony Benn, *Speeches By Tony Benn* (Nottingham, Spokesman Books, 1974).
34 E. Varley, in *Hansard*, 977 (4 November 1974), p. 825.
35 Cmnd. 5710, p. 2; also Department of Industry, *The Contents of a Planning Agreement* (London, 1975); 'Progress on Industrial Strategy', in *Economic Progress Report* (August 1976).
36 E. Mishan, *Costs of Economic Growth* (Harmondsworth, Penguin, 1969); also E. Mishan, *Twenty-one Popular Economic Fallacies* (London, Allen Lane, 1969), pt 5.
37 See Chapter 1 for an example of different growth rates using a production possibility boundary. Society's preferred growth rate can be shown by a set of indifference curves for the community, reflecting its preferences between present and future consumption: society will aim to maximise utility.

Chapter 8   *Price Controls, Markets and Income Distribution*

1 Football is an example of private price-fixing in the form of the annual FA Cup Final and the (now abolished) players' maximum wage.
2 In Figure 8.1, S_m, S_S and S_L are the market, short- and long-run supply curves, respectively.
3 J. M. Currie *et al.*, 'The Concept of Economic Surplus and Its Use in Economic Analysis', in *Economic Journal* (December 1971).
4 Speech by E. Short for the Labour Opposition in a debate on housing, reported in *Daily Telegraph* (14 March 1973).
5 See, for example, K. J. Arrow, 'Economic Welfare and the Allocation of Resources for Invention'; also H. Demsetz, 'Information and Efficiency: Another Viewpoint', both in D. M. Lamberton (ed.), *Economics of Information and Knowledge* (Harmondsworth, Penguin, 1971).
6 R. L. Harrington, 'Housing – Supply and Demand', in *National Westminster Bank Quarterly Review* (May 1972). Real rates of interest are money rates adjusted for inflation and tax relief. They were negative in 1955–7 and in 1969.
7 Alex Henney, 'The Housing Situation in the UK', in *Moorgate and Wall Street* (Autumn 1974).
8 See, for example, E. H. Phelps-Brown and J. Wiseman, *A Course in Applied Economics* (London, Pitman, 1964).
9 Rent collectors allocating houses on the basis of a tenant's willingness to pay a capital sum for the key, or for 'good quality' decorations, fixtures and fittings.
10 *Committee on the Rent Acts* (Francis), Cmnd. 4609 (London, HMSO, 1971).
11 NIESR, 'The Price of Accommodation', in *Economic Review* (August 1964).
12 *Daily Telegraph* (17 October 1974), p. 11.
13 *Fair Deal on Housing*, Cmnd 4728 (London, HMSO, 1971).
14 ibid.
15 See, for example, M. Cooper and A. K. Maynard, *The Price of Air Travel*, IEA, Hobart Paper No. 53 (London, 1971), p. 49.
16 A. P. Ellison and E. M. Stafford, *The Dynamics of the Civil Aviation Industry* (Farnborough, Saxon House, 1974).
17 K. Hartley, *A Market for Aircraft*, IEA, Hobart Paper No. 57 (London, 1974).
18 The oil cartel of the mid-1970s (OPEC) faced similar competition from substitutes. Higher oil prices have stimulated alternative sources of energy,

such as coal and nuclear power, as well as the search for new oil fields outside the OPEC area.

19   E. G. West, 'Britain's Evolving Minimum Wage Policy', in *Moorgate and Wall Street* (Autumn 1969). Also Cmnd. 4648 NBPI *General Problems of Low Pay* (London, HMSO, 1971): this Report refers to contract cleaning as a low-paid industry where keen competition exists and where '. . . the workforce is used relatively efficiently and it would not be practicable to devise . . . schemes for raising pay and productivity' (p. 35).

20   A. A. Alchian and W. R. Allen, *University Economics*, 3rd edn (London, Prentice-Hall, 1974), p. 439. Even if there are monopsonistic markets, the employment predictions of the competitive model will remain valid so long as there are *some* labour markets which are competitive in the economy. Can you name a British monopsonist in the labour market, other than conscription for the armed forces?

21   *General Problems of Low Pay*, op. cit., p. 41.

22   C. Mulvey, 'Collective Agreements and Relative Earnings in UK Manufacturing in 1973', in *Economica* (August 1976).

23   For surveys of the evidence, see E. West, op. cit., and Cmnd 4648, op. cit.

24   Cmnd 4648, op, cit.

25   ibid., pp. 41–3. It has been estimated that human capital explains 30 per cent–50 per cent of earnings inequality.

26   For a summary of the evidence, see R. B. McKenzie and G. Tullock, *The New World of Economics* (Illinois, USA, Irwin, 1975), p. 82.

27   If information has externality – public good characteristics – the appropriate public policies might include the subsidisation of women's employment in higher paid jobs traditionally confined to men and the state provision of more information about the quality of women's work.

28   To the extent that monopsony exploitation exists, its abolition will result in an improvement in resource allocation, assuming monopsony is the only constraining sector. See also B. Chiplin and P. Sloane, 'Sexual Discrimination in the Labour Market', in *British Journal of Industrial Relations*, vol. 12, no. 3.

29   This can be shown using standard iso-quant and iso-cost diagrams. On one diagram show capital and labour inputs with a rise in female wage rates raising the relative price of labour. A second diagram can be used to show male and females as factor inputs with a rise in the latter's wage rates changing the slope of the iso-cost curve. In both cases, there are substitution and scale effects.

30   With the subsidy, H_2 involves individual expenditure of RY_2. Without the subsidy, H_2 would have cost the individual RY_0: hence Y_2Y_0 is the amount of the subsidy.

31   Alternatively, if society wishes to achieve U_2, cash payments are a lower-cost method than price subsidies. The analysis can be extended to payments-in-kind, for example, coupons entitling pensioners to 'free' beef, bus rides or TV viewing. If the recipients do not consume any of the free commodities and are not allowed to sell their coupons, they will not benefit from the policy. Others might gain but could be even 'better off' if they were allowed to exchange their tokens for cash. The analysis can also be extended to foreign aid and the issues of cash assistance, tied aid and gifts of capital equipment. See, for example, M. Pauly, 'Efficiency in the Provision of Consumption Subsidies', in *Kyklos*, Vol. 23 (1970). Also A. Peacock and J. Wiseman, *Education for Democrats* IEA, Hobart Paper No. 25 (London, 1964).

32   G. Tullock, 'The Costs of Transfers', in *Kyklos*, Vol. 24 (1971).

33 L. Godfrey, *Theoretical and Empirical Aspects of the Effects of Taxation on the Supply of Labour* (Paris, OECD, 1975), p. 126.
34 ibid., ch. 5.
35 C. V. Brown and E. Levin, 'The Effects of Income Taxation on Overtime', in *Economic Journal* (December 1974).
36 The result being a backward-bending supply curve for the individual worker.

Chapter 9   Large Firms, Mergers and Public Policy

1 See *Census of Production Reports* (London, HMSO). Figures for small firms exclude some 50,000 units with under eleven employees.
2 E. H. Chamberlin, *Theory of Monopolistic Competition* (Harvard University Press, 1938).
3 *The Industrial Reorganisation Corporation*, Cmnd. 2889 (London, HMSO, January 1966).
4 W. McClelland, 'The Industrial Reorganisation Corporation', in *Three Banks Review* (June 1972), p. 27.
5 H. Demsetz, 'Information and Efficiency', in *Journal of Law and Economics*, vol. 12 (1969); reprinted in D. Lamberton (ed.), *Economics of Information and Knowledge* (Harmondsworth, Penguin, 1971).
6 An outcome which means that when comparing competition and monopoly, it is logically invalid to argue that the monopolisation of a previously competitive industry will be advantageous because the monopoly will benefit from greater scale economies. This is not to deny that a monopolist might operate under decreasing costs, in which case competition will not be a technical possibility. Such a technical monopoly will still misallocate resources if price exceeds MC and the policy issue then involves the appropriateness of a MC pricing solution.
7 Methodologically, questions arise as to whether the model yields alternative predictions compared with the extremes of monopoly and perfect competition. See D. Dewey, *The Theory of Imperfect Competition* (London, Columbia University Press, 1969), p. 79.
8 In conventional analysis, the LAC rises because of the limitations of management or managerial diseconomies of scale. These arise because eventually the managerial task of co-ordination becomes increasingly difficult and, in the last resort, the top decision-maker has only a limited capacity for assimilating information and making decisions of a given quality. However, there is a logical inconsistency since management is regarded as 'fixed', and yet in the long run all factors are supposed to be variable!
9 The evidence relates to technical economies; see C. Pratten, *Economies of Scale in Manufacturing Industries* (Cambridge University Press, 1971).
10 A. Silberston, 'Economies of Scale in Theory and Practice', in *Economic Journal* (March 1972) (Supplement).
11 J. K. Galbraith, *American Capitalism* (London, Hamish Hamilton, 1957), pp. 86–7.
12 Demetz, op. cit.
13 The range of discontinuity in MR means that, over a range, variations in MC will not lead to price–output changes. The difficulty is to known how *OP* is *initially* established!
14 J. Jewkes *et al.*, *The Sources of Invention* (London, Macmillan, 1969). Invention refers to the creation of ideas and innovation to their commercial production.
15 C. Kennedy and A. Thirlwall, 'Technical Progress', in *Economic Journal* (March 1972), p. 49.

16   A. Singh and G. Whittington, *Growth, Profitability and Valuation*, Department of Applied Economics, Occasional Paper No. 7 (Cambridge University Press, 1968), ch. 8. This study is based on four UK industries in the period 1948–60: non-electrical engineering, clothing and footwear, food, tobacco.

17   ibid., p. 189. A 1 percentage point increase in a firm's post-tax profitability on equity assets could result in a 0·7 percentage point increase in its growth rate. However, it must be stressed that the relationship between profitability and firm size is dependent on how profits and size are measured; see D. G. Smyth *et al.*, *Size, Growth, Profits and Executive Compensation in the Large Corporation* (London, Macmillan, 1975).

18   A. Singh, *Take-Overs* (Cambridge University Press, 1971), p. 44. This study is based on take-overs in five industries, 1955–60 (food, drink, electrical and non-electrical engineering, and clothing and footwear). Also, A. Singh, 'Take-Overs, Natural Selection and the Theory of the Firm', in *Economic Journal* (September 1975).

19   A. Singh, *Take-Overs*, op. cit.; also A. Singh, 'Take-Overs, Natural Selection and the Theory of the Firm', in op. cit. The evidence has implications for the hypothesis that the threat of take-over is expressed as a valuation ratio constraint (ratio of stock market value of a firm's equity to its book value) – that is, unless a firm achieves a certain minimal valuation ratio it is almost certain to be acquired but, having achieved this value, it is more or less safe from acquisition. The *Take-Overs* study by Singh found that about 40 per cent of the acquired firms had above average valuation ratios whilst some of the units not taken over had valuation ratios below their industry averages. Such evidence refutes the strong version of the valuation ratio constraint hypothesis.

20   A. Singh, *Take-Overs*, op. cit., p. 151. UK evidence shows that 'in so far as the neo-classical postulate of profit maximisation relies on the doctrine of economic natural selection in the capital market (via the take-over mechanism), the empirical base for it is very weak'. A. Singh in *Economic Journal* (September 1975), p. 514.

21   A. Cosh, 'The Remuneration of Chief Executives in the UK', in *Economic Journal* (March 1975). For quoted companies 1969–71, size (net assets) 'explained' 49 per cent of the variation in pay; the addition of profitability raised the 'explanation' to 54 per cent. It was estimated that in a company of £10m. net assets, the chief executive's remuneration would only vary between £12,230 and £16,470 as the rate of return varied between 0 per cent and 30 per cent; increased size from £1m. to £100m., with constant profitability, raised pay from £7,790 to almost £26,000 (1971 prices).

22   A. Singh, *Take-Overs*, op. cit., p. 166; M. A. Utton, 'On Measuring the Effects of Industrial Mergers', in *Scottish Journal of Political Economy* (February 1974), p. 26.

23   G. Newbould, *Management and Merger Activity* (Liverpool, Guthstead, 1970), pp. 161–75; also P. G. Devine, *et al.*, *An Introduction to Industrial Economics* (London, Allen & Unwin, 1974), ch. 5. K. Hartley, 'The Export Performance of the British Aircraft Industry', in *Bulletin of Economic Research* (November 1972), p. 84.

24   Even if product markets are not perfect, competition in the capital market will ensure that only those who maximise (monopoly) profits survive. Thus, the capital market is an alternative method of promoting competition. A. Alchian and R. Kessel, 'Competition, Monopoly and the Pursuit of Pecuniary Gain', in *Aspects of Labour Economics* (Princeton, NBER, 1962), p. 160.

Chapter 10   Monopoly, Mergers and Public Policy

1   M. Friedman, *Competition and Freedom* (Chicago, University of Chicago Press, 1962), p. 120. The marriage market is a good example of a competitive market.

2   H. Leibenstein, 'Allocative Efficiency *v*. X-Efficiency', in *American Economic Review* (June 1966). It must be stressed that X-efficiency is a necessary but not a sufficient condition for allocative efficiency. The distinction has caused some confusion with suggestions being made (incorrectly) that the welfare losses of X-inefficiency exceed those of allocative inefficiency. For evidence on X-inefficiency, see various reports of NEDO and National Board for Prices and Incomes.

3   There are beliefs that it is relatively greater in Britain. Even if X-inefficiency is greater in Britain, this might be a 'preferred' position for society. Also, adjustments in the exchange rate can be used to maintain the UK's international competitiveness. For a critical assessment of the X-inefficiency concept see G. Stigler, 'The Xistence of X-efficiency', in *American Economic Review* (March 1976).

4   O. E. Williamson, *Economics of Discretionary Behavior* (Chicago, Illinois, Markham, 1964); see Chapter 5, Figure 5.4 in this text.

5   C. Rowley, *Anti-Trust and Economic Efficiency* (London, Macmillan, 1973).

6   Between 1948 and 1973, monopoly was defined as one-third of the market. The new definition was introduced in the 1973 Fair Trading Act. However, the definition is only used to identify a monopoly: the Monopolies and Mergers Commission then has to determine whether a monopoly is acting against the 'public interest'.

7   An alternative concentration measure is the Herfindahl index (H) which takes account of both the number of firms and their size differences: it is based on summing the squares of the market shares of all firms in the industry. H tends to 1 when there are few firms and/or greater degrees of inequality in market shares. The H index can give a reverse ordering compared with a five-firm concentration ratio, see, for example, J. F. Pickering, *Industrial Structure and Market Conduct* (London, Martin Robertson, 1974), pp. 3–7.

8   S. Aaronovitch and M. Sawyer, 'Concentration of British Manufacturing', in *Lloyds Bank Review* (October 1974).

9   A. Armstrong and A. Silberston, 'Size of Plant, Size of Enterprise and Concentration in British Manufacturing Industry', in *Journal of Royal Statistical Society*, vol. 128 (1965), pt 3.

10   Pickering, op. cit., p. 21.

11   J. Meehan and T. Duchensneau, 'The Critical Level of Concentration', in *Journal of Industrial Economics* (September 1973).

12   P. Hart, 'Competition and Rate of Return on Capital in UK Manufacturing Industry', in *Business Ratios*, vol. 2 (1968).

13   For a summary of evidence see, for example, W. Reekie, 'Advertising and Market Structure', in *Economic Journal* (March 1975).

14   ibid.

15   Vertical mergers involve firms at different stages of production and distribution within an industry – for example, a car assembly firm merging with a tyre company and/or a distributor. Conglomerates are firms involved in a variety of apparently unrelated product markets (diversified), for example, a car firm acquiring a food manufacturer; see Department of Trade and Industry, *A Survey of Mergers 1958–1968* (London, HMSO, 1970).

16   M. Utton, 'The Effects of Mergers on Concentration', in *Journal of Industrial Economics* (November 1971); also K. George, 'Changes in Industrial Concentration in the United Kingdom', in *Economic Journal* (March 1975).

17   M. Utton, 'British Mergers Policy', in K. George and C. Joll (eds), *Competition Policy in the UK and EEC* (Cambridge University Press, 1975), p. 98.

18   G. Meek and G. Whittington, 'Giant Companies in the UK', in *Economic Journal* (December 1975).

19   G. Whittington, 'Changes in the Top 100 Quoted Manufacturing Companies in the United Kingdom, 1948–1968', in *Journal of Industrial Economics* (November 1972).

20   M. Utton, 'Aggregate Versus Market Concentration', in *Economic Journal* (March 1974).

21   P. Hart *et al.*, *Mergers and Concentration in British Industry* (London, Cambridge University Press, 1973).

22   Monopolies Commission, *Household Detergents* (London, HMSO, August 1966).

23   K. Hartley, *A Market for Aircraft*, IEA Hobart Paper No. 57 (1974), p. 48; also A. Sutherland, *Monopolies Commission in Action* (Cambridge University Press, 1970).

24   Board of Trade, *Mergers: A Guide to Board of Trade Practice* (London, HMSO, 1969), p. 9.

25   ibid., pp. 10f.

26   O. E. Williamson, 'Economies as an Anti-Trust Defence', in *American Economic Review* (March 1968).

27   See previous chapter for a comment on the source of scale economies available under a merger but not under competition.

28   D. Swann *et al.*, *Competition in British Industry* (London, Allen & Unwin, 1974).

29   ibid., p. 195. Resource allocation is defined to embrace static, dynamic and X-efficiency.

30   Rowley, op. cit.

Chapter 11   Monopoly, Bureaucracy and Competition in the Public Sector

1   In Figure 11.1, OQ_c is twice OQ_m and OQ_b is twice OQ_c: an assumption which simplifies the analysis. See J. A. Stockfisch, *The Political Economy of Bureaucracy* (New York, General Learning Press, 1972). This chapter presents the results of a research project undertaken by the author, assisted by Janet Cubitt, as part of the SSRC-financed Public Sector Studies Group at York. See Chapter 3.

2   If the technically efficient cost schedule gives a budget less than the entire area under the demand curve, the bureau will respond by increasing its estimated expenditures required for Q_b in Figure 11.1. As Figure 11.1 is drawn, $OP_cBQ_b = ORQ_b$.

3   J. Stockfisch, op. cit., p. 16; also, R. McKenzie and G. Tullock, *The New World of Economics* (London, Irwin, 1975), ch. 17. G. Tullock, *The Vote Motive* (London, Institute of Economic Affairs, Hobart Paperback, 1976).

4   See, for example, K. Hartley, 'Programme Budgeting and the Economics of Defence', in *Public Administration* (Spring, 1974).

5   Proposals for education vouchers allow state finance and private provision. See, for example, A. K. Maynard, *Experiment with Choice in Education*, IEA Hobart Paper No. 64 (London, 1975).

6   Reputable insurance brokers and the established medical profession behave in a similar way and confine themselves to advice about the 'reputable' (that is, in their view, 'safe') policies and treatments; the consumer is rarely given any indication of the risks and prices associated with less reputable (risky?) policies and treatments. The so-called medical 'quacks' are an example of a riskier treatment for ailments which cannot be 'solved' with established medical techniques.

7   National Joint Consultative Committee of Architects, *Code of Procedure for Selective Tendering, 1972* (London, RIBA Publications, 1972).

8   In some cases (for example, defence; DHSS), competition is multi-dimensional involving both price and non-price factors such as delivery, technical performance of a weapon and reliability. The standing orders of local authorities also specify circumstances under which competition is not required – for example, monopoly, where no local or national competition exists; emergencies such as the collapse of a sewer or flooding.

9   C. Turpin, *Government Contracts* (Harmondsworth, Penguin, 1972), p. 244.

10 Ministry of Defence Procurement Executive, *The New Quality Requirements for. Defence Procurement* (London, HMSO, 1973), para. 3.

11 Ministry of Public Building and Works, *The Placing and Management of Contracts for Building and Civil Engineering Work* (London, HMSO, 1964), p. 8.

12 Difficulties arise since costs are subjective and reflect the decision-maker's valuation of alternatives foregone through selective tendering. Analysis can contribute to the debate by estimating the magnitudes being placed on the valuations.

13 Complete elimination of the risks of default is too costly. The policy model implies a negative relationship between the price level and the probability that the contractor will fail to complete the work satisfactorily: Ministry of Public Building and Works, op. cit.

Chapter 12   Subsidy Policy and the Regions

1   A. Whiting (ed.), *The Economics of Industrial Subsidies* (London, HMSO, 1976), ch. 1.

2   See K. Hartley, *A Market for Aircraft*, IEA, Hobart Paper No. 57 (London, 1974).

3   See Chapter 5 for an example of profit controls and utility-maximising firms.

4   Whiting (ed.), op. cit., ch. 1.

5   The TES was £20 per week per job in mid-1976; the school-leaver's subsidy was £10 per week per job for six months.

6   See A. J. Brown, *The Framework of Regional Economics in the UK* (Cambridge University Press, 1972).

7   'Exports' and other autonomous expenditures will have regional multiplier effects. The regional multiplier shows the extent to which a rise in autonomous expenditure in a region will raise the region's income levels and hence local employment. Estimates of regional multipliers are relatively low, probably about 1·2 to 1·3, due to the substantial 'leakages' of expenditure to other regions in the UK. A. J. Brown, 'Regional Economics', in *Economic Journal* (December 1969).

8   'The Economics of North Sea Oil', in *Midland Bank Review* (May 1975).

9   These are equivalent to changing the price and shifting labour demand or supply curves at the ruling wages. Location policy aims to increase labour demand at the existing wage rates, whilst mobility policy will shift the supply curve to the left. See Chapter 6 for an application to exchange rates and Chapter 8 on minimum wages.

10   For simplicity, we concentrate on the problems of labour mobility and ignore other sources of labour market failure resulting from monopolies, entry barriers and information 'gaps'. Training and re-training should also be considered in any treatment of labour mobility. They have been ignored because they raise no new general principles about the failure of the capital market to finance human investments: see K. Hartley, 'Industrial Training and Public Policy', in A. Culyer (ed.), *Economic Policies and Social Goals* (London, Martin Robertson, 1974).

11   See, for example, M. Friedman, *Capitalism and Freedom* (Chicago, University of Chicago Press, 1962), ch. 6.

12   See, L. Needleman, 'What Are We to Do About the Regional Problem?' in *Lloyds Bank Review* (January 1965); also, H. Richardson and E. West, 'Must We Always Take Work to the Workers?', in *Lloyds Bank Review* (January 1964).

13   See, for example, A. Hobson, 'The Great Industrial Belt', in *Economic Journal* (September 1951).

14   R. Nicholson, 'The Regional Location of Industry', in *Economic Journal* (September 1956).

15   W. Luttrell, *Factory Location and Industrial Movement* (London, NIESR, 1962).

16   A comparative statics approach would examine the price–output responses of firms to changes in demand and costs due to lump-sum taxes and profits taxes: this is a method of assessing the predictive accuracy of alternative models of firm behaviour.

17   The situation is similar to the marriage market where there are substantial search costs: where further search is unlikely to be worthwhile, the partners will make exchange decisions without the costly searching of the whole market! See Chapter 4.

18   In Figure 12.1, AR and MR are average and marginal revenue curves, respectively; AC and MC are average and marginal cost curves, respectively. Profit-maximisation is assumed. Firm N receives REP, leading to a downward shift in its MC curve and hence a lower price and higher output.

19   Iso-quants are labelled Q and they relate to the output levels shown in Figure 12.1. The iso-cost lines are the budget lines C_1 and C_2. The broken budget line is parallel to C_2 and tangential to Q_1: it shows the substitution effect – that is, the effect of a change in relative factor prices, output being unchanged.

20   R. MacKay, 'The Impact of the REP', in Whiting (ed.), op. cit.

21   The estimates assumed a constant pressure of demand and included indirect multiplier effects in the service industries. The period taken was 1960–71. B. Moore and J. Rhodes, 'A Quantitative Analysis of the Effects of the REP and Other Regional Policy Instruments', in Whiting, op. cit.

22   D. Metcalf, 'Urban Unemployment in England', in *Economic Journal* (September 1975).

23   Expenditure Committee, *Public Money in the Private Sector*, HC 347, (London, HMSO, 1972), p. 57.

Chapter 13   Subsidy Policy and Lame Ducks

1   A. Whiting (ed.), *The Economics of Industrial Subsidies* (London, HMSO, 1976).

2   See also A. Prest, 'The Economic Rationale of Subsidies to Industry, in Whiting (ed.), op. cit.

3   Expenditure Committee, *Public Money in the Private Sector*, HC 347, (London, HMSO, 1972).

4 These include chemicals, electricals, instruments, mechanical engineering and vehicles. See, for example, K. Hartley, *A Market for Aircraft*, IEA, Hobart Paper No. 57 (London, 1974).

5 I. Byatt, Comment, in Whiting (ed.), op. cit., p. 75.

6 See, for example, F. Cripps, 'The Economics of Labour Subsidies', and K. Hartley, Comment, in Whiting (ed.), op. cit.

7 M. Peston, 'The Nationalised Industries', in R. Grant and G. K. Shaw (eds), *Current Issues in Economic Policy* (London, Philip Allan, 1975); also H. Phelps-Brown and J. Wiseman, *A Course in Applied Economics* (London, Pitman, 1964).

8 See Chapters 2 and 10 as well as Figure 8.2 in Chapter 8. Where marginal costs are zero, as with bridge crossings, the appropriate price is zero.

9 See, for example, I. M. Little, *A Critique of Welfare Economics* (Oxford, University Press, 1960); also R. Turvey, *Economic Analysis and Public Enterprise* (London, Allen & Unwin, 1971).

10 What is meant by fixed costs? If costs are sacrifices, no current sacrifices are incurred by using 'fixed' assets; the sacrifices were incurred in the past and are irrelevant for current decision-making: hence fixed cost is contradictory! The associated short- and long-run distinction is also dubious since *all* inputs can be varied in any interval but, for some inputs, the costs of adjustment will be lower for delayed variations. See, for example, A. Alchian and W. Allen, *University Economics* (London, Prentice-Hall, 1974), ch. 15.

11 Taxes, especially progressive income taxes, interfere with optimum allocation. Only poll taxes are unlikely to affect the marginal conditions, but they are probably unacceptable on equity grounds.

12 See, for example, J. Wiseman, 'Nationalisation', in *International Encyclopaedia of the Social Sciences*, Vol. 1 (1968); also K. Hartley, 'Estimating Military Aircraft Production Outlays', in *Economic Journal* (December 1969).

13 *Nationalised Industries: A Review of Economic and Financial Objectives*, Cmnd. 3437 (London, HMSO, 1967); also various reports of the House of Commons Select Committee on Nationalised Industries (for example, 1968 and 1974). On investment, the 1967 policy proposed social cost benefit analysis, with a test discount rate of 8 per cent, later raised to 10 per cent.

14 House of Commons Select Committee on Nationalised Industries, *Capital Investment Procedures, 1973–1974* (HMSO, 1974), para. 108.

15 See also J. Meade, 'The Theory of Labour-Managed Firms and of Profit-Sharing', in *Economic Journal* (March 1972) (Supplement); also J. Shackleton, 'Is Worker's Self-Management the Answer?', in *National Westminster Bank, Quarterly Review* (February 1976).

16 Meade, op. cit., p. 403. Worker-managed enterprises exist in Yugoslavia; other UK examples include lawyers, accountants, doctors, consultancy partnerships and orchestras.

17 ibid., p. 415. Discriminatory fiscal policies of the tax-subsidy type can be used to induce a LMF to raise employment in the short-run: J. Suckling, 'Employment, Fiscal Policy and the Labour-Managed Firm', in *Public Finance*, No. 1 (1974).

18 K. Walker, 'Workers' Participation in Management: Problems, Practices and Prospects', in *International Institute for Labour Studies Bulletin*, No. 12, p. 29.

19 See, for example, F. Cripps, op. cit., p. 107.

20 J. S. Mill, *Principles of Political Economy* (London, Longman, 1883), p. 552.

Further Reading and Questions

CHAPTER 1

Reading

A. Coddington, 'Positive Economics', in *Canadian Journal of Economics* (February 1972)

R. Lipsey, *An Introduction to Positive Economics* (London, Weidenfeld & Nicolson, 1975)

E. V. Morgan and A. D. Morgan, *The Economics of Public Policy* (Edinburgh University Press, 1972)

E. S. Phelps (ed.), *Economic Justice* (Harmondsworth, Penguin, 1973), Introduction.

A. R. Prest and C. D. Coppock (eds), *The UK Economy* (London, Weidenfeld and Nicolson, 1976)

G. K. Shaw, *An Introduction to the Theory of Macro-Economic Policy* (London, Martin Robertson, 1971), ch. 1

R. Turvey, 'How Rational Economic Decisions are Made', in *Lloyds Bank Review* (January 1968)

Questions

1 What is the objective function of the present British Government? Does the Government have a sufficient range of policy instruments to achieve its objectives?

2 'Whilst economic factors determine the size of the Budget, political factors determine its composition.' Discuss.

CHAPTER 2

Reading

S. Brittan, *Government and Market Economy*, IEA (London, 1971), Hobart Paperback

D. Collard, *Prices, Markets and Welfare* (London, Faber, 1972)

D. Dewey, *Micro-Economics* (London, Oxford University Press, 1975), chs 1, 13 and 14

G. Mrydal, *Against the Stream*, Critical Essays on Economics (London, Macmillan, 1972), chs 4, 7 and 10

C. K. Rowley and A. T. Peacock, *Welfare Economics: A Liberal Restatement* (London, Martin Robertson, 1975)

Questions

1 Does a knowledge of welfare economics enable you to determine whether the Industrial Revolution in Britain was a desirable change?

2 The RAF proposes to introduce night flying in the Vale of York. Is this desirable?

3 Does market failure explain state intervention in education, health and transport in the UK?

4 What are the economic arguments for the state *provision* (as distinct from finance) of (i) health services, (ii) education, (iii) employment exchanges?

CHAPTER 3

Reading

A. Downs, *An Economic Theory of Democracy* (New York, Harper, 1957)
W. A. Niskanen, *Bureaucracy: Servant or Master?*, IEA (London, 1973), Hobart Paperback

Questions

1 Which theory of firm behaviour under which market conditions best explains the behaviour of British political parties?
2 What would constitute a refutation of the Downs model?
3 (i) What is a public service?
   (ii) Are state agencies (bureaucracies) the most efficient suppliers of public services?
4 Consider the merits of a proposal to allow private firms to bid to supply the postal services, refuse collection, fire protection and local police services.

CHAPTER 4

Reading

J. Burton *et al.* (eds), *Readings in Labour Market Analysis* (London, Holt, Rinehart & Winston, 1971)
J. D. Farquhar, *The National Economy* (London, Philip Allan, 1975)
B. McCormick, *Wages* (Harmondsworth, Penguin, 1969)

Questions

1 Using a model of national income determination, predict the effects on output employment and the balance of payments of:
   (i) a fall in private investment;
   (ii) an increase in exports;
   (iii) a fall in the average propensity to save at all levels of national income.
2 What is the speculative motive for holding money? What are the policy implications of the existence of this motive?
3 Does the 'real wage' have any significance for current UK economic policy?
4 Does job search explain UK unemployment in the mid-1970s?

CHAPTER 5

Reading

R. Gill, *Economics: A Text with Included Readings* (London, Prentice-Hall, 1974), chs 12–14
D. Laidler, *The Demand for Money: Theories and Evidence*, (Pennsylvania, International Textbook Company, 1969)
S. Morley, *The Economics of Inflation* (Illinois, Dryden Press, 1971)
F. Paish, *Rise and Fall of Incomes Policy*, IEA, Hobart Paper No. 47 (London, 1971)

Questions

1 Does the Phillips curve provide a satisfactory explanation of inflation in postwar Britain?

2   How would the inclusion of a cost of living clause in *all* wage negotiations affect prices, output and employment in the UK?
3   Is inflation always and everywhere a monetary phenomenon which can only be controlled by monetary measures?

CHAPTER 6

Reading

P. Curwen and A. Fowler, *Economic Policy* (London, Macmillan, 1976), ch. 6
R. Levacic, *Macro-Economics* (London, Macmillan, 1976), ch. 8

Questions

1   What would be the implications for the economic policies of the British Government of a commitment to maintain a fixed exchange rate between pounds and dollars? Are there any reasons why the British people should want their government to have this objective?
2   Which is the most appropriate policy for solving a nation's balance of payments deficit: a devaluation, floating exchange rates, a domestic deflation, an incomes policy or import controls? Relate to British experience.

CHAPTER 7

Reading

C. V. Brown (ed.), *Economic Principles Applied* (London, Martin Robertson, 1970), pt 7
The National Plan, Cmnd. 764 (London, HMSO, 1965)
B. McCormick *et al.*, *Introducing Economics* (Harmondsworth, Penguin, 1974), ch. 38
A. Sen (ed.), *Growth Economics* (Harmondsworth, Penguin, 1970), Introduction

Questions

1   Can any growth theory explain the UK's post-war growth experience?
2   What were the theoretical foundations of (i) the UK National Plan and (ii) the White Paper on the Regeneration of British Industry?

CHAPTER 8

Reading

K. Lyall, *Micro-Economic Issues of the 1970s* (London, Harper & Row, 1974)
B. McCormick *et al.*, *Introducing Economics* (Harmondsworth, Penguin, 1974), ch. 10
E. Mansfield, *Micro-Economics: Theory and Applications* (New York, W. Norton, 1970), ch. 8
R. Turvey, *Demand and Supply* (London, George Allen & Unwin, 1971)

Questions

1   Does the concept of consumers' surplus have any relevance to economic policy?
2   Predict the effects of UK price and wage controls on the behaviour of firms and households. Does a knowledge of welfare economics enable you to

determine whether such controls will result in an improvement in the welfare of the community?

3 Compare the behaviour of IATA with that of trade unions.

CHAPTER 9

Reading

M. Gilbert (ed.), *The Modern Business Enterprise* (Harmondsworth, Penguin, 1972), pts 2 and 3

B. Hindley, *Industrial Mergers and Public Policy*, IEA, Hobart Paper No. 50 (London, 1970)

E. Mansfield, *Micro-Economics* (New York, W. Norton, 1970), chs 6, 9–11

D. Needham, *Economic Analysis and Industrial Structure* (London, Holt, Rinehart & Winston, 1969), ch. 10

B. S. Yamey (ed.), *Economics of Industrial Structure* (Harmondsworth, Penguin, 1973)

Questions

1 Why is a public policy towards mergers needed?

2 Is British government policy towards mergers inconsistent with other aspects of industrial policy?

3 Write a job specification for the NEB

CHAPTER 10

Reading

J. Blair, *Economic Concentration* (New York, Harcourt Brace, 1972)

P. Curwen and A. Fowler, *Economic Policy* (London, Macmillan, 1976)

M. Utton, *Industrial Concentration* (Harmondsworth, Penguin, 1970)

Questions

1 Does economic analysis suggest any policy rules for the control of mergers, monopolies and imperfect competition? Relate your analysis to current British policy.

2 How would you measure the competitiveness of a market structure? What are the implications of your discussion for UK monopoly policy?

CHAPTER 11

Reading

J. Buchanan, *Cost and Choice* (Chicago, Markham, 1969), chs 5 and 6

D. Coombes, *State Enterprise: Business or Politics?* (London, George Allen & Unwin, 1971)

J. R. Galbraith, *The New Industrial State* (Harmondsworth, Penguin, 1967)

R. Gill, *Economics: A Text with Included Readings* (London, Prentice-Hall, 1974), chs 3–5

Questions

1 Does the economics of politics and bureaucracies explain the development of British regional policy since 1945?

2   How can economic analysis be used to assess local expenditure programmes?
    Illustrate with reference to highways and health.

CHAPTER 12

Reading

A. J. Brown, *The Framework of Regional Economics in the UK* (London, Cam-
    bridge University Press, 1972)
H. Richardson (ed.), *Regional Economics: A Reader* (London, Macmillan, 1970)

Questions

1   Must we always take work to the workers?
2   Can the UK's regional problem be explained in terms of international trade
    theory?
3   Consider the case for state support to labour-managed firms (workers' co-
    operatives) as a means of tackling the British regional problem.

CHAPTER 13

Reading

Expenditure Committee, *The Motor Vehicle Industry*, 14th Report (London,
    HMSO, 1975)
I. Little, *A Critique of Welfare Economies* (London, Oxford University Press,
    1960), ch. 11
C. Rowley (ed.), *Readings in Industrial Economics*, Vol. 2 (London, Macmillan,
    1972), chs 2, 5, 6, 9–12 on X-efficiency, public utilities and regulation
M. Webb, *The Economics of Nationalised Industries* (London, Nelson, 1973)

Questions

1   (a) Examine the economic logic of state support for (i) a firm and (ii) an
        industry.
    (b) What are the main alternative forms of government support?
    (c) How does the state select a particular form of support as 'appropriate'?
2   Should British Leyland and/or Chrysler (UK) have received state support?
3   What improvements, if any, in the economic performance of the nationalised
    industries would you expect to follow from an instruction to relate prices to
    long-run marginal costs?

Index